JOURNAL FOR THE STUDY OF THE NEW TESTAMENT SUPPLEMENT SERIES
224

Executive Editor
Stanley E. Porter

Editorial Board
Craig Blomberg, Elizabeth A. Castelli, David Catchpole,
Kathleen E. Corley, R. Alan Culpepper, James D.G. Dunn,
Craig A. Evans, Stephen Fowl, Robert Fowler,
George H. Guthrie, Robert Jewett, Robert W. Wall

CLASSICS IN BIBLICAL AND THEOLOGICAL STUDIES SUPPLEMENT SERIES
1

Selected and Edited by
Craig A. Evans and Stanley E. Porter

Sheffield Academic Press

Trinity Academic Press

Holy Word

The Paradigm of New Testament Formation

J. Arthur Baird

Selected and Edited by
Craig A. Evans and Stanley E. Porter
with the assistance of Scott N. Dolff

Journal for the Study of the New Testament
Supplement Series 224

Classics in Biblical and Theological Studies
Supplement Series 1

Dedicated to my father
Jesse Hays Baird
Who first introduced me to the Holy Word

Copyright © 2002 Sheffield Academic Press
A Continuum imprint

Published by Trinity Academic Press,
a wholly owned imprint of Sheffield Academic Press Ltd
The Tower Building, 11 York Road, London SE1 7NX
370 Lexington Avenue, New York NY 10017-6550

www.SheffieldAcademicPress.com
www.continuumbooks.com

All rights reserved. No part of this publication may be reproduced or transmitted in any form or by any means, electronic or mechanical, including photocopying, recording or any information storage or retrieval system, without permission in writing from the publishers.

British Library Cataloguing-in-Publication Data

A catalogue record for this book is available from the British Library

Typeset by Sheffield Academic Press
Printed on acid-free paper in Great Britain by Bookcraft Ltd, Midsomer Norton, Bath

ISBN 0-8264-6025-9

'Inasmuch as many have undertaken to compile a narrative of the things which have been accomplished among us, just as they were delivered to us by those who from the beginning were eyewitnesses and ministers of the word, it seemed good to me also, having followed all things closely for some time past, to write an orderly account for you, most excellent Theophilus, that you may know the truth concerning the things of which you have been informed' (Lk. 1.1-4 RSV).

'You have been born anew, not of perishable seed, but of imperishable, through the living and abiding word of God… That word is the good news which was preached to you' (1 Pet. 1.23, 25 RSV).

'For I supposed that things out of books did not profit me so much as the utterances of a voice which lives and abides' (Papias, *apud* Eusebius, *Hist. Eccl.* 3.39.4).

'Let us walk in obedience to his hallowed words' (*1 Clem.* 13.3).

CONTENTS

Editors' Foreword   9
Preface   11
Abbreviations   14

Chapter 1
A CRITICAL INTRODUCTION: HISTORICAL REALISM
AND THE PARADIGM OF THE WORD   15

Chapter 2
HOLY WORD: THE STARTING POINT OF THE DEVELOPMENT   46

Chapter 3
HOLY NARRATIVE: THE CONTEXT OF THE WORD   64

Chapter 4
HOLY GOSPEL: THE THEOLOGICAL INTERPRETATION
OF THE WORD   81

Chapter 5
HOLY TRADITION: THE APPLICATION OF THE WORD   107

Chapter 6
HOLY APOSTLES: THE CUSTODIANS OF THE WORD   120

Chapter 7
HOLY SCHOOLS: THE ENVIRONMENT OF THE WORD   130

Chapter 8
HOLY ΓΡΑΦΗ: THE REPOSITORY OF THE WORD   160

Chapter 9
HOLY FATHERS: THE TRANSMITTERS OF THE WORD   186

Chapter 10
THEOLOGICAL TRAJECTORY: IMPLICATIONS OF THE
PARADIGM FOR THEOLOGY   209

Chapter 11
HISTORICAL TRAJECTORY: IMPLICATIONS OF THE
PARADIGM FOR HISTORY   230

Index of Ancient Sources   256
Index of Authors   266

Editors' Foreword

In 1995, J. Arthur Baird died after a lengthy and distinguished career as a scholar and teacher. At the time of his death, Professor Baird left a major unpublished manuscript, which in several ways brings together many of the significant themes and ideas that defined both his scholarly and his ecclesiastical careers. Mrs Mary Baird asked the editors to assist her and her family in the publication of her late husband's manuscript. She believed that it had significant merit and deserved to be published, not only as a final memorial to her husband's work but as a contribution to New Testament scholarship in its own right. We were only too happy to assist in this task, and are pleased to present this volume as the first in the new series, Current Issues in Biblical Theology, under the imprint of Trinity Academic Press, and as a volume of the JSNT Supplement Series of Sheffield Academic Press.

Professor Baird will already be well-known to many, if not most, New Testament scholars, and rightly so on the basis of the significant and ground-breaking work of scholarship that he produced. For those unfamiliar with the man or his work, a brief recounting of several pertinent biographical facts are in order. Professor Baird was a native Californian. He graduated with the B.A. from Occidental College in Los Angeles in 1943, and then served in the United States Navy. At the end of the Second World War, he studied at San Francisco Theological Seminary and became an ordained Presbyterian minister, serving a church in California, before returning to higher education. In 1953, he received the Ph.D. from the University of Edinburgh, and in the fall of 1954 began his lengthy teaching career at Wooster College in Wooster, Ohio, becoming Synod Professor of Religion in 1972. Professor Baird is the author of numerous books and articles, several of which books have paved new ways in New Testament study, especially in the area of historical Jesus research. He also served as general editor for The Computer Bible series. The monographs that he authored include the following:

The Justice of God in the Teaching of Jesus (London: SCM Press; Philadelphia: Westminster Press, 1963)

Audience Criticism and the Historical Jesus (Philadelphia: Westminster Press, 1969)

Rediscovering the Power of the Gospels: Jesus' Theology of the Kingdom (Wooster, OH: Iona Press, 1982)

A Comparative Analysis of the Gospel Genre: The Synoptic Mode and Its Uniqueness (Lewiston: Edwin Mellen Press, 1991)

We are pleased now to offer the final monograph from Professor Baird, *Holy Word: The Paradigm of New Testament Formation.* Sensitively written and profoundly thoughtful, Professor Baird's *Holy Word* is first and foremost a study in New Testament theology. As such, we believe that it will make a lasting contribution to the subject, but it is much more than that. It should serve to re-awaken biblical scholars, especially New Testament experts, to the theological function of Scripture in the life of the early Church. We have essentially presented the work as Professor Baird prepared it, making only the necessary adjustments to make it ready for publication, but resisting for the most part the desire to alter wording or even references. As a result, there is some duplication, which Professor Baird himself probably would have eliminated, but which we have left, since to thoroughly revise the manuscript would have run the risk of altering what is his book. At a few points, however, we have added a few pertinent references to relevant secondary literature. Professor Baird has also referred extensively to his own writings, both published and unpublished. We have left those references in this book, since they seemed to us to provide the necessary foundation for this important volume. Most biblical quotations are taken from the Revised Standard Version.

Craig A. Evans	Stanley E. Porter
Trinity Western University	McMaster Divinity College
Langley, B.C.	Hamilton, ON

Preface

The wellspring of the New Testament was a fountain of collective memory that found its origin in the life and teachings of Jesus. Papias called it 'a voice that lives and abides'. This voice found its channel in the apostles, but preceded them, and gave general consensus to their preaching and teaching. Behind the written memoir lay the oral word as the voice of Jesus, living and active within the minds and experience of his eye witnesses, as of the ongoing church from the very beginning.

There is an abundance of evidence to support the thesis of this book that the teachings of Jesus, what the author of 1 Peter called 'the living and abiding word of God... the good news which was preached to you' (1.23, 25), and which some in the early Church came to call 'the Holy Word', functioned as the basis of Christian doctrine and practice from the beginning of the Christian era, and continues so today. This study documents this phenomenon at least as far as Eusebius in the fourth century. The key to it all seems to have been the sanctity with which these teachings were regarded, treasured and used within the early Church. They believed he was the son of God, and they treated his words accordingly. As the author of 2 Peter aptly summarized it: 'Remember...the commandments of the Lord and Savior through your apostles' (3.2). Clement of Rome echoed the same message: 'Let us walk in obedience to his hallowed words' (*1 Clem.* 13.3); and Papias characterized himself as one who 'took delight in those who recall the commandments given to the faith by the Lord' (*Hist. Eccl.* 3.39.2-4). The evidence to follow will establish that the Church was the Church of the Holy Word; and the New Testament is the written record of that word as it found expression in the life and thought of the Church. In the light of these data, it can be truly said that the history of the Church and the history of the Word are one and the same history.

This book is then a study of the origin and development of the New Testament canon at the earliest and most basic level of its genesis. The criteria for canonization emerged directly and naturally from the nature of the situation itself, and found their formulation in what I shall be describing in the pages to come as the paradigm of the Word. The crucial insight that guides these pages is that in understanding the process of New Testament formation and canonization, theology precedes historical process. They go together in the emergence of the Christian story, but in terms of priority and historical development, the Holy Word about God and his Kingdom came first. Much of the work on the canon has in recent years been done from the reverse assumption—that it is out of the process of historical development that the theological consensus of the church emerged. What my evidence suggests is that it was the earliest consensus of the Church around the nexus of the Holy Word of Jesus that provided the impetus and guiding principle for the formation of the Gospels and then the New Testament. This, then, was the foundation stone for the life and thought of the early Church from the time of Jesus at least until that of Eusebius. It is this understanding more than any other single thing that unlocks the mystery of Gospel formation and New Testament canonization.

The implications of this paradigm of the Word for biblical hermeneutics, the Church's understanding of its own theology and history, and its assessment of the historical character of the New Testament, are great, and may cause some confusion, some opposition, and hopefully some excitement and support: confusion, because it is the fifth in a series of books dealing with various aspects of these questions which the reader may not have read, most of which challenge some commonly held critical axiom or point of view, and use methods not generally understood or accepted; opposition, because it will challenge several widely held critical presuppositions of what David Hall has recently called 'modern critical orthodoxy';[1] and possible excitement, because some of these insights may be, and indeed have been, called 'breakthroughs' in New Testament critical research.[2]

Throughout I shall refer to God in Synoptic terms, using the male gender as Jesus did. My purpose in doing this is not to prejudice an important contemporary discussion, but to avoid confusion in dealing

1. D.R. Hall, *The Seven Pillories of Wisdom* (Macon, GA: Mercer University Press, 1990), p. vii.
2. J.W. Ellison ('In Pursuit of the Ipsissima Verba', *Computers in the Humanities* 4.3 [1970], review of J.A. Baird, *Audience Criticism and the Historical Jesus* [Philadelphia: Westminster Press, 1969]) comments: 'This study should mark a turning point in studies of the Synoptic Gospels as significant as the introduction of Form Criticism over thirty years ago'.

carefully with the text of these Gospels. What one does with these data theologically will probably be a function of other criteria.

It remains only to acknowledge the many teachers, friends and colleagues in the United States and Europe whose insight and advice are evident on every page, and the many institutions where this lengthy project was carried out. Among these are San Francisco Theological Seminary, the University of Edinburgh, the Universities of Marburg, Princeton, Yale, and Harvard, where the bulk of the research was done, the Ecumenical Institute for Advanced Theological Study in Jerusalem, and especially the College of Wooster, whose indulgence and facilities have always implemented its dedication to scholarly research. And of course there is Mary, whose dedication to the author is only matched by her commitment to the cause we both serve.

J. Arthur Baird
Wooster, Ohio

ABBREVIATIONS

AB	Anchor Bible
ASNU	Acta seminarii neotestamentici upsaliensis
BBR	*Bulletin for Biblical Research*
BZ	*Biblische Zeitschrift*
CSR	*Christian Scholar's Review*
ETL	*Ephemerides theologicae lovanienses*
FBBS	Foundation Books in Biblical Studies
FRLANT	Forschungen zur Religion und Literatur des Alten und Neuen Testaments
ICC	International Critical Commentary
Int	*Interpretation*
JAAR	*Journal of the American Academy of Religion*
JBL	*Journal of Biblical Literature*
LCL	Loeb Classical Library
MNTC	Moffatt New Testament Commentary
NovTSup	*Novum Testamentum*, Supplements
NTS	*New Testament Studies*
NTTS	New Testament Tools and Studies
PL	J.-P. Migne (ed.), *Patrologia cursus completus... Series prima [latina]* (221 vols.; Paris: J.-P. Migne, 1844–85)
SBLDS	Society of Biblical Literature Dissertation Series
SBLSP	Society of Biblical Literature Seminar Papers
SBT	Studies in Biblical Theology
SE	*Studia Evangelica*
SNTSMS	Society for New Testament Studies Monograph Series
TDNT	Gerhard Kittel and Gerhard Friedrich (eds.), *Theological Dictionary of the New Testament* (trans. G.W. Bromiley; 10 vols.; Grand Rapids: Eerdmans, 1964–76).
TU	Texte und Untersuchungen
TWNT	Gerhard Kittel and Gerhard Friedrich (eds.), *Theologisches Wörterbuch zum Neuen Testament* (11 vols.; Stuttgart: Kohlhammer, 1932–79).
TS	*Theological Studies*
WUNT	Wissenschaftliche Untersuchungen zum Neuen Testament
ZTK	*Zeitschrift für Theologie und Kirche*

Chapter 1

A CRITICAL INTRODUCTION:
HISTORICAL REALISM AND THE PARADIGM OF THE WORD

The Basic Problem

The degree of seriousness with which scholars take the New Testament, the manner in which they interpret it, the authenticity they accord to it, all depend to a large extent on their understanding of two things: first, the historical process out of which the New Testament emerged, and secondly, the relation between the historical person of Jesus and the Gospel message; that is, between narrative and theology, between the process and the word. C.H. Dodd put his finger clearly on the first: the major problem in New Testament historical research, he said is 'to discover the starting point of the development which the New Testament writings exhibit'.[1] C.K. Barrett expressed the second particularly well: 'We are confronted in primitive Christianity with two traditions, one the almost purely theological tradition that we meet in Paul, the other the curious mingling of historical recollection and theological conviction that we encounter in the Gospels; and we have so far been able neither to identify them nor to explain the relation between them'.[2] This present volume attempts to address these two interrelated questions: (1) What is the starting point and primary control of the development which produced the Synoptics, the New Testament and the early Church? (2) What is the guiding principle in the interaction of the early Church's historical recollection and its theological conviction?

These are both in their own way the same historical question, and our answer will depend to a large extent upon our understanding of the nature of biblical history. Every book on the New Testament must

  1. C.H. Dodd, *History and the Gospel* (London: Nisbet, 1947).
  2. C.K. Barrett, *Jesus and the Gospel Traditions* (Philadelphia: Fortress Press, 1968), p. 12.

somehow relate itself to the problem of historical authenticity; and a book like this, dealing with the teachings of Jesus, has a special need to treat certain critical historical questions. The problem is that in this, the most creative age in the history of biblical scholarship, so much critical research has been done that it is difficult to get through the mass of secondary data to the basic underlying questions. Each scholar is operating on a set of presuppositions to such an extent that it is almost impossible to talk to one another. We are divided into schools of thought, factions, research groups, and critical ghettos. As a result, the progress of scholarship is threatened with 'gridlock' from the amount of new data, and the commitment to past research becomes assumption, and then critical dogma. This is confusing to anyone trying to understand the conclusions of someone whose entire publishing program may not have been read or is not available for consultation. In order to mitigate, if not to solve, the problem, it should be helpful to spell out the major critical assumptions lying behind any particular conclusion and give as much of the evidence as is reasonable. At least then one can recognize for himself or herself the source of the presupposition, and direct the discussion constantly to the rational bases of any conclusions. These need to be constantly re-examined, and possibly abandoned as just another station along the way. Only thus can the cause of biblical scholarship be advanced since, hopefully, we are not in the business of defending set 'positions', but rather in pursuing the truth, wherever it may lead.

The Problem of Historical Skepticism

The problem of history is of course an old one for biblical scholarship, and well-known to many; but perhaps it would be useful to introduce and summarize the matter with a brief historical review. This historical skepticism is traceable at least as far back as the Reformation to Martin Luther, who was able to call James 'an epistle of straw', or John Calvin who rejected 2 Peter, and recognized such discrepancies in Scripture as Matthew's slip in attributing to Jeremiah a quotation that really comes from Zechariah (Mt. 27.9). This nascent criticism gathered momentum during the seventeenth and eighteenth centuries as the scientific method being developed in secular research commended itself to biblical scholars. It was Johann Gottfried Eichhorn (1752–1827) who is said to have first secured a place for a critical method of biblical study in

European Protestant university circles. But it was in the twentieth century that the critical method really began to come into its own. In 1901, William Wrede, in his classical work, *Das Messiasgeheimnis in den Evangelien*, asserted that Jesus' Messiahship was a theory imposed by Mark upon the narrative. Julius Wellhausen, in his commentaries produced between 1905 and 1911, pursued this early objectivity by concluding that the oldest tradition consisted mostly of small individual fragments of the sayings of Jesus which did not originally present a continuous story. K.L. Schmidt, in *Der Rahmen der Geschichte Jesu* (1919), took the next obvious step by insisting that all descriptions of place or time which connect the individual Gospel fragments are due to editorial redaction.

This skepticism was carried to its most creative extreme in the work of Martin Dibelius, in *Die Formgeschichte des Evangeliums* (1919), and most especially Rudolf Bultmann, whose classic work, *Die Geschichte der Synoptischen Tradition* (1921), has represented a watershed in New Testament history. Bultmann represented on the one hand an extension of the work of these nineteenth-century scholars; but on the other hand he was reacting to the Jesus of History movement in Europe which wanted to reduce Jesus to a truly historical figure by stripping away all theological accretions. In that sense, Bultmann's work was an attempt to retrieve the Christ of faith from the profane hands of the Jesus of History movement. Bultmann was a noted eclectic and his book is filled with references to the work of others upon which he leaned heavily. Basically this book is the application of the concept of 'form' to the Synoptic Gospels, derived from his colleague Martin Dibelius, and more basically from the Old Testament work of Hermann Gunkel. The idea is that every culture has its own *Sitz im Leben*. It thinks and acts in a particular way in terms of its faith. It is this way of living, as Gunkel said, that determines the form of the literature stemming from such a culture. Form, then, tells us something about the culture that produced it. When one approaches the Synoptics, one must be sensitive to this fact. For Bultmann, this was a basic axiom that needed no proof, and none was given. From Wellhausen and others he derived the insight that the Synoptic Gospels are divided up into individual *Einzelstücke* which circulated independently in the earlier tradition. Bultmann then spent much time in this book identifying the seams between the various units and classifying them according to form. The narrative, therefore, as Schmidt insisted, was of secondary historical value. Wellhausen provided the source for Bultmann's belief that the early oral tradition within the Church was constantly producing new sayings of Jesus. The early Church thus became a major and original source of much Synoptic material. From Wrede, Bultmann obtained the conviction that Jesus did not consider himself to be the Messiah, and so whenever we find him so doing, we have evidence that the early Church is superimposing this image upon him. Again, this needed no more support than what Wrede had given it.

The more original and creative work in Bultmann's book is his thesis concerning the 'ideal scene'. He notes that some scenes, like that of the widow's mite, have a kind of ideal character ('how did Jesus know that this was her all?'). The Evangelist has been indulging in some artistic creation to set up the sayings of Jesus imbedded therein. He compares this to rabbinic passages where some rather bizarre narration has been created to set off a saying. He pursues this idea by applying it to such scenes as the calling of the twelve, which he says was probably the turning of some original saying of Jesus about becoming fishers of men into an ideal scene where actual fishermen were being called beside the sea. The Gospel editor then became an artistic creator, and a primary source of much of the Gospel material.

The result of this century of critical scholarship, especially as it came to focus in Bultmann's work, is what he wryly described as *meine vielgetadelde Skepsis*. Just how skeptical he was continues to be a matter of debate, since he persisted in making much use of the Gospel material in developing his New Testament theology. I must confess that I am still most impressed by his comment to the effect that all he could really know about the historical Jesus was *das dass*, the fact that he lived. His practice of continuing to use the teachings of Jesus as if he knew what Jesus said, and his assumption that the early Church was essentially accurate in thus creating stories and sayings of Jesus out of whole cloth, remains for me a classic illustration of trying to have your cake and eat it too. What he has done is canonize the entire Palestinian church, which is a peculiar form of fundamentalism for a critical scholar. This represents a basic contradiction within Bultmann's mind that remained unresolved to his death, and which continues within the circle of his followers.[3]

---

3. In significant ways this radical skepticism continues to be in evidence in recent works, such as B.L. Mack, *A Myth of Innocence: Mark and Christian Origins* (Philadelphia: Fortress Press, 1988).

1. *Historical Realism and the Paradigm of the Word*

There was of course a strong reaction to Bultmann's skepticism both within and outside of Germany. The first reaction came from a group of scholars who rejected with varying degrees of vehemence the negative thrust of form criticism, while accepting many of its critical insights. Emil Fascher, in his book *Die formgeschichtliche Methode*, roundly condemned Bultmann's excessive skepticism, and complained that 'form is not in itself an historical tool; by itself it can tell us nothing of the truth or falsity of the events narrated'.[4] This same criticism was stressed in 1927 by L. Koehler in *Das Formgeschichtliche Problem des Neuen Testaments*. A host of others, like B.S. Easton, Vincent Taylor, Donald Baillie, Oscar Cullmann, Joachim Jeremias, Paul Althaus, C.H. Dodd, John Wick Bowman, and Basil Redlich, objected to the battery of questionable assumptions that formed the core of this negative estimate of Gospel historicity. Jeremias warned of grave dangers from the widespread conviction that the historical Jesus and his message have no decisive significance for Christian faith, stressing the kerygma of the early Church at the expense of the message of Jesus.[5]

Another more sympathetic, but also strong, reaction came from a group of Bultmann's students and other disciples whom James Robinson immortalized as 'Post-Bultmannians' in *A New Quest of the Historical Jesus*. This group, including men like Ernst Käsemann, Hans Conzelmann, and Günther Bornkamm, occupying some of the most distinguished New Testament chairs in Germany, were concerned to follow Bultmann's methodology, but were much more interested in recovering the historical Jesus. Gerhard Ebeling of Zürich expressed this concern in a now famous rhetorical question: 'Who shall forbid us to ask the historical question concerning the historical Jesus? This defeatism has no justification...either as to the state of the actual historical sources available to us or in relation to the possibility of historical understanding in general.'[6] According to Robinson, who is chiefly responsible for bringing this trend to the attention of American scholarship, as a method, form criticism has largely passed out of vogue among these scholars; but the basic critical orientation of form criticism, going back to

---

4. E. Fascher, *Die formgeschichtliche Methode* (Giessen: Alfred Töpelmann, 1924), p. 223.

5. See J. Jeremias, 'The Present Position in the Controversy Concerning the Problem of the Historical Jesus', *ExpTim* 69 (1958), p. 333.

6. G. Ebeling, 'Die Frage nach dem historischen Jesus und das Problem der Christologie', *ZTK* 56 (1959), p. 20.

Wellhausen and Wrede, still remains. History has survived only as kerygma, the 'messianic secret' in Mark is thoroughly established, and Schmidt's work showing the non-historicity of the order of events in Jesus' life remains unchallenged. The old nineteenth-century liberal, positivistic question of the historical Jesus has been made impossible for this group by the new kerygmatic approach to the Gospels. It is the kerygmatic movement that produced what Fuchs, following M. Kähler, called 'passion narratives with long introductions'. The Synoptics are therefore really theologies of history with little historiographic interest. This means then that the burden of proof lies with the scholar who sees objective, factual source material in the primitive Church's 'book of common worship'. Robinson notes within this group, however, a new emphasis on the historical reliability of the Gospels which is in effect a criticism of the earlier kerygmatic approach that failed to see Jesus as a concrete, historical incarnation and led to a mythical Christ. For the 'post-Bultmannians', the record of the life and words of Jesus derives from the Church, but following Bultmann, the Church was essentially correct in its understanding.[7]

Modern Critical Orthodoxy

In the last generation, within New Testament circles there has been a virtual tyranny of this point of view, which David Hall with great good humor has recently characterized as 'Modern Critical Orthodoxy'.[8] Martin Hengel was less humorous as he complained of this 'radical historical skepticism', which is still widespread within a number of areas of German scholarship. He charged that it is 'often coupled with flights of imagination which suggest a retreat from any historical research worthy of taking seriously'.[9]

Beginning as a bold move to protect the New Testament from the late nineteenth- and early twentieth-century liberal European historical critics, and to help usher biblical scholarship into the scientific age, this critical movement has in my opinion had widespread value and introduced into

---

7. J.A. Baird, *The Justice of God in the Teaching of Jesus* (London: SCM Press; Philadelphia: Westminster Press, 1963), p. 20.

8. D.R. Hall, *The Seven Pillories of Wisdom* (Macon, GA: Mercer University Press, 1990).

9. M. Hengel, *Acts and the History of Earliest Christianity* (Philadelphia: Fortress Press, 1979).

modern scholarship many new and liberating ideas. But it has also proven to be a Trojan Horse that has for many become just another form of fundamentalism that can be a serious deterrent to creative new research.

More recently, the scholarly pendulum has been swinging away from this establishmentarian orthodoxy toward a more critical assessment of Bultmann and radical historical skepticism, and toward a more flexible, varied, open, and, one dares to hope, even more truly scientific, approach to the Bible. Since 1959 when Robinson summarized the situation in terms of the post-Bultmannian school, there has been a continuous stream of concern for the historical Jesus, especially in Germany, Britain, Scandinavia and the United States. The extreme historical skepticism of Bultmann has, with some exceptions, been generally repudiated, and most books and articles on the subject seem to be attempting to validate the essential historicity of Jesus' life and teachings to one degree or another. The tyranny of the criterion of dissimilarity as the single test for authenticity has come under increasing attack, especially when used negatively to say that if something in the Gospels is not dissimilar to the known kerygma of the Church, then it cannot be relied upon. There is in this large body of literature since 1959 an almost universal concern to see Christianity as an historical religion, and an increasing insistence that there is a genuine historical interest on the part of the Gospel editors and the early Church.[10] The existential, kerygmatic approach continued with post-Bultmannians like Käsemann, Braaten, Harrisville, James Robinson, and others, but even those like Fuchs and Ebeling wanted to talk seriously about the objective facts of the historical Jesus. As Van Harvey and Schubert Ogden pointed out, there was really little 'new' in the 'New Quest'.[11] It was not a breakthrough, but only a modification of the old Bultmannian position.

---

10. [C.A. Evans, 'The Historical Jesus and Christian Faith: A Critical Assessment of a Scholarly Problem', *CSR* 18 (1988), pp. 48-63; *idem*, 'Authenticity Criteria in Life of Jesus Research', *CSR* 19 (1989), pp. 6-31; *idem*, 'Life-of-Jesus Research and the Eclipse of Mythology', *TS* 54 (1993), pp. 3-36.—Eds.]

11. V.A. Harvey and S.M. Ogden, 'How New is the "New Quest of the Historical Jesus"?', in C.E. Braaten and R.A. Harrisville (eds.), *The Historical Jesus and the Kerygmatic Christ: Essays on the New Quest of the Historical Jesus* (Nashville: Abingdon Press, 1964), pp. 197-242, esp. pp. 239-41.

Bultmann crystallized the problem for the twentieth century in his well-known distinction between *Historie,* the objective data of history,[12] what Collingwood called 'outer history', and *Geschichte,* the history of mind, what Collingwood called 'inner history'.[13] As is well known, Bultmann stressed the importance of the latter, while C.H. Dodd,[14] Butterfield,[15] D.M. Baillie[16] and others stressed the former. My own research, however, points to the importance of both in the discipline of historiography, without necessary contradiction or equivocation. This turning in an existential direction actually slowed down the progress of historical Jesus research, since it rejected the importance of historiography and re-defined the problem as the search for the philosophy or theology of the historical Jesus. Stephen Neill's call for 'real historians' seems to have been a more prophetic insight; and it is the question of historiography, not the philosophy of history, which is predominant in the work of most of those researching the historical Jesus in the last twenty five years.[17] I am calling this 'A New Paradigm Community', and will be describing it as we move along through the chapters of this book.

Foundations of a Cautious Historical Optimism

At this point we must deal more exactly with the issues raised in the above historical review. We must find some critical foundations in this morass of debate which will act as bases for the research that is to follow. Only as we lay out and defend our presuppositions will we have the right to propose the very large conclusions which are the thesis of this book. I want to stress that these are only the critical issues most significant for the theme under discussion. They do not pretend to be a complete coverage of the subject or final in their present form. They

---

12. R. Bultmann, *History and Eschatology* (Edinburgh: Edinburgh University Press, 1957).

13. R.G. Collingwood, *The Idea of History* (New York: Oxford University Press, 1956).

14. Dodd, *History and the Gospel.*

15. H. Butterfield, *Christianity and History* (London: G. Bell, 1949).

16. D.M. Baillie, *God Was in Christ* (New York: Charles Scribner's Sons 1948).

17. It is now widely referred to as the 'Third Quest'. [See the recent summary and evaluation of the latest phase of Jesus research in M.A. Powell, *Jesus as a Figure in History: How Modern Historians View the Man from Galilee* (Louisville, KY: Westminster/John Knox Press, 1998).—Eds.]

must remain open to question, and will no doubt continue to be debated for many years to come by others more competent than myself. I make bold to offer these here as the result of a lifetime of critical study and the product of several new lines of investigation which have revealed new evidence and critical insights that I believe will be helpful in moving along the discussion of the formation of the New Testament, and the place of the teachings of Jesus in that process.

a. *Bultmann and Beyond*
In the light of what has been written above, we must first of all face the challenge of what is being called 'Modern Critical Orthodoxy', especially as it comes to focus in the work of Rudolf Bultmann and the form-critical movement, as well as in its most recent manifestation—the Jesus Seminar of North America. My debt to Bultmann is great, and my respect for him as a person is real. A semester in Marburg reading everything he had written, and talking with him in his home on Calvinstrasse was one of the great experiences of my scholarly pilgrimage. The positive side of my appreciation includes many things: his unrelenting honesty and courage in the pursuit of an objective methodology; his insights, along with Dibelius and others, into the independent unit character of the Synoptics; his concept of 'form' in so far as it provided a useful typology for distinguishing these units; his awareness of the part played by the kerygma in the formation of the New Testament; his concern to understand the meaning of history, defined by him along the lines pursued by Collingwood, Dilthey and others, where the distinction was made between *Historie* and *Geschichte*. One of his most helpful contributions was this awareness of the 'inner history' of mind that stressed the manner in which the original reporters entered into the history they were reporting, and the ways in which the modern historian must also become existentially involved in that history. This distinction has proven useful for an initial attack upon the problem, and the recognition that any history is inevitably interpreted history.

Unfortunately, these benefits have also been accompanied by a number of problems in Bultmann's work which have caused much unnecessary opposition, and directed Synoptic scholarship into several critical blind alleys. The brilliance of the man and his many lasting insights have unfortunately blinded almost two generations of scholars to these more sinister aspects of Bultmann's work, which have formed the crux of the critical 'orthodoxy' we have been describing, and which have been challenged through the years, and even more vigorously today. I cannot go into much detail in this short introduction, but I shall list those issues which are most crucial for the research of this book, and give a brief critique and defense.[18]

(1) The first has to do with the concept of form itself. Bultmann took this useful idea and turned it into a tool for making historical decisions. He interpreted these data to mean that the form of the λόγια is the result of the 'use' to which they were put by the community in preaching, teaching and debate. Form is therefore a 'sociological result', and has been regularly assumed to be an historical barrier to what Jesus himself may have actually said.[19] This interpretation of form is superficially defensible in explaining the way in which the early community standardized legends and miracle stories about Jesus, but it runs into logical problems when examined in terms of the Sayings material itself. These phenomena could possibly mean that the Evangelists in order to make them 'useful' created the legends and miracle stories out of whole cloth.

More realistically it could also mean that by their very nature these λόγια demanded a particular form, which in turn required a particular context for that form to have meaning.[20] The standardizing would suggest then an early stabilizing of the wording through oral repetition or early fixing in writing, or both. But form gives us no real data for deciding the historical question, which must be resolved with different kinds of evidence. This leads to a quite different interpretation of the data. A legend suggests a certain written form, including a clear historical context because of the nature of those data. There is a naturalness to this which would have commended itself to those recording legends. The apophthegm demands a rounding off at the end within a brief narrative because that is the necessary way to reproduce such a saying. The parable and the saying stand alone by their very natures and need no narrative setting, although at times a brief context is helpful for understanding. A better explanation for the phenomenon of the form of the tradition, rather than seeing it as the product of the early

---

18. The full details of this critique are found in my unpublished manuscript entitled, 'Historical Skepticism and Gospel Renewal'.

19. J.A. Baird, *Audience Criticism and the Historical Jesus* (Philadelphia: Westminster Press, 1969), p. 146.

20. Baird, *Audience Criticism*, pp. 145-49.

community, lies in its intrinsic nature, as it would have naturally occurred in the mind of the originator, and would have commended itself to those who recorded the tradition. Form is a valid literary category, but not a useful historical tool. At this point, using Wittgenstein's terminology, the form critics have mixed up their 'language game'. It is a problem of epistemology. If this is true, then the category of form does not prevent us *necessarily* from going beyond it to the original historical situation. As far as form is concerned, historicity is a wide open question. Other kinds of data are needed for a valid historical judgment.[21]

(2) Beyond form, there are several other critical issues that have supported the Bultmannian historical skepticism, and comprise the negative structure of what we are calling 'critical orthodoxy'. One of these has been the doctrinaire insistence on a 'strictly oral' period of Gospel transmission for at least 20–30 years before there was any writing down of the Jesus material. Bultmann recognized fully that to admit early recording of the data would seriously challenge his skepticism. There are several problems with this argument:

(a) The first is that this is a method out of its proper context. Bultmann's form criticism was an extension into Gospel studies of the Old Testament form-critical thesis of Hermann Gunkel, whose conclusions depended on hundreds of years of transmission time during which certain oral and literary conventions developed. With the Gospels, however, we are dealing with a very short period of time, and to apply this method to the New Testament demanded a rigid insistence on a 'strictly' oral period. Without that, Gunkel's Old Testament form criticism would not work with the Synoptics as an historical tool. Here is a case where a method out of place and an a-priori thesis have skewed the evidence.

(b) This argument was further based on Bultmann's work on what he called 'the laws of folk tradition' which operated to change the original data. Bultmann based this on the primitive work of the early German folklorists. The problem is that such scholars have never been able to agree on the 'laws' of folk tradition. As Thorlief Boman has shown, more sophisticated research has revealed that when folk material like the Gospel story is circulated orally, it tends to be passed on not by a 'community' but by individual story tellers whose capacity for memory

---

21. Baird, *The Justice of God in the Teaching of Jesus*, pp. 23-24. See Chapter 11 below.

preserved, rather than distorted, the original.[22] My own work on the *Gospel of Thomas* has shown the inadequacy of Bultmann's insistence that during the earliest period the laws of oral tradition required oral material to 'develop' necessarily in transmission from small units to larger and more complex ones. For example, in comparing *Thomas* with the Synoptics, 88 verses of *Thomas* have some clear parallel to the Synoptics, and 54 as close a parallel as one Synoptic to another.[23] Some of the *Thomas* sayings are longer, but even more are shorter than the Synoptics. For example *Thomas* 75 is a case where a rather long Synoptic parable (Mt. 25.1-2) has become a one sentence λόγιον: 'Jesus said: Many are standing at the door, but the solitary are the ones who will enter the bridal chamber'. If this is any indication, within the primitive process of transmission, whether oral or written, both shortening and lengthening took place, but shortening would probably have been the more common.

(c) Another basis for this 'strictly oral' argument is the assumption that since the first disciples were uneducated people, one must not attribute much literary activity to them. But here again is a debater's argument based on a polemical point that is unrelated to the evidence. Aside from the fact that Matthew was probably a literary person, my studies have shown that the larger group of disciples would have had many who had an interest in writing, including priests, scribes and Pharisees, as well as wealthy supporters who could certainly have afforded writing materials.[24]

(d) It has also been popular among the last generation of scholars to point to an unwritten prohibition among Jewish rabbinic students against writing down the sayings of the rabbis. Jesus' disciples would therefore not have done so. On the contrary, more recent evidence has shown that the Jews were people long accustomed to recording the words and deeds of their great figures, often during or immediately after the lifetime of those persons.[25] H.L. Strack, G.F. Moore, and others have shown that rabbis regularly composed written collections of Haggadoth

---

22. T. Boman, *Die Jesus-Überlieferung im Lichte der neueren Folkskunde* (Göttingen: Vandenhoeck & Ruprecht, 1967).

23. Cf. J.A. Baird, *A Comparative Analysis of the Gospel Genre: The Synoptic Mode and Its Uniqueness* (Lewiston: Edwin Mellen Press, 1991), pp. 109-10. The evidence points to the Synoptics as being the earlier material.

24. Baird, *Audience Criticism*, pp. 37-43.

25. Baird, *The Justice of God in the Teaching of Jesus*, p. 24.

to refresh their memories, and the remoter sources of the Mishnah were probably in writing. Perhaps most significant for this study is the positive evidence of Chapters 8 and 11 that the writing down of the words and deeds of Jesus played a very important part in the life of early Christianity from the very beginning. One really must take Luke seriously when he writes, 'Many have undertaken to compile a narrative of the things that have been accomplished among us' (Lk. 1.1).

(e) A further objection to early Christian writing is the matter of 'motive'. As E.F. Scott paraphrased it: 'It was believed...that the Lord would return at any moment to bring in the Kingdom, and there would be no purpose in writing down a record of him for a future age which would never come'. I have shown elsewhere the problem with this logic. Detailed exegesis of the λόγια does show Jesus to be an eschatologist, but he also warned so constantly against the perversion of this into apocalypticism that it is difficult to imagine all of his disciples misunderstanding him so thoroughly.[26] Even with those like Paul, who clearly expected the end soon, there was no lack of motive to write down what he had seen and heard.[27] As far as my research is concerned, this 'strictly oral' argument is not sober historical evidence, but rather a polemical invention designed to win an argument. It has been thoroughly discredited, and needs to be decently buried. As we shall be seeing in detail, both oral and written transmission were active within the early Church from the beginning.

(3) The analysis of parables has been one of the chief supports for the Bultmannian skepticism. Here, perhaps more than anywhere, there is a need to re-examine the critical data if one is to take the Jesus of history seriously. There are three typical bases for the skepticism of modern critical orthodoxy:

(a) The first is the argument from 'development'. This is usually based upon the assumption that certain 'motives' operated within the early Church to change the tradition: the 'messianic secret' motive, the 'paranetic' motive, the parousia motive, the motive for generalizing the particular, and the 'Christ myth' motive.[28] The one line of argument used to support this theory of development is to show that two or more

---

26. J.A. Baird, *Rediscovering the Power of the Gospels: Jesus' Theology of the Kingdom* (Wooster, OH: Iona Press, 1982), pp. 229-37; idem, *The Justice of God in the Teaching of Jesus*, chap. 12.

27. Baird, *The Justice of God in the Teaching of Jesus*, pp. 23-24.

28. Baird, *The Justice of God in the Teaching of Jesus*, p. 26 n. 23.

similar parables were originally the same parable, with the differences being due to the activity of the early Church. Of the ten examples usually given to support this argument, there are only two that can be supported on objective grounds.[29] For the rest, one must accept a wholesale changing of detail and major imagery that is extremely difficult to justify on anything but a-priori grounds. The argument from 'development' usually runs aground on the simple suggestion that such development could have taken place within the mind of Jesus himself. As I see it, the evidence points more objectively to the fact that Jesus was fond of certain basic illustrative images and had several major items of teaching which he gave in many different ways, as does any effective itinerant teacher.[30] There is a lack of 'realism' in this development argument that suggests a modern European classroom where the lecture is read from the same manuscript each time it is given, rather than the more realistic practice of any itinerant oral teacher or preacher of varying his or her presentation for a number of reasons, like audience, circumstance, variety, or the development of the theme and imagery within the mind of the speaker. Jesus was not a twentieth-century scholar, but a first-century preacher and teacher, and we must allow him to be such if we are to understand his history accurately.

(b) A second common support for the argument from development is the axiom that a parable is a means of analogy which, according to the classical Greek usage, can have only one point. When we find any of Jesus' parables having more than one point, then the extra is the product of early Church intrusion. Adolf Jülicher made this argument popular in his book *Die Gleichnisreden Jesu* (1888). This practice of going to classical Greek literature and imposing its conventions upon the Synoptics is a relic of a bygone age when most New Testament scholars were also classics scholars, and this was a natural thing to do. In more recent years, Gospel scholarship has discovered that the Hebrew tradition is a more accurate guide to understanding Jesus.[31] In the Hebrew use of the *mashal*, one finds many different points, and common sense suggests that Jesus should be evaluated on the basis of

---

29. Baird, *The Justice of God in the Teaching of Jesus*, p. 26 n. 23.
30. [See B.F. Meyer, 'How Jesus Charged Language with Meaning: A Study in Rhetoric', in B. Chilton and C.A. Evans (eds.), *Authenticating the Words of Jesus* (NTTS, 28.2; Leiden: E.J. Brill, 1998), pp. 81-96.—Eds.]
31. Baird, *A Comparative Analysis*, pp. 24-25.

1. *Historical Realism and the Paradigm of the Word*

his own Hebrew background and orientation, not that of classical Greek usage. Enunciated in 1888, this old polemic must surely be abandoned.[32]

(c) A third argument often employed in support of a widespread 'development' is Jülicher's insistence that a teacher like Jesus who expressed himself without great deliberation would probably not have used a form as highly artificial and rhetorical as allegory. Again, this is an extension of the same problem of forcing a Greek model upon one who had essentially a Hebrew mind. The Hebrew *mashal* made abundant use of allegory.

A more flexible and exhaustive examination of this material reveals some interesting things. There are eleven parables in the Synoptics which contain explanations of the various symbols within the parables, usually at the end as a separate unit. I would call these 'semi-allegories', since every symbol within them is not interpreted. In Mark, Jesus comments on this to the effect that he explained his parables to his disciples, and left them unexplained to the others (Mk 4.10-12). Jülicher insisted that this was an unacceptable illustration of allegory, and Mark must have been mistaken. On the contrary, my study has shown that there were not just these semi-allegorical explanations, but other types as well: thematic, contextual and internal.[33] The new factor in my study was that of the audience to which these parables were given. Jülicher paid no attention to this, even though Mark gave him the clue. It was a matter of audience. If one correlates the four major audiences[34] with these four types of explanation, what appears is that among the 71 different Synoptic parables, 42 are explained in one of these four ways and 21 left unexplained. To the disciples, 30 were explained, and seven unexplained. To those who opposed him, 12 were explained, but 14 left without explanation. The evidence suggests that Jesus did both. Here is a clear pattern cutting across all the sources supporting Mark's generalization that it was Jesus' custom to explain parables to the disciples and leave them unexplained to those 'outside'. This is not a perfect pattern, but one cannot expect classroom consistency from a series of editors describing a public figure speaking in the heat of a busy ministry, whose continuous output must have been prodigious. The reporting of this pattern is too consistent and widespread across the sources to have originated with the redactors or early Church.

32. Baird, *The Justice of God in the Teaching of Jesus*, p. 26.
33. Baird, *Audience Criticism*, pp. 104-109.
34. Baird, *Audience Criticism*, p. 105.

(4) A final weakness of the Bultmann tradition that needs to be mentioned is one of the most crucial to our discussion, and indeed to the entire critical understanding of the Synoptics. This is the phenomenon which I have called 'discontinuity'.[35] There are several lines of evidence pointing to the distinct probability that a line must be drawn between the original writing of the editors and the λόγια of Jesus. If one assumes, as Bultmann did, that all of the Synoptic material is the product of the early Church in general and the redactors in particular, then there is no such distinction that can be drawn. It is all one, what Bultmann called 'a sociological product'. This has been the prevailing view among Synoptic critics for two generations. But if one is not tied to such critical orthodoxy, then a fascinating new line of evidence opens up. I find at least four types of discontinuity between the obvious editorial material and the λόγια that sets the two strains apart in a very significant way, and opens up a whole new area of possibilities:

(a) To begin with, there is a clear discontinuity between the wording of these two bodies of material.[36] This is based on the observations of patterns of word usage, a 'pattern' being defined as an occasion when a particular word in the text exhibits some distinct usage or some high degree of correlation that makes it stand out. The category of audience as a correlation factor is especially revealing. There are 309 words within the λόγια showing distinct patterns of correlation between audience and wording. These can be called 'characteristic' of the teachings of Jesus as recorded in this material.[37] In comparison, there are only 121 words characteristic of the clearly redactional material, whether narrative, connective words and phrases or editorial comment. More exactly, the λόγια group reveals 95 pattern words which occur exclusively or almost so within that stratum cutting 'horizontally' across all sources and through all Gospels. The list of 121 redactional words contains only 55 words which occur almost exclusively in the clearly editorial material, running 'vertically' down through a source, Gospel or some particular audience.[38] The fact is that the overwhelming number of verbal patterns run horizontally across the sources rather than vertically down through

---

35. Baird, *Audience Criticism*, pp. 74-89.
36. Baird, *Audience Criticism*, pp. 74-89.
37. Baird, *Audience Criticism*, p. 75.
38. Baird, *Audience Criticism*, p. 76. There is some evidence for the intrusion of the Evangelist into the wording of the λόγια. The clearest fact about these data is their scarcity. Cf. *Audience Criticism*, pp. 78-79.

any particular one. This discontinuity is further sharpened when we see the almost complete absence in the editorial list of words with Christian, theological overtones, which stands in sharp contrast with the λόγια. Most of the redactional list consists of words with the kind of rational, legalistic, political orientation peculiar to first-century Judaism like 'festival', 'unclean', 'unleavened', 'truth', 'it is permitted', 'bill of divorce', 'Caesar', 'soldier', etc.[39] The few that might be called theological, such as δοξάζω, ἀρνέομαι, αἰτέω, φοβέομαι, are used mostly in a non-religious way. If these editors, redactors and narrators had been as theologically active as many have insisted, there should be evidence of this in the words characteristic of clearly redactional material. This is simply not the case. Christian theological terms are almost exclusively limited to the λόγια.

(b) A very subtle indication of verbal and grammatical discontinuity has long been observed in the Aramaic flavor of the λόγια as contrasted with the Greek quality of the narrative and redactional material. Matthew Black's work is well known. His conclusion is to the point: 'Where any one Semitic or Aramaic construction could be observed recurring, its distribution showed that it tended to be found most frequently, and sometimes exclusively, in the words of Jesus... A sayings-tradition, cast in translation Greek and reflecting faithfully the Aramaic construction, has been utilized by the Evangelists.'[40] My own computer-assisted research turned up a curious support for Black's thesis. An exhaustive study of every word in the Synoptics in every one of its usages, cross-correlated for the λόγια and the redactional traditions, shows a regular absence of the imperfect and aorist tenses in the Greek of the λόγια, but an abundance of these as well as other tenses in the editorial material.[41] The λόγια and the clearly editorial narration are unmistakably different in wording and grammatical structure, with the former reflecting a Semitic orientation, and the latter a Greek one.

(c) A third type of discontinuity occurs in the identification of the audience to which Jesus is recorded as speaking. The Evangelists mostly describe the audiences as μαθηταί, πολύς...ἄλλων οἳ ἦσαν μετ' αὐτῶν, ὄχλος, Φαρισαῖοι, etc., with only a rare designation that has theological

39. Baird, *Audience Criticism*, p. 76.
40. M. Black, *An Aramaic Approach to the Gospels and Acts* (Oxford: Clarendon Press, 3rd edn, 1967), p. 6.
41. Baird, *Audience Criticism*, p. 80.

overtones (Lk. 7.29; 10.29-37). On the other hand, in the λόγια, Jesus is regularly recorded as describing the audience in a rich variety of terms, almost every one of which has deep theological meaning.[42] Furthermore, the editors refined this audience tradition into four clear categories, the twelve, the larger group of disciples, the small hard core group of opponents, and the larger opponent crowd, depending on their superficial relation to Jesus.[43] In contrast, Jesus in the λόγια seems to have viewed the audience theologically in basically a dual sense in terms of their relation to God: they are either sheep or goats, wheat or tares, sons of the Kingdom or sons of the evil one, etc.[44]

(d) The uniqueness of the λόγια comes to special focus when we see the theology of the λόγια differing significantly from that of the editorial tradition. For example, along with the common practice in that generation, the Evangelists pictured Satan as a personal being, who is in effect a rival God. If one contrasts the editorial stratum with that of the λόγια, it is surprising to find Jesus seemingly very reluctant to do so.[45] Instead the λόγια show him using Satan as a symbol for men in a problem-ridden and sinful condition typified by his comment to Peter: 'Get thee behind me, Satan, for you are not on the side of God but of *men*' (Mk 8.33, my emphasis).[46] There are many illustrations of this phenomenon. Another would be the contrast in the use of the phrase Kingdom of God. In the λόγια, Jesus presents the Kingdom as intensely spiritual, both personal and social, embracing both the present and the future eschaton. When the Evangelists are clearly giving their own summaries of this concept, they speak of the Kingdom in general terms, remarkably lacking in interpretation: 'He welcomed them and spoke to them of the kingdom of God' (Lk. 9.11; cf. also Lk. 8.1; Mt. 4.23; Mk 1.14-15; etc.). Every other occurrence in this editorial tradition reflects the use of the Kingdom in highly Jewish terms (Mt. 3.2; Lk. 1.33; Mk 11.10; etc.) as an imminent political (Mk 11.10) or eschatological reality (Mk 15.43; Lk. 23.42). Both of these concepts Jesus in the λόγια soundly rejected.[47] As Luke indicates in a brief editorial summary: 'They

42. Baird, *Audience Criticism*, p. 82.
43. Baird, *Audience Criticism*, pp. 32-53.
44. Baird, *Rediscovering the Power of the Gospels*, pp. 95-115.
45. Baird, *Audience Criticism*, p. 85.
46. Cf. Baird, *The Justice of God in the Teaching of Jesus*, pp. 187-92.
47. Baird, *Audience Criticism*, pp. 86-87; idem, *The Justice of God in the Teaching of Jesus*, pp. 169-70; idem, *Rediscovering the Power of the Gospels*, pp. 223-37.

supposed that the Kingdom of God was to appear immediately' (Lk. 19.11).[48]

b. *The Scientific Method and Content Analysis*
Any approach to the historical Jesus is an exercise in historiographic method. Despite one hundred years of supposed scientific biblical study, many biblical critics, with notable exceptions, are still operating in a nineteenth-century atmosphere of deductive thinking, replete with aprioris, impatient with evidence, and unwilling to be tied down to the drudgery of a truly scientific discipline.[49] As science is being defined today, there are two aspects to scientific study. The first is method, the second is what James Conant called 'policy'.[50] As is well known, the scientific method consists of empirical observation, controlled experiment, inductive reasoning, and the constant testing and retesting of theory. Conant described 'policy' as a dynamic undertaking aimed at 'lowering the degree of empiricism'.[51] This means the taking of isolated data and relating them to the whole in coherent theories to the extent that new concepts arise from experiments and observations. A truly scientific theory then represents a breakthrough into a new dimension of research.[52] This book is dedicated to that kind of research, and unless the reader understands this, he or she will not be able to follow the logic of my thesis.

More exactly, the method here used includes a variety of familiar methodologies: form criticism, redaction criticism, source criticism, genre criticism, historical criticism, structural analysis to name but a few.[53] The novel addition is that of content analysis. This can be defined as the application of the scientific method to the study of literary text. I have

---

48. See also the contrast between λόγια and redactor in the use of οὐρανός, ἄγγελος, and γενεά; cf. Baird, *Audience Criticism*, pp. 87-88.
49. Baird, *Audience Criticism*, p. 21.
50. J.B. Conant, *Modern Science and Modern Man* (New York: Doubleday, 1959).
51. Conant, *Modern Science and Modern Man*, p. 44.
52. Baird, *Comparative Analysis*, p. 113.
53. I count at least fifteen different criteria for assessing the historicity of the Synoptic Gospels. See my unpublished manuscript, 'Historical Skepticism and Gospel Renewal'; see also 'Criteria for Historical, Authenticity in Recent Scholarship: The Continuing Quest for the Historical Jesus' (unpublished manuscript).

described it at length elsewhere,[54] but perhaps a word here is in order. Content analysis 'aims at a statistical classification of a given body of content in terms of a system of categories devised to yield data relevant to that particular content'.[55] Perhaps the most unique principle is what is called 'The Manifest Content'. One begins by assuming that the text is meaningful as it is and on its own terms. The text is then allowed to describe itself, and through exhaustive empirical study hypotheses are drawn, which are then tested in every way against the various assumptions made and categories used. This is called 'the limited feedback loop'. The principle is to test the validity of one's categories and hypotheses by applying them to some data to see how well they operate in a practical situation. The 'loop' then goes from theory to application and back to theory; and if the theory produces some understandable and cogent bit of information, then it can be said to 'work', unless it is contradicted by other tests being applied. As an application of this 'loop', I have suggested at least six tests in the content analysis of the Synoptic Gospels: checking the research model, coder reliability, mathematical probability, internal compatibility, external comparison, and, finally, the principle of greatest limitation.[56] The problem of so much biblical study in what we have been calling 'Modern Critical Orthodoxy' is that when we go to the text, we have already surrounded it with so many rigid presuppositions that the text cannot speak for itself. Our results are then either skewed, or merely the confirmation of the assumptions with which we started. We have no way to test our conclusions. The phrase, 'it seems to me', is a substitute for rigorous and exhaustive documentation, and taking opinion polls is as close as we get to empirical research. 'Skewed theology' is one of the products of two generations of this only 'partially' scientific approach to the Bible. We are on the right track, but we need to go further methodologically lest we destroy the subject of our research. We have removed the 'brakes' on biblical study in our initial application of the scientific method, but have failed to apply the needed restraints that go with that method. As a result, in the last two generations, biblical theology has been out of control. What the more rigorous application of

54. See esp. Baird, *Comparative Analysis*; idem, *Rediscovering the Power of the Gospels*.
55. Baird, *Comparative Analysis*, p. 117.
56. J.A. Baird, 'Content Analysis and the Computer: A Case Study of the Scientific Method to Biblical Research', *JBL* 95 (1976), pp. 255-76, esp. pp. 273-75.

1. Historical Realism and the Paradigm of the Word

the scientific method in content analysis does is allow for genuine and controlled breakthroughs in biblical study, opening up entire new avenues of research. This is what is desperately needed in a discipline that is stalled in its own inadequate and partially documented presuppositions.

c. *The Kerygma as Method*

The strongest support for 'Modern Critical Orthodoxy' and the greatest barrier to what I am calling 'Historical Realism' is what is loosely called 'kerygmatic theology'. It is here that the influence of Wrede and Bultmann is most active, even among those who have long since given up the details of form criticism. There are many descriptions of the kerygmatic approach to the New Testament. One of the earliest and still most dominant voices is that of William Wrede.[57] The basic principle, he said, is always what the report in the Gospels says *aus ihrem eigenen Geist*, what the *Erzähler* in his own time would say to his readers. Behind this principle for Wrede lay four assumptions: (1) the priority of the *Gemeinde* in understanding the Synoptic Gospels, (2) the significant activity of the reporter in the recounting of the data, (3) the decisive difference in time between the original written report and the historical Jesus, and (4) something special that the author would convey to the reader other than mere factual knowledge. From these assumptions he then built his theory of the 'messianic secret', which he believed Mark superimposed upon the narrative. The later account of the life of Jesus is therefore not identical with the *Sache selbst*. He did feel that at times certain *stosse* break through, and there we can be sure that we stand on the ground of the *Leben Jesu selbst*. These are where there are striking *Wunderhaften*, or open contradictions in the same source, or when one report strikes against another, that is, the criterion of dissimilarity. Basically, however, there is an impenetrable barrier between the Gospels and the historical Jesus. This I shall call the 'kerygma barrier'. It is probably the most determinative set of critical assumptions operating in New Testament scholarship today, especially in Gospel studies and with regard to contemporary Christology. Jesus did not consider himself to be the Messiah, and this was a theory superimposed upon him by the early Church in general and Mark in particular. John Hick's book, *The Myth*

---

57. W. Wrede, *Das Messiasgeheimnis in den Evangelien: Zugleich ein Beitrag zum Verständnis des Markusevangeliums* (Göttingen: Vandenhoeck & Ruprecht, 1901); ET: *The Messianic Secret* (Cambridge and London: James Clarke, 1971).

of God Incarnate,[58] or some widely publicized statements in the United States coming out of the so-called 'Jesus Seminar'[59] reflect the tenacity of this thesis. As James Robinson said in his book, *A New Quest of the Historical Jesus*, even though form criticism has largely passed out of vogue, the basic critical orientation of form criticism, going back to Wellhausen and Wrede, still remains. History has survived only as kerygma, and the 'messianic secret' in Mark is thoroughly established.[60]

In my opinion, there is much truth in this kerygmatic approach to the New Testament. For example, I have long observed the influence of the redactors in the Synoptic Gospels. I have shown elsewhere how the Evangelists went out of their way to indicate the audience to which Jesus' teachings were directed. Wherever we find a collation on the basis of audience, we have testimony to the redactor's belief in the importance of this selective principle.[61] We see this in summarizing generalizations where the Evangelists clearly give their own opinions (Lk. 19.11), or theological comments like that of Mk 12.12, where he interprets a parable and affirms Jesus' audience orientation, or Luke's insertion of δοκεῖ in 8.18, or Matthew's explanation of the λόγιον in 16.12, or his interpretation of an obscure figure of speech in 12.28, or the explanation of a parable with the addition of one word, σχολάζοντα, in 12.44. The patterns of word usage peculiar to any one redactor are clear, and one must accept considerable stylistic and literary activity on their part. Their theological activity, however, would seem to be at a minimum. My own work suggests that the primary evidence of redactional activity is as transmitter, rather than as author/theologian. A defensible application of source criticism suggests that 'Where the redactor is most surely at work, he is most clearly at work, and this tends to be mostly literary, rather pedantic, and theologically innocuous'.[62]

The theological activity of the transmitting community can be more clearly observed and less dependent upon critical presuppositions in what

---

58. J. Hick, *The Myth of God Incarnate* (London: SCM Press; Philadelphia: Westminster Press, 1977).

59. See, e.g., *Time* (10 January 1994), pp. 35-36. [See the stinging criticism of the Seminar's tactics and pronouncements in L.T. Johnson, *The Real Jesus: The Misguided Quest for the Historical Jesus and the Truth of the Traditional Gospels* (San Francisco: HarperCollins, 1996).—Eds.]

60. J.M. Robinson, *A New Quest of the Historical Jesus* (SBT, 25; London: SCM Press, 1959; repr. Missoula, MT: Scholars Press, 1979).

61. Baird, *Audience Criticism*, pp. 137-38.

62. Baird, *Audience Criticism*, pp. 137-42.

1. *Historical Realism and the Paradigm of the Word* 37

I shall be calling in this book the 'shift' within the New Testament from the words 'of' Jesus to the words 'about' Jesus, and then to the words that interpret and apply those words to the needs of the early Church.[63] It is in this kind of evidence that the concept of a 'kerygma' can indeed be seen, and I shall be developing at length the evidence for this under the concept of the 'theological trajectory' of the New Testament and early Christian community.

Once one has said this, however, it is necessary to apply the same critical methodology to the work of Wrede and the kerygmatic approach to the New Testament in general, and to that of redaction criticism in particular. Despite Wrede's anticipation of such contemporary axioms as the priority of Mark, the entire kerygmatic program of New Testament research based upon him and supporting a radical historical skepticism must be called into question. Wrede himself, writing in 1901, was concerned to lead New Testament study out of the nineteenth century, to get rid of what he called 'psychology', which he would permit only between *festen Punkten*. He railed against exegetical guessing and subjectivity.[64] In many ways he was one of the fathers of modern scientific biblical study. But I think it is now clear that his was nevertheless a very primitive understanding and use of the scientific method, and some of the very warnings he leveled against psychology and the subjectivity that so plagued nineteenth-century scholarship were his own problems as well. His was still a nineteenth-century mind, relying on intuition and what I would call 'declamation exegesis'. All four of his major assumptions rely upon intuition unsupported by evidence and dogmatically proclaimed. This reminds one of Bultmann's constant use of the phrase *meines Erachtens* ('it seems to me') as a major source of what he used as evidence. In effect, Wrede was saying that the *Gemeinde* is prior to the Gospel λόγια simply because the *Gemeinde* must be prior to the Gospel λόγια. His insistence upon the significant activity of the reporter, the necessary difference in time between the original written report and the historical Jesus, or the influence of special motivation upon the redactor are all based upon what would seem to be pure assumption, or at best the work of others which he took for granted. He seems to have drunk deeply of the spirit of skepticism essential to the scientific method, which was strong in Europe at the time, but he was too far ahead of his time to have gained

63. See Chapter 10 below.
64. Wrede, *Das Messiasgeheimnis* (2nd edn), p. 3.

the disciplined tools of the scientific method which restrain the radical bounds of such skepticism and allow for creative new research.

On the basis of these assumptions, Wrede then begins his 'scientific' case for the 'messianic secret'. He first shows the 'planned' development of the 'messianic secret' in Mark, assuming that this was Mark's motive and could not have had any origin in the historical Jesus. Then he attempts to show the misconstrual and abandonment of that 'secret' in Matthew, based on the work of Ritschl and others. He then goes one step further to find therein the historical course of events themselves. Here is a sign of what he calls the inner *Geschlossenheit* of the total. This would seem to have been Wrede's big insight, and the question is, how valid is this logic and this historical 'one step' further? My own exegesis suggests that this is a case where the conclusion is merely a proof-texting of his prior assumption.[65] The research in this present book further supports the conclusion that in his thesis of the 'messianic secret' and its historical application he is guilty of circular logic, or 'begging the question'.

Even more exactly, one must criticize Wrede's method of argument within a limited range of possibilities. In the first place, he ignores many types of evidence within the text which do not suit his purpose, but which would, I shall attempt to show, challenge his conclusions. Then he sets up a very limited number of possibilities for explaining the secret sayings in Mark, and goes through them, arguing logically for the one which seems to him to be the most cogent. The fact that there are many other possible explanations does not seem to occur to him, and so he loads the case by setting up a select list of 'straw men' and proceeds to knock them down—all but the one he favors. This is good homiletics, but not good scientific method, unless there is hard evidence that goes beyond clever logic. For example, he concludes that Mark shows what he does not say, through a row of 'certain examples'. Mark himself had no awareness of the historical interpretation attributed to him that Jesus began to teach about his death only after Peter's confession. Since Mark cannot give us a clear picture of the development, and since Matthew seems to have had such an understanding (16.21), Wrede conjectures that a reviser must have given this schematic idea to Mark which then Matthew picked up and wrote into his Gospel. This is possible, but the range of other logical possibilities is almost endless:

65. See Baird, *The Justice of God in the Teaching of Jesus*, Chapter 14; *idem*, *Rediscovering the Power of the Gospel*, Chapter 9.

(1) It is possible that Wrede makes too much of this, or that Matthew does not mean this as an absolute principle but only that Jesus taught more about his death after Peter's confession.

(2) Or it is possible that Jesus did urge a certain secrecy, but not dogmatically or absolutely but with many exceptions; and for many possible reasons he kept some things which he taught only to the disciples, as it was accurately preserved in Mk 4.10-12. My audience criticism research has turned up a rather large amount of evidence that this was Jesus' common practice.[66]

(3) Or he remained silent about his impending death because of what this would (and did) do to fuel apocalyptic speculation, and he knew he would be misunderstood.

(4) Or perhaps he did not want to be associated with current pictures of the Jewish Messiah, and there is also evidence for this. Wrede's ingenious explanation of the data surrounding Jesus' reluctance to proclaim his Messiahship offends against three basic principles of the scientific method: simplicity, obviousness to many interpreters, and a comprehensive examination of all possibilities. Those mentioned above are merely a few alternatives. The method breaks down in its own subjectivity.

(5) I would add one other possibility, which comes from a more inductive and comprehensive examination of the Synoptic λόγια: Jesus talked about himself in his own terms, which were those of the Son of Man and a series of metaphors and parables which included but went far beyond the first-century concept of the Messiah. The refusal to allow Jesus to be himself, and to use his own language and thought frames, which were not limited to those of Jewish messianism, is a problem of Wrede's set of assumptions which forbade him to talk of the self-consciousness of Jesus. I cannot demonstrate this here in a short introductory chapter, but I have argued it at length elsewhere.[67]

Furthermore, there is a psychological problem involved in this method of historical motivational conjecture. To be so certain about the motives of any one editor or redactor 2000 years later, and on the basis of such a paucity of sources, is completely unrealistic, and contrary to a century of psychological research. Any psychologist knows that motivation is so complex, so hard to discover, so difficult to assess, that to use it as a

---

66. Baird, *Audience Criticism*, pp. 103-108.
67. Baird, *The Justice of God in the Teaching of Jesus*; idem, *Rediscovering the Power of the Gospels*; idem, *Comparative Analysis*.

basis for a method that is trying to be scientific is to mistake subjective conjecture for evidence, and nineteenth-century idealism for twentieth-century science. This method of historical conjecture, where Wrede attributes motives to Jesus, the editors, the redactors, the disciples, or people in Jesus' audience, and uses these conjectures as hard evidence for drawing very radical and far-reaching conclusions about Jesus' Messiahship, is epistemological nonsense, and a reversion to the worst of nineteenth-century subjectivism. To set up a series of restrictions for Jesus based on our own conjectural imagination, and then forbid him any other motivation than those we have already set up is what I call 'thesis exegesis', directing the analysis on subconscious and apriori grounds. I would guess that Wrede was so adamant about 'psychology' because unconsciously he knew that that was his greatest methodological weakness. But that is my conjecture, and not to be misconstrued as evidence. The insistence that Jesus be perfectly consistent according to Wrede's own professional scholarly reasoning is a form of exegetical tyranny that was popular in certain circles in Wrede's time, and continues today in the spirit and assumptions of what we have called 'Modern Critical Orthodoxy'. As a bottom line to this critique, I would say that there is some validity to Wrede's method, but only as a support for many other more objective methods that would chasten and correct his singular and heavily outdated one.

The principal casualty of Wrede's methodology is the loss of the self-consciousness of Jesus, which his presuppositions forbid him even to mention. In my opinion, this is the chief weakness of Wrede, and of those who have taken the kerygma method as their guide. I shall have much more to say about this as we proceed.

d. *Beyond the Kerygma Barrier*
Once one has gotten Wrede in perspective, been willing to distinguish the Synoptic λόγια from the narrative tradition, and applied a more modern scientific concern to allow the text to speak for itself, we are in a much more 'open' situation with regard to our research. We do not begin by assuming the historicity or non-historicity of the Synoptic Gospels, but rather accept the 'possibility' of one or the other at any singular point, depending on the evidence. With this kind of approach, a whole new set of possibilities for understanding the so-called kerygma emerges.

1. *Historical Realism and the Paradigm of the Word*   41

What immediately appears is the probability that the kerygma concept is too crude a method, too blunt a tool, for sorting out anything as complex as New Testament theology, and the history of its formation. It is valid as far as it goes, but it does not go nearly far enough. The most basic insight of my research along these lines is that we must distinguish between the λόγια and the narratives in the Synoptics, which suggests that the kerygma must be evaluated differently for each body of material. This keeps us from begging the messianic question, and opens the possibility that the picture of Jesus in the λόγια might be necessarily different from that in the narrative, something that can be hypothesized and tested against all the available data.

Following this possibility, in the work to come I will demonstrate the 'trajectory' of the Word, which begins with the teachings of Jesus, and then moves outward from that focus to the narratives about Jesus and the Church, the Gospel interpretation of the Word of Jesus, and the traditions that applied the Word to ethical and ecclesiastical concerns. At each level we shall see subtle changes in the theology of the Church which most probably represented not sinister alterations in theology from the Word of Jesus, but rather the natural and inevitable growth of the message of and about Jesus due to the changing needs, purposes, functions, time and circumstance of the Church. Running throughout the process for the first three centuries, one can detect a basic consensus around the Word of Jesus, along with this shift or trajectory which was the logical working out of the understanding and application of the life and teachings of Jesus. All of this could be called 'kerygma', but I shall not use the term. It is too crude, and too loaded with the negative skepticism of early twentieth-century Gospel criticism, to be an accurate category for research. Did the Church alter the life and theology of Jesus in this process? That is the subject for another book, although I shall touch upon it as we go along, and bring some evidence to focus in Chapter 11. In this study, my concern is to develop the nature and function of the Word of Jesus as it operated within the process of the formation of the New Testament and the early Christian Church.

Historical Realism as Method

As far as I can see, there is no valid barrier, whether form, kerygma, or otherwise, to presenting such a thesis and testing it against the evidence. This is basically an approach to the Synoptics, and through them to the rest of the New Testament, which takes these Gospels seriously as potential sources of genuine history. They are 'sufficiently' defensible, within all the reservations one must have in historical research, to be used as bases for the authentic thought and life of the historical Jesus. This method then opens up various creative alternatives to the rigid closed door on historicity demanded by a generation of critical hyper-skepticism. Each alternative must of course be constantly tested and re-tested against all available evidence, and using every relevant historical method. What happens with such 'cautious optimism' is that whole new dimensions of data emerge as further evidence for or against historical authenticity. I will attempt such an approach in this book. The evidence suggests that what Jesus is recorded as saying and doing in the Synoptics, with some notable exceptions, forms a realistic source of actual history that can be relied upon within the degree of authenticity common sense tells us is possible and necessary for such a highly sensitive subject 2000 years old. Mine is therefore a different research stance from what Rudolf Bultmann called his *vielgetadelde Skepsis*. Healthy and necessary skepticism, yes. But for the extremes to which some 'modern critical orthodoxy' has carried normal scientific skepticism, this I think is a healthy and defensible answer. What this historical introduction says is that many questions thought by those within the contemporary critical community to be closed, are really, from a research point of view, still wide open.[68]

The Paradigm of the Word

One more tool for the research in this book is the awareness of the part played in science, and indeed in all of knowledge, by what Ian Barbour has called 'myths, models and paradigms'.[69] Thomas Kuhn, in *The Structure of Scientific Revolutions*, has opened a new understanding for science of its dependence on models and paradigms in its use of the scientific method.[70] Kuhn maintained that the thought and action of a scientific community are dominated by its paradigms, defined as

---

68. This theme of 'Historical Realism' is developed at length in 'Historical Skepticism and Gospel Renewal'.

69. I.G. Barbour, *Myths, Models and Paradigms: A Comparative Study in Science and Religion* (New York: Harper & Row, 1976).

70. T. Kuhn, *The Structure of Scientific Revolutions* (International Encyclopedia of Unified Science, 2; Chicago: University of Chicago Press, 2nd edn, 1970).

'standard examples of scientific work which embody a set of conceptual methodological and metaphysical assumptions'. This means that observational data and criteria for assessing theories are all 'paradigm-dependent'. These are essential ingredients in any research, whose validity is then a function, among other things, of the adequacy of one's theoretical constructs. This would seem to be true for the task of historiography as well as that of physical science, especially in view of the ways in which the modern study of history is thoroughly involved with such physical sciences as archaeology, paleontology, paleo-botany, geology, and many others. In the discipline of New Testament and early Christian historiography, what is needed is an historical 'paradigm' adequate to explain the data of Christian, and especially New Testament, history.

Barbour, in his extension of Kuhn's thesis into 'the process of assessment in religion', points to three criteria for evaluating scientific theories: *simplicity* both as a practical advantage and an intellectual ideal, *coherence* with other accepted theories, and, most importantly, the number and variety of supporting *experimental observations*. What this says to the scientist as well as the philosopher and the historian is that theoretical myths, models and paradigms are inevitable and indeed necessary for the operation of human thought, just so long as we do not become too attached to them; for models and paradigms shift, and must be constantly upgraded to fit the primary data.

In the task of biblical historiography, in understanding the origin, production and interrelational development of the New Testament, we have in recent years been operating on the basis of a continuing series of theoretical constructs which have been competing for dominance: historical, source, form, audience, redaction, genre, rhetorical, structural, oral folklore, rabbinic, and more recently prophetic criticisms, to name but a few. Each has its usefulness, and its limitations, and each is based on a complicated theory structure and also certain models which are necessary for its understanding and application. If what Kuhn and others are saying is correct, irrespective of their individual adequacy, these 'myths, models, and paradigms' are not only epistemologically inevitable, but perfectly legitimate, and practically useful, providing we keep them in their place, and constantly test them with new data. The problem is that most of these theories are too limited in their conception to deal with the historical process in its entirety. What is needed is a theoretical construct of sufficient scope to include all the data. As

Barbour points out, 'a theory of great generality is usually abandoned only in favor of an alternative theory, not just because of conflicting data'.

In this study, I am offering a paradigm for Christian origins that employs many models and paradigms, but which proposes to provide a guiding principle for the interaction of the early Church's historical recollection and its theological conviction. The thesis of these pages is that in dealing with the special phenomena of Christian history, we need a different approach from secular history. *On its own terms*, we are dealing initially and primarily with the Word of God which intruded into the world of men and women in the unique words and person of Jesus Christ. Whether or not we agree that this is true is irrelevant. For accurate historiography we must allow the data of Christian history to speak for itself. It is my contention that this is what the early Christians believed, and the basis on which they lived and acted. They were first and foremost a community of faith. What this demands is a paradigm that adequately reflects this situation. The evidence of this approach points to one clear historiographic principle: in this peculiar, Christian, historical situation, theological substance precedes the formation process. The Word precedes the narrative.

The problem with much Christian historiography is that we have been doing it backwards. We have been pursuing the search by beginning with the process of New Testament 'development', and from those data going on to the emergence of the Word of theology out of the process. In the Bultmannian model, the Synoptic Gospels, and within them the words of Jesus, are the last link in the chain of linear development, what he called a 'sociological product', where the process precedes the word. In secular historiography, this may be an adequate agenda; but the Christian story is different. The evidence of the New Testament text and the literature of the early Church demand that we reverse this model and begin with the incursion of the Word into the historical process, and from that 'starting point' go on to the understanding of the development of the Gospels, the New Testament canon and the history of the Church. This I think will provide us with a paradigm which is simpler, more coherent and much more in keeping with the empirical evidence.

What has emerged from this study is a paradigm for Gospel formation active within the early Church that began with the Holy Word of Jesus, surrounded it with the Holy Narrative of his life, death and resurrection, interpreted it with the Holy Gospel, and applied it to every aspect of

Church life in a growing body of Holy Traditions. It is this paradigm which provides us with the starting point and primary control of that which produced the Synoptics, the New Testament and the early Church, and gives us a guiding principle for understanding the interaction of the early Church's historical recollections and its theological convictions.

Chapter 2

HOLY WORD:
THE STARTING POINT OF THE DEVELOPMENT

The term λόγος is the natural tool for probing beneath the gospel to lay bare the deeper substance of theological validation within the early Church. Like any large concept, there are many levels of meaning to this word and its correlates as one traces its occurrence from the Synoptic Gospels to that in the later New Testament and the writings of the Fathers. The following schema has emerged from this research, giving ten layers of meaning in the Church's use of λόγος from Jesus to Eusebius. As we list these, we note the development of this concept from plural to singular, from oral to written, from informal to formal, from a reference to the teachings of Jesus to a more comprehensive description of his life and person, and eventually to the theological understanding and ethical application of that word.

The Words of Jesus

The most primitive use of λόγος in the New Testament seems to be the reference to 'the words of Jesus', always in the plural, and possessing a directness and vividness bespeaking the belief of the author that he is dealing with the actual words of an historical person. The method of direct discourse is the most graphic display of this phenomenon. The use of λόγος occurs most often in the Synoptics, where Jesus himself is pictured referring to his teachings collectively as his 'words': 'heaven and earth will pass away, but my words will not pass away' (Mk 13.31; Mt. 24.35; Lk. 21.33; cf. Lk. 24.44). These are said by him to possess very heavy crisis significance: 'Whoever is ashamed of me and my words...of him will the Son of man be ashamed...' (Mk 8.38; Lk. 9.26). The editors also use the term in this way to summarize the sayings of Jesus as an authoritative and definable body of teaching: 'When Jesus

2. The Starting Point of the Development 47

finished these sayings (λόγους), the crowds were astonished... he taught with authority' (Mt. 7.28; cf. Mt. 19.1; 26.1; Lk. 4.22, 32; 9.28; 10.24).

Several patterns in this material are worth noting. The plural form occurs in all four sources, but most often (6 of 13) in the Markan source. Furthermore, there is an audience pattern reflected in all sources showing Jesus giving these words always to the disciples, mostly to the twelve (10 times), and never to the opponents. This concurs with the audience-critical observation, that Jesus gave his most characteristic teaching to the twelve.[1]

One further pattern is visible, and that is the way references to 'collections' of Jesus' words cluster about the twelve disciple audience: 'When Jesus had finished all these sayings (πάντας τοὺς λόγους), he said to his disciples...' (Mt. 26.1; cf. Mt. 7.28; 11.1; 13.53; 19.1; Lk. 9.28; cf. 1.4). There is a regularity and compatibility among these various subtle patterns that cuts across all the early Synoptic sources, and argues for the primitive authenticity of this use of λόγος in the plural within the Synoptics. The 'words' of Jesus, pictured as an historical person, seem to form the most basic layer of the trajectory of the word.

The same plural usage occurs in the later New Testament, where Paul in Acts introduces a new saying of Jesus in just this fashion: 'remembering the words of the Lord Jesus, how he said...' (Acts 20.35). There is an interesting indication of a later development in 1 Tim. 6.3, where the author seems to need to distinguish between what he calls 'the sound words of our Lord Jesus Christ', and 'the διδασκαλία that accords with godliness', a seeming reference to the apostolic 'tradition', both of them being standards for what one should teach. Then in 2 Tim. 1.13, we see an even further development as the author summarizes Paul's gospel in terms of 'the pattern of sound words (ὑγιαινόντων λόγων) which you heard from me'; and we are dealing with the words of Jesus in the larger context of the εὐαγγέλιον. This further underscores the more primitive character of this phenomenon in the Synoptic Gospels.[2]

---

1. J.A. Baird, *Audience Criticism and the Historical Jesus* (Philadelphia: Westminster Press, 1969), p. 126.
2. H. Riesenfeld points to the Synoptic λόγοι as 'Holy Words' with Old Testament authority. He compares them to the words of the rabbis in the Mishnah, and the prophetic discourses in the Old Testament. My work I think supports this insight, but I would say that the λόγοι are more exactly comparable to the God sayings in the Old Testament and to Torah, that is, to 'written' rather than to 'oral'

The Word of Jesus

The next stage in the developing use of λόγος comes where the term is singular only, and refers to the 'word' of Jesus as something with special redeeming significance. The λόγος continues to have the sense of a collective reference to the actual words of Jesus, but the use of the singular gives them a more formal coherence. It would seem by the very logic and nature of the difference that 'word of Jesus', in this more formal sense, is later than the more vividly historical 'words of Jesus'. The Jews were 'astonished at his teaching for his word (λόγος) was with authority' (Lk. 4.32), 'Peter remembered the word of the Lord' (Lk. 22.61), 'a prophet mighty in deed and word' (Lk. 24.19; cf. 7.7; 10.39; etc.).

Several patterns are visible. On one occasion, this more formal sense is placed on the lips of Jesus: 'When anyone hears the word of the kingdom' (Mt. 13.19). All other references, however, are editorial, which would seem to argue for its later character. If one pays close attention to the correlation of source and the various λόγος categories, a subtle pattern is observable in the shift from 'words of Jesus', strongest in Mark (6 Mark, 0 Q, 2 M, 3 L) to 'word of Jesus', predominant in Luke (1 Mark, 3L). This same progression can be detected in the movement within the comparative sources, where 'the word' in Mk 4.14 becomes 'the word of the kingdom' in Mt. 13.19 and then 'the word of God' in Lk. 8.11, seemingly a later rendering. Mark, Matthew, Luke would appear to be the chronological progression at this point. What seems to be emerging here is a development within the mind of Jesus or the early community, from 'words of Jesus' to 'word of Jesus', but referring in either case to that message, given by Jesus primarily to the twelve and then to the larger group of disciples.

This early usage occurs at least once in Paul where 'the word of the Lord' in 1 Thess. 4.15 could be a paraphrase of Jesus' teaching about the eschaton (Mt. 24.31; cf. 1 Cor. 15.51; 1 Thess. 1.8). Paul's references to the teachings of Jesus are so intertwined with his concept of 'gospel', however, that it is difficult to separate them.

There is a much more certain use of λόγος in this way in the Johannine material, for example in 1 Jn 2.3-5, where the 'commandments' of Jesus are immediately characterized as 'his word'. This is not

---

tradition. H. Riesenfeld, *The Gospel Tradition* (Philadelphia: Fortress Press, 1970), pp. 17-19.

2. The Starting Point of the Development

unlike the general practice of John in this theological Gospel where the λόγος continues its formal reference to the teaching of Jesus as a body of material with special significance. John summarizes Jesus' experience in Samaria by saying 'many...believed because of his word' (4.41), and then later in the same chapter points to the official in Capernaum whose son was healed because 'the man believed the word that Jesus spoke to him' (4.50); 'if we say we have not sinned...his word is not in us' (1 Jn 1.10). Mostly, however, John places this particular usage of λόγος into the words of Jesus, for whom λόγος is the epitome of his entire teaching: 'If you continue in my word, you are truly my disciples' (8.31); 'you are already made clean by the word which I have spoken to you' (15.3); 'remember the word that I said to you' (15.20; cf. 15.25; 8.37; Rev. 3.10); 'he who hears my word and believes him who sent me, has eternal life' (5.24). The 'words' of Jesus have become the 'word' of Jesus, and the process of theological formalization has begun. The important thing to note is that whether 'words' or 'word', the teachings of Jesus possess a centrality and sanctity that is a reflection of their intrinsic power and effectiveness for salvation.

At a slightly more sophisticated level, λόγος becomes formally parallel to Scripture without necessarily reflecting written documents. John places the λόγος of Jesus on a par with the Old Testament: 'they believed the scripture and the word which Jesus had spoken' (2.22). He also puts this same parallel in the words of Jesus: 'you cannot bear to hear my word... he who is of God hears the words of God' (8.43, 47); 'the word that I have spoken will be his judge on the last day...' (12.48; cf. 14.23-24).

The Word

Thus far, the orientation of λόγος has been toward the person of Jesus: 'the word of Jesus... his word... the word which Jesus had spoken'. But now we must recognize another usage of λόγος in the singular where the orientation shifts from the person to the Word. The word of Jesus has become simply 'the Word'. Mark summarizes Jesus' teachings in this fashion: 'with many such parables he spoke the word (τὸν λόγον) to them' (4.33). Jesus identifies the seed in the parable of the sower as 'the word' (Mk 4.14, 16, 18, 19, 20). The disciples in Luke's resurrection account characterize Jesus as 'a prophet mighty in deed and word' (Lk. 24.19); and at this point we see his word taking on the character of the

Kingdom and the power of God, capable of generating the new life of the Kingdom, and healing the servant of the centurion: 'Say the word, and let my servant be healed' (Lk. 7.7). This is the apex of the formalized and sanctified expression of λόγος in Jesus' teaching and the Synoptic narration, and we are on the threshold of the Church's theology of the word, where the person of Jesus, the content of his teaching and the power of God are all united in one concept called gospel.

The Word about Jesus: The Gospel

By far the most abundant use of λόγος in the New Testament is where the Church describes itself rightly handling 'the word of truth' (τὸν λόγον τῆς ἀληθείας; 2 Tim. 2.15; cf. 1 Tim. 6.5; 2 Cor. 6.7). At this point, λόγος takes on most of the rich quality of the various other synonyms for gospel, like εὐαγγέλιον, ἀλήθεια, διδαχή, σοφία, with one special emphasis: the immediate, intimate and substantive relation between what the Church was proclaiming about Jesus, and what he had proclaimed about himself and the Kingdom of God, that is, between the Gospel and the Holy Word. The use of λόγος in this way underscores the teachings of Jesus as the basis of the gospel.

As one might expect, this usage never occurs in the Synoptics except for two late summary statements describing the activity of the disciples as 'ministers of the word' (Lk. 1.2) and evangelists for whom the word they were proclaiming called gospel would be confirmed 'by the signs that attended it' (Mk 16.20). It is also instructive to note that this usage of λόγος is absent from the Gospel of John, although it does occur in the later Johannine epistles as 'the word of life' (1 Jn 1.1), or 'the word of truth' (1 Jn 1.10). This is an application of λόγος arising out of the reflection of the Church upon the life and teachings of Jesus, and describes the major task of those going beyond the primitive presentation found in the Synoptics.

In the Acts of the Apostles, on the other hand, this meaning for λόγος occurs 23 times, and two things are apparent: the transition to gospel is all but complete; nevertheless, the 'words of Jesus', 'the word' as the message of Jesus, stands immediately behind the λόγος as gospel.[3] This

---

3. Acts 8.25; 10.36; etc. The 'word of God' and 'the word of the Lord', referring to Jesus, are often hard to distinguish (Acts 13.10, 48; 15.36). Regularly (22 times) κύριος occurs with reference to an authoritative body of Christian teaching that

2. The Starting Point of the Development 51

is what was being proclaimed by the disciples as they went about the ministry of the word (6.2, 4), 'the Holy Spirit fell on all who heard the word' (Acts 10.44; cf. 11.19; 17.11). They called the gospel 'the word' (8.4; 10.36; 11.19; etc.), 'the word of God' (4.29; 6.2, 4; 11.1; etc.), 'the word of the gospel' (5.7), all referring to the Holy Word of Jesus as expressed in the κήρυγμα.

John Meagher calls Acts 19.36-37 the 'Little Gospel' because it so well summarizes what was being preached by the apostles, what he calls the 'quintessential Gospel'.[4] This is described as 'the word... good news of peace by Jesus Christ... proclaimed throughout all Judea', and has a broad range of meanings, including Jesus' baptism, his healing ministry, all that he did in Galilee and Jerusalem, his teaching, his death and resurrection, the Old Testament witness to his advent, and forgiveness through faith in him (cf. Acts 10.36-37, 44; 11.1, 19). The emphasis here is typical of the rest of the New Testament description of the gospel: on the word proclaimed and on his death and resurrection.

In his farewell address to the Ephesian elders, Paul summarizes his message as one of 'repentance to God', of 'faith in our Lord Jesus Christ' (Acts 20.21), a ministry which he 'received from the Lord Jesus, to testify to the gospel of the grace of God' (v. 24); 'preaching the kingdom' (v. 25); 'the word of his grace' (v. 32); 'remembering the words of the Lord Jesus'. Here the 'word of God's grace' and 'the words of Jesus' form the two poles of Paul's message. At this stage, the word of Jesus about the Kingdom, and the word of the Kingdom about Jesus as understood by the Church are seen to interpenetrate, and we are observing the genesis of a very natural and inevitable transition from the 'words... word... WORD' of Jesus (as in the first three sections above) to the 'word about Jesus' (as in the present section). The shift is so subtle as to be almost indiscernible. Acts no doubt came from the third quarter of the first century; but what I have described above would seem to represent a primitive transition from the earliest Synoptic situation, which testifies to the earliness of Luke's material.

'Let him who is taught the word share all good things with him who teaches' (Gal. 6.6). With the epistles of Paul, the λόγος becomes another

---

is to be equated either with the teachings of Jesus or with the εὐαγγέλιον in the larger sense (Acts 12.24; 13.12; 28.31; 1 Cor. 14.37; Eph. 4.17; Col. 3.16; 1 Thess. 1.8; etc.).

4. J.C. Meagher, *The Way of the Word: The Beginning and the Establishing of Christian Understanding* (New York: Seabury Press, 1975).

of the main terms he uses to describe the gospel. It is not his most frequent,[5] but it is one of the best to show the connection of his thought with the more primitive levels of the Christian message. One is struck immediately with the variety of ways Paul describes the λόγος, and also his characteristic interweaving of parallel terms. This is the 'word of God' (Rom. 9.6), the 'word of the cross' (1 Cor. 1.18), 'the testimony to Christ',[6] the 'word of wisdom', the 'word of knowledge'[7] (1 Cor. 12.8), a 'command of the Lord' (1 Cor. 14.37), the 'gospel' (1 Cor. 15.1), 'the gospel of the glory of Christ' (2 Cor. 4.4), 'the word of reconciliation',[8] 'the word of truth' (Eph. 1.13; Col. 1.5), 'the mystery of the gospel' (Eph 6.19), 'the word of life' (Phil. 2.16), 'the mystery hidden for ages' (Col. 1.25), 'the word of Christ' (Col. 3.16), 'the mystery of Christ' (Col. 4.3).

For Paul, the λόγος is the content of what is being taught and preached, and this is an interplay between the theological and the spiritual which represents one of the chief characteristics of his thinking about the gospel. This dialectic comes to special focus in 1 Cor. 1.5–2.16 where the intellectual-theological word of the cross which Paul is preaching, the 'foolishness', the 'secret and hidden wisdom of God', on the one hand, is counterbalanced on the other with the word which is itself the spirit and power of God. At this point Paul is stressing with this Greek audience that the 'wisdom of God', which he is proclaiming in Christ, is different from the 'lofty words of wisdom' more common to the Greek understanding of the term, in that not only is it a rational word about God in Jesus Christ, but it is also the incursion into their midst of the very power of God himself. Here is that deeper dimension of 'wisdom', 'mystery', and 'knowledge' which runs throughout Paul's thought as it does through the Hebrew understanding of 'faith' in

---

5. Paul's use of the nine most frequent synonyms is as follows: λόγος, 35; ἀλήθεια, 28; πίστις, 100; μυστήριον, 13; κηρύσσω, 17; διδαχή, 4; γνῶσις, 18; σοφία, 11; εὐαγγέλιον, 52.

6. 1 Cor 1.5: ἐν παντὶ λόγῳ. The translation, 'with all speech', in the RSV is misleading.

7. RSV obscures the meaning of λόγος by translating it as 'terms'. I see no sharp distinction between λόγος σοφίας and λόγος γνώσεως. There seems to be some distinction in Paul's mind, but it is too subtle, and is not consistently used. The words are used interchangeably. They both refer to the intellectual and spiritual content of faith, but with a slight stress on the intellectual.

8. 2 Cor. 5.19. Again RSV obscures the meaning by translating λόγος as 'ministry'.

2. The Starting Point of the Development

general,⁹ summarized in Paul's contention that 'we have the mind of Christ' (2.16). In this case, Paul is referring to the entire argument from 1.5 to 2.16, which is the 'gospel of Christ', including the teachings of Jesus and the teaching of the Church about Jesus, as well as the experience of the 'glory of God', his presence and power, in the 'face of Christ' (2 Cor. 4.6).¹⁰

At this point Paul represents the original transition of the gospel from the Hebrew-oriented Palestinian faith to a Greek-oriented Hellenistic faith, from πίστις as *emunah* to πίστις as both a trusting experience of the Holy Spirit and a believing knowledge about the justice of God in Jesus Christ. We must never sell Paul short on either side of this gospel equation. One can perhaps see a subtle distinction between the λόγος as primarily the theological content of what was taught, and σοφία as the rational-existential-spiritual 'condition' of those who have the word; but ultimately such subtleties fade away in the powerful, driving comprehensiveness of Paul's gospel which was both theological and spiritual, but where the primary emphasis was rational and theological.

Behind the λόγος always lay the teachings of Jesus. The *Grundlage* behind Paul's gospel was the 'words of Jesus... the word of Jesus... the Word'. Whatever else it meant with regard to the Christ experience, 'the mind of Christ' always had behind it the actual mind of Jesus and his teaching about the Kingdom of God. It is true, however, that in his use of λόγος, the more vividly historical reflections of Jesus' actual words are less strong than in Acts, remaining more as an echo and an authoritative substratum. Paul's λόγος of the Gospel stresses more the 'Gospel of the cross' than 'the Gospel of the Kingdom', more the resurrection than the life of Jesus, more the faith of the Church than the nature and justice of God; and there is some justification for asking again the question as to whether or not Paul has radically shifted the grounds of the gospel. At this point I think it is fair to say that for Paul this shift was more a matter of emphasis, orientation and vocabulary than it was of substance. Paul was commenting on the historical Jesus, his life and teachings, from the other side of the cross and resurrection, and also in

---

9. See M. Buber, *Two Types of Faith* (London: Macmillan, 1951; repr. New York: Harper & Brothers, 1961).

10. Meagher (*The Way of the Word*, p. 21) expresses this very well when he says that to have the Spirit is to have the mind of Christ. The problem is that he does not seem to see this other more rational-theological side to Paul's understanding of the 'mind of Christ'.

the light of his own dramatic spiritual experience. He was writing for the Hellenistic world, and for a developing Church in which matters of faith and ethics were paramount. In the light of all this, his particular theological commentary seems quite natural and probably inevitable. Whether his influence caused the Church to veer from the original intention of Jesus is an extremely important matter, but beyond the scope of this study.

The Pastoral Epistles continue this same emphasis on what the author of 1–2 Timothy calls 'the word of truth' (2 Tim. 2.15), 'the word of God' (Tit. 1.3; 1 Tim. 4.5), or the word that is 'faithful and worthy of full acceptance' (πιστὸς ὁ λόγος; 1 Tim. 1.15). We find here the same linkage of λόγος with ἀλήθεια, πίστις, and εὐαγγέλιον that one finds in the rest of the Pauline epistles describing the gospel of salvation in Christ (1 Tim. 1.15). This is the manifestation of the grace of God, abolishing death and bringing immortality to light (2 Tim. 1.8-14), and is based on the 'sound words of our Lord Jesus Christ' (1 Tim. 6.3; cf. 4.6; 2 Tim. 1.13). Such is the theological substance of the preaching of those 'who labor in the word' (1 Tim. 5.17), and it is distinguished from the 'διδασκαλία that accords with godliness' (1 Tim. 6.3), which is the ethical application of this word. The point to note here is the strength of the 'words of Jesus' lying behind the λόγος within the Pastoral Epistles,[11] and the crucial distinction being made between the gospel as theological substance, and the διδασκαλία as its ethical extension.

The rest of the New Testament continues this pattern, with a strong use of λόγος for gospel in James, 1 Peter, 1 John and Revelation. It is 'the word' (Jas 1.22; cf. 1 Jn 1.10) which is able to save their souls, 'the word of life' (1 Jn 1.1), the 'word of God' (1 Pet. 1.23; Rev. 1.9; 20.4), and is closely connected with the 'commandments', 'the word' and 'the name' of Jesus (1 Jn 1.10; Rev. 1.9; 3.10).

In summary, the patterns are clear. With varying emphases and in varying degrees, but using a surprising number of the same terms, all of the major segments of the New Testament present the λόγος as a coherent body of teaching, containing the substance of the Church's theology about Jesus and the Kingdom, distinct from the παράδοσις application of this gospel, and thoroughly and immediately grounded on the primitive teachings of Jesus. The λόγος is parallel then to the many other terms used in the New Testament to describe the gospel, but with

---

11. Cf. 1 Tim. 1.15, which parallels Lk. 5.32; Jn 12.47; cf. also 1 Tim. 4.6; 6.3.

this special characteristic: λόγος serves to underscore the place of the teachings of Jesus as the immediate foundation of that Gospel.

The Word is Jesus: The Holy One

Within this active Christian exploration of the λόγος concept, we must also understand the identification of Jesus as 'the word made flesh' (Jn 1.14), 'the word of life' (1 Jn 1.1), 'the word of God' (Rev. 19.13), deriving as much from Christian usage as it did from that of Hellenistic writers, Philo or the Old Testament. There is a thoroughgoing λόγος doctrine in the New Testament aside from John, who seems to have exploited what was already well developed within the Christian community, and brought it to focus in the service of the developing Christology of the Church. We can see this especially well in the use of the term ἅγιος. John calls him 'the Holy One of God' (6.69; cf. 1 Jn 2.20), and this is echoed in Acts, where Peter condemns the people for denying 'the Holy and Righteous One' (3.14). It is this belief which gave the strong sense of importance to those days, the awareness of being involved in the very καιρός of God;[12] and it is this awareness which lifted his words out of obscurity into the level of 'the Holy Word'. As Hennecke put it, 'these words are holy not because they are written in a holy book, perhaps in a proto Gospel, but because they are words of Jesus, the risen one, and consequently words of God'.[13]

The Word is Spirit and Power

The spiritual connotation of these many gospel terms emerges again and again in this study, and the same is true with the Church's use of λόγος.

---

12. Meagher (*The Way of the Word*, p. 191) calls this 'the Principle of kairological coherence'; cf. J.A. Baird, *The Justice of God in the Teaching of Jesus* (London: SCM Press; Philadelphia: Westminster Press, 1963), p. 97.

13. E. Hennecke and W. Schneemelcher (eds.), *New Testament Apocrypha* (2 vols.; Philadelphia: Westminster Press, 1963), I, p. 29. Meagher (*The Way of the Word*, pp. 192-93) puts it well: 'Jesus as the One is the fundamental conditioning determinant of kairology, and is the common denominator of early Christian kerygma. The kerygma was derived by the application of the early disciples' sense of coherence and appropriateness to the conviction that Jesus is the one within the framework of their recognition and recollections on the one hand, and the resources of pre-Christian kairology on the other. The key facts and interpretations thus discerned become the core of the Gospel.'

Paul links this term with many others like 'mystery', 'wisdom' and 'faith'; and when placed in the total context of his teaching, there is a dialectic in his thought which brings the theological into constant dialogue with the spiritual. The interesting thing is that in the direct use of the term λόγος throughout the New Testament, the theological so far outweighs the spiritual that I find only eight such references, of which four are in the Gospel of John. A subtle indication of John's purpose in this Gospel emerges where the word of Jesus is closely related to the word of God (17.14), the will of God (17.6), the word which ultimately is God himself in the beginning (1.1-2). This word then becomes the presence of the Spirit and power and love of God abiding within them (5.38). To believe in this word is a source of eternal life (5.24), and this indwelling word becomes a morally cleansing power (15.3). To keep the word is to love Jesus and to be in communion with him and the Father (14.23, 24).

The spiritualization of the λόγος is certainly in keeping with the Old Testament and the teachings of Jesus. Its adoption by Paul (1 Cor. 1.4–2.16) and the apostles (Acts 11.1) as a way of bringing together the kerygma as a word about Jesus, and the power of God, the presence of the risen Christ 'by which you will be saved' (Acts 11.1, 14). This reflects the developing awareness within the Church that somehow the word about God and the word who is God are inseparable. Out of this awareness was emerging, inevitably and necessarily, the doctrines of the incarnation, of sanctification and of scriptural revelation, where the word of God was seen as 'living and active, sharper than any two-edged sword' (Heb. 4.12).

The Word 'Applies' Jesus: Tradition

The ethical use of λόγος is late, and found almost exclusively in the Pastoral Epistles. The phrase πιστὸς ὁ λόγος occurs six times in these epistles to refer to the application of the gospel and the teachings of Jesus to the practical and liturgical life of the Church toward the end of the first century. The one occurrence in James vividly makes the point that they are to be 'doers of the word' (1.22), not merely hearers. A second adaptation within this developing παράδοσις is ὑγιαινόντων λόγων, referring to the 'pattern of the sound words' of ethical instruction which the author of 2 Timothy is distinguishing from the 'gospel' and the 'truth' in that passage (2 Tim. 1.11, 13, 14; cf. 1 Tim.

2. The Starting Point of the Development

6.3). A third phrase often translated 'sound doctrine', ὑγιαινούσῃ διδασκαλίᾳ (1 Tim. 1.10; cf. 2 Tim. 4.3; Tit. 1.9; 2.1) makes the same point, where the 'traditions' of the Church, called παράδοσις, διδασκαλία, πιστὸς ὁ λόγος, that is, the liturgical and ethical applications of the teachings of Jesus, existed alongside their more theological extension in the 'gospel'.

The Ministry of the Word

In Acts we are given a graphic picture of the beginnings of the structure and mission of the Church. One of the first things that emerged according to Luke was a distinction between the ministry of service and 'the ministry of the word' (διακονία τοῦ λόγου), which in this case meant 'preaching the word of God' (6.1-4). This office, which Paul called a 'gift' of the Spirit (1 Cor. 12.4, 8), seems to have been concerned with the special preservation and proclamation of the life and teachings of Jesus (Lk. 1.1-4), then with the gospel, what Paul called 'the word of wisdom' and 'the word of knowledge' (1 Cor. 12.8), and eventually with the ethical and liturgical traditions. As the author of 1 Timothy put it, ἐν λόγῳ καὶ διδασκαλίᾳ (1 Tim. 5.17).

It was originally an oral ministry, 'preaching the word of God' (Acts 6.2), with the apostles acting as models, but with many others taking part. The term διακονία was regularly used to designate this office. Very quickly, however, it involved the writing down of the 'memoirs' of Jesus; and the word ὑπηρέτης describes this more specialized ministry. The important observation here is that these indications of special 'ministries of the word', whether oral or written, whether apostle, prophet or Christian scribe, all point to the particular concern of the Church to preserve and proclaim this word with fidelity and care. As Luke put it, 'having followed all things closely...that you may know the truth...' (Lk. 1.1-4). For the author of 2 Timothy it meant 'rightly handling the word of truth' (2 Tim. 2.15).

The Word of God

At times the early Church used λόγος to refer to the word of God, either in the Old Testament or in the life of the community. For John, this was both the 'word written in their law' (15.25; cf. 10.35) and the will of God operating in the lives of the early Christians (17.6, 17). Jesus' comment that he had 'given them thy word' (17.14) established a close relationship between the Old Testament, the living word of God and his own teachings, which of course is tied in with John's overriding christological purpose. Paul makes the same threefold use of λόγος, identifying the 'word of God' (Rom. 9.6) as God's 'purpose of election' which he finds in the 'promise' of Scripture (v. 9), a reference to Gen. 18.10. Later in Romans he sums up the commandments of God in 'this word' (λόγος), 'you shall love your neighbor as yourself', which may well be a reference to both the Old Testament and the teachings of Jesus (Rom. 13.9; cf. Gal. 5.14).

It is in the later Epistles that λόγος occurs most often in this fashion, to refer to either the 'prophetic word' of Scripture (2 Pet. 1.19; cf. 1 Jn 2.7), or the creative act of God (2 Pet. 3.5, 7), the word which 'abides in you' (1 Jn 2.14). Most characteristically, this λόγος for the Christian community was described by the author of Hebrews as the 'first principles' of God's 'word of righteousness' (5.13), 'the elementary doctrine of Christ' (τὸν τῆς ἀρχῆς τοῦ Χριστοῦ λόγον; 6.1) which Christians are to leave behind if they would go on to maturity. The point is to bring 'just' men and women who have an Old Testament faith to a new 'perfection' in the Christian gospel (12.23) by seeing the presence of Christ in the Old Testament, and then going on to the understanding of Christ as the fulfillment of the law (2.10; 9.11; 10.11).

It is instructive to see the many times in which the Christian gospel is simply called 'the word of God' (Heb. 13.7). For the early Church, the continuity within God's creative word, seen in creation, contained in Scripture, incarnate in the life of Jesus and revealed in his words, is one of the most important aspects of the gospel. The prologues to the Gospel of John, the epistles to the Colossians and the Hebrews, and the Old Testament orientation of Synoptic infancy narratives, all make this clear for the early Church.

A study of κύριος in the New Testament reveals the same pattern. Regularly (22 times) 'the word of the Lord' occurs with reference to an authoritative body of Christian teaching that is to be equated either with the teachings of Jesus, or with the Gospel. Although in Paul's letters κύριος refers mostly to Jesus, throughout the New Testament the term refers in about equal measure to Jesus or to God, and at times it is difficult or even unnecessary to distinguish.

2. The Starting Point of the Development 59

The Word in Written Form

The latest form in which λόγος appears is as part of written Christian γραφή. The λόγος itself was the oral dimension of the earliest Christian substance, but on a very few occasions we find it used to describe the content of written material. Paul, in what is the earliest such reference, warns against any one who 'refuses to obey what we say (τῷ λόγῳ) in this letter' (2 Thess. 3.14). He repeats this same idea later when he defends himself to the Corinthians by insisting that 'what we say by letter (τῷ λόγῳ δι' ἐπιστολῶν) when absent, we do when present' (2 Cor. 10.11). It was γραφή, however, which was used in the New Testament for the written vehicle, and this was carefully distinguished from the oral form of the Jesus material. Later, for example, with Polycarp, we begin to see λόγος as written 'oracles (τὰ λόγια) of the Lord', but these he distinguishes clearly from the teachings of Jesus, 'the word which was delivered to us from the beginning' (Polycarp, *Phil.* 7.1-2). Theophilus of Antioch identifies written γραφή with 'the divine word', but here he is talking about Pauline letters (1 Tim. 2.2; Rom. 13.7), and distinguishes these from the teachings of Jesus, which he calls 'the voice of the gospel'. The lateness and scarcity of these references would serve to underscore the primarily oral conception of the λόγος within the early Church.

The Holy Word in the Apostolic and Ante-Nicene Fathers

In the first century the teachings of Jesus dominated the minds of the Fathers, and the more informal references to his 'words' predominate. Clement of Rome makes a very interesting distinction between the 'holy word' (ἅγιος λόγος), referring to the Old Testament and the 'holy words' of Jesus: 'let us...walk in obedience to his hallowed words (ἁγιοπρεπέσι λόγοις)... paying close attention to his words, you stored them up carefully in your heart... remembering the words of the Lord Jesus...' (*1 Clem.* 13.1-4; 2.1).

Papias is aware of 'books' describing 'what Andrew or Peter or Philip or Thomas or James or John or Matthew or any other of the Lord's disciples had said...' But he is more interested in 'the word of a living and abiding voice', that is, the oral stream which carries the voice of Jesus. It would seem that this is what he is examining in the 'five treatises' which Eusebius describes as 'interpretation of the oracles of the Lord', λόγιον κυριακόν, using the term τὸ λόγιον, generally reserved for the God sayings of the Old Testament, or for the teachings of Jesus in the somewhat stylized sense of a body of written material with a peculiar sanctity (*Hist. Eccl.* 3.39.1).

Ignatius contains many echoes of Paul and the Gospels, and when he quotes Jesus it is seemingly done from memory. He makes no reference to the λόγοι of Jesus, preferring to call them 'commandments', or 'charters', ἀρχεῖα (*Phld.* 8.2). One thing is certain: for Ignatius the teachings of Jesus, taken singly, or as a definable body, are absolutely central to the Christian faith: 'Do nothing...but after the teaching of Christ (χριστομαθίαν)' (*Phld.* 8.2).

Diognetus, writing perhaps in the early second century of what had been handed down (παραδοθέντα) to those who were becoming 'disciples of the truth', describes himself as 'a disciple of the apostles', a 'lover of the word'. He is learning plainly 'the things which have been clearly shown by the word to the disciples, to whom the word appeared' (*Diogn.* 11.1). His reference to 'the faith of the Gospels' in this same context, and his quotation or allusion to various portions of the New Testament, show that he possesses written portions of the New Testament as the basis for this 'word' he is learning. One finds the same sense of the teachings of Jesus as the source of Christian doctrine in the *Didache*, but there ἐντολή or διδαχή is used instead of λόγος in its more formal sense of 'gospel'. This is also the case with *2 Clement*: 'when we have gone home, let us remember the commandments of the Lord' (*2 Clem.* 17.3); and with Aristides of Athens, 'they have the commandments of the Lord Jesus himself graven upon their hearts' (*Apology*). The author of the *Shepherd of Hermas* refers to the apostolic preaching and teaching in more formal terms as 'the word of the Lord' (*Sim.* 9.25.2). Justin Martyr at this time points to the miracles and passion of Jesus as proof that he is the New Covenant predicted by Jeremiah; but it is the teachings of Jesus that are central to his thinking: 'I would wish that all...do not keep themselves away from the words (λόγους) of the savior' (*1 Apol.* 8). These are 'the teachings which have come from Christ himself' (*1 Apol.* 14). Polycarp in his *Letter to the Philippians* illustrates two levels of meaning within the same paragraph: 'whoever perverts the oracles (λόγια) of the Lord... let us turn back to the word (λόγον) which was delivered to us in the beginning...' (7.1-2). In all these second-century Fathers, one finds the constant theme that the teachings of Jesus, in both written and oral form, are the center of

2. The Starting Point of the Development

the Christian faith. The concept of this λόγος occurs in its more formal sense as the 'word' of the gospel, but it is evident that the less formal reference to the 'words' of Jesus is more prominent than in the third century.

In the latter half of the second century, the *Martyrdom of Polycarp* gives us a clear indication of λόγος in its more formal sense: 'Walk according to the gospel, in the word of Jesus Christ' (22.1). Theophilus of Antioch reflects the later identification of λόγος with written γραφή when he quotes four sections from Matthew (5.28; 5.32; 5.44, 46; 6.3) as 'the voice of the gospel', and then 1 Tim. 2.2 and Rom. 13.7-8 as 'the divine word'. Clement of Alexandria reveals in his writings the sense of a constant, intimate, running consciousness of the teachings of Jesus as the heart of his theology. These he describes as 'the laws of the word' (*Instructor* 3), the 'unwritten rendering of the written' Scripture which is 'inscribed' on men's hearts (*Strom.* 6.15). These are the 'divine words', the source of his teaching, the heart of 'the tradition of the Lord' (*Strom.* 7.16-17). He is also able to refer to Jesus as 'the word of God... the instructor' (*Instructor* 1–2). Irenaeus also places the 'words of the savior' in the center of Scripture, what he calls 'the gospel of God' (*Adv. Haer.* 3.1; 3.2.2), and then goes on to identify the parables as the center of Jesus' teaching (*Adv. Haer.* 2.10.2; 3.2.2).

Moving out to the first half of the third century, we find the more formal conception of the word in 'the rule of faith' referred to in Novation (*On the Trinity* 16) as the extension and formalization of the gospel, or what Tertullian calls the 'sacred deposit' in the apostolic churches (*Against Marcion* 4.4). There is a more primitive use in Origen (*Contra Celsus* 5.63), who refers to those 'who are followers of the word of Jesus', and then an even more primitive reference to the 'words' of Jesus in Cyprian who talks about the 'evangelical precepts' as 'nothing else than divine teachings' (λόγοις), referring to the teachings of Jesus (*Treatise* 4).

In the fourth century, Eusebius is primarily concerned to tell the story of what he called 'the ambassadors of the word' (*Hist. Eccl.* 1.1). This Jesus material came to him through the 'succession of the apostles' in two forms: 'by speech or pen'. He is much involved with the written gospel, 'the divine books' (*Hist. Eccl.* 7.19.1), but seems especially interested in the oral stream, what Papias called 'the living and abiding voice' (*Hist. Eccl.* 3.39.4). This 'divine word', oral and then written, was for Eusebius a body of sacred material which had been 'Holy

Word' from the early days of Clement of Rome (*Hist. Eccl.* 3.34) and Peter, whose 'teaching given them verbally' was written down by Mark at the urging of 'Peter's followers' (*Hist. Eccl.* 2.15.1). The Church then had only one teaching from the beginning as far as Eusebius was concerned, and this was the 'divine word' (τοῦ θείου λόγον; *Hist. Eccl.* 3.37.3), 'the sound standard of the preaching of salvation' (*Hist. Eccl.* 3.32.7). This was the heart and substance of such schools as that of Pantaenus, dedicated to the διδασκαλείου τῶν ἱερῶν λόγων (*Hist. Eccl.* 5.10.1). It was Eusebius's view that the Church from earliest times had been concerned to preserve true and accurate accounts of the life and teachings of Jesus. We can detect the lateness of this highly 'orthodox' history by the fact that all of the uses of λόγος, with the exception of one quotation from Papias (*Hist. Eccl.* 3.39.14), refer to the more formal 'divine logos' as a synonym for gospel, the 'saving seeds of the Kingdom', 'broadcast through the whole world' (*Hist. Eccl.* 3.37.1-2; cf. 2.1.13; 2.15.1; 3.4.3). He does refer to Jesus as 'the saving λόγος' (*Hist. Eccl.* 2.1.1), and the Gospels as οἱ θεῖοι λόγοι (*Hist. Eccl.* 7.19.1), but generally for Eusebius, the λόγος refers to 'the dogmas of the Christian life according to the gospel' (*Hist. Eccl.* 2.1.1).

In summary, the Apostolic Fathers from Papias to Eusebius are unanimous in their view that the teachings of Jesus as 'words', 'Word', 'WORD', are the basic substance of apostolic preaching and the heart of the Christian gospel. The life, death and resurrection, the miracles and the virgin birth, all augment the divine authority of the holy words of Jesus. This λόγος formed the heart of catechetical schools like that of Pantaenus in Alexandria, and had a wide range of meanings. The primitive 'words of Jesus' occur throughout but are stressed with earlier fathers like Papias and Clement of Rome, while the more formal references to 'the word of Jesus' or 'the Word' are more common to the later fathers and Eusebius. After Polycarp, and rising to a crescendo with Eusebius, the gospel use of λόγος to refer to the Church's theology about Jesus becomes increasingly prominent.

One thing is clear: throughout this entire range of history, in the New Testament and the Fathers, whether plural or singular, informal or formal, oral or written, preached or inscribed on the heart of memory, the concept of the λόγος was founded upon a body of sayings of Jesus that had a peculiar sanctity and theological centrality for the Church.

They were 'Holy Word', and were remembered, cherished and passed on with an apparent carefulness consonant with their sanctity.

Chapter 3

HOLY NARRATIVE:
THE CONTEXT OF THE WORD

So far we have discussed at length the place of the Holy Word in the life of the early Church, but have deferred the examination of the Jesus story until the evidence for the word was in. Now we can face this very important question: what was the function of the narrative concerning Jesus in the Church's quest for theological validation; and how does this relate to the Holy Word?

Current 'Narrative Fixation'

The discussion of the Synoptic genre in recent years has emphasized the narrative biographical character of the Synoptic Gospels as opposed to Bultmann's insistence that they represent the preaching (κήρυγμα) of the early Church in narrative form, what Charles Talbert called the 'consensus' of critical scholarship for over a generation. As early as 1863 Ernst Renan in his *La Vie Jesu*[1] called the Synoptics 'legendary biographies'. Clyde Weber Votaw[2] has likened them to popular biographies like Philostratus's *Life of Apollonius of Tyana*. Morton Smith termed them aretalogies, a type of biography, Charles Talbert has shown the close parallels between the Gospels and certain types of Greco-Roman biographies, and W.S. Vorster writes that it is 'proved beyond doubt' that the Gospels are narratives, made-up stories with a distinctive point of view.[3] Klaus Baltzer believes that the Gospels are

---

1. E. Renan, *The Life of Jesus* (New York: Doubleday, 1863), p. 136.
2. C.W. Votaw, *The Gospels and Contemporary Biographies in the Greco-Roman World* (FBBS, 27; Philadelphia: Fortress Press, 1970).
3. M. Smith, 'Prolegomena to a Discussion of Aretalogies, Divine Men, the Gospels and Jesus', *JBL* 90 (1971), pp. 188-89; C.H. Talbert, *What is a Gospel? The Genre of the Canonical Gospels* (Philadelphia: Fortress Press, 1977). For my

akin to the Old Testament biography of the prophet.[4] Even more recently David Aune has insisted that the Evangelists wrote with historical intentions, and calls them 'a sub-type of Greco-Roman biography'.[5] Werner Kelber has done a selective analysis of Gospel apophthegmata, which he calls 'didactic stories', focusing entirely on the narrative.[6] Philip Shuler attempts to identify a suitable genre for the Evangelists, and proposes what he calls an 'encomium biography'. This he compares to similar biographies by Isocrates, Xenophon, Philo, Tacitus, Lucian, Josephus and Philostratus, where a distinction can be made between historical biography and encomium biography, which he characterizes as being 'biased' in favor of the one being described.[7]

analysis of Talbert's book, see J.A. Baird, *A Comparative Analysis of the Gospel Genre: The Synoptic Mode and Its Uniqueness* (Lewiston: Edwin Mellen Press, 1991), pp. 14-18; cf. W.S. Vorster, 'Kerygma/History and the Gospel Genre', *NTS* 29 (1983), pp. 81-93.

4. K. Baltzer, *Die Biographie der Propheten* (Neukirchen-Vluyn: Neukirchener Verlag, 1975).

5. D.E. Aune, *The New Testament in Its Literary Environment* (Philadelphia: Westminster Press, 1987), p. 64. Biographical approaches to the Gospels have in recent years gained in popularity. See also A. Dihle, 'The Gospels and Greek Biography,' in P. Stuhlmacher (ed.), *The Gospel and the Gospels* (Grand Rapids: Eerdmans, 1990), pp. 361-86; R.A. Burridge, *What Are the Gospels? A Comparison with Graeco-Roman Biography* (SNTSMS, 70; Cambridge: Cambridge University Press, 1992).

6. W. Kelber, *The Oral and the Written Gospel* (Philadelphia: Fortress Press, 1983), p. 56.

7. P. Shuler, *A Genre for the Gospels: The Biographical Character of Matthew* (Philadelphia: Fortress Press, 1982), pp. 54-55. Shuler begins well by insisting that the genre patterns must emerge from the written text (p. 31). But he goes on to reduce the Synoptics to just another Greek genre, which is the old deductive method of approaching this question (cf. Baird, *Comparative Analysis*, pp. 1-2). His encomium genre illustrates a biography for a special purpose, which is an important advance in this discussion, but he denies any creative uniqueness to the Synoptics, which negates this insight. To assume that Jesus or the authors of the Synoptics were familiar with and followed closely the literary conventions of Greco-Roman rhetoricians is very dubious, especially in view of the evidence that they are a blend of Greek and Hebrew modes, a unique genre, *sui generis*, which developed out of the necessities of the Jesus situation, was confined to the Christian community, and lasted about 300 years after which the Gospel genre disappeared completely. Shuler gives some good new evidence for the old observation that there are striking similarities between the Synoptic birth narratives and some in the Greco-Roman literature, which puts them in a secondary historical class; but he fails to allow any distinction between these

Mary Ann Tolbert has suggested that the Gospels are a form of Greek novel,[8] while Adela Yarbro Collins speaks of Mark as an 'apocalyptic historical monograph'.[9] All of these and other recent studies stress the narrative element within the Synoptics almost to the exclusion of the teachings of Jesus.

The Importance of the Narrative

In response to this, the first thing that must be said is that the narrative of Jesus' life, death and resurrection obviously formed an important part

narrative units, and the teachings material, or even other narrative material of a quite different type. He insists on comparing the Synoptics on a par with other Greco-Roman literature, without allowing the authors of the Synoptics any uniqueness in their assessment of Jesus as Son of God. This one conviction, whether justified or not, puts their efforts at preserving his life and teachings in a special category. No one would contend that Demonax or Socrates or Apollonius was considered by his followers to be the Son of God, savior of the world. Whether we accept this as fact or not, we must accept their *belief* that this was so, and interpret the data on the text's own terms, not ours. What Shuler has basically said is that Matthew shares certain concerns for praise, commendation and vindication with many Grace-Roman authors. This is no doubt true. But the problem is that he begs several basic questions, which put his conclusions more into the category of special pleading than that of inductive, empirical scholarship: (1) He assumes the Synoptics are Grace-Roman in their orientation. (2) He assumes the validity of the method of finding an external genre, in this case a very 'slippery one', and working hard to make the Synoptics fit. (3) He assumes without discussion that there is really nothing unique or *sui generis* about the Synoptics, and so we can compare them on a par with this Grace-Roman encomium literature. My recent study of this question has, I think, at least challenged each of these assumptions. What I think I have demonstrated is that the Synoptics represent a very special kind of biography, with no significantly close parallel in the literature of the ancient world, Grace-Roman, Hebrew or Christian. Perhaps most importantly, while correctly seeing the biographical character of the Synoptics, Shuler, along with others mentioned above, has almost completely ignored the teachings of Jesus in his concentration on the narrative. If the evidence of this book says anything, it is that the biographical character of the Synoptics is a function of the Holy Word of Jesus, and must be understood on those terms.

8. M.A. Tolbert, *Sowing the Gospel: Mark's World in Literary-Historical Perspective* (Minneapolis: Fortress Press, 1989), pp. 55-79.

9. A.Y. Collins, *The Beginning of the Gospel: Probings of Mark in Context* (Minneapolis: Fortress Press, 1992), pp. 26-28.

of first-century Christianity.[10] This is especially true of the passion narrative, whose importance needs no documentation. It has long been noted that there is an unusually high agreement between the four Gospels on the details of the passion narrative, suggesting that this was something so often recounted that it had achieved a polished form by the time of its inclusion in these edited Gospels.[11] Furthermore, with the publication of Hennecke–Schneemelcher's *New Testament Apocrypha*, we are more certain than ever of the multiplication of Gospels in the late first to third centuries. In some, like the *Gospel of Peter*, and *The Protevangelium of James*, the narrative element is particularly strong, however believable.

Another illustration of narrative importance comes from my genre study of the Synoptics. In that work I identified nine modal qualities which are characteristic of all three of these Gospels. They are typified by short, independent units, couched in direct discourse, easily remembered, with a clearly identified audience closely related to the content of the saying, containing that 'oracular quality' so typical of Jesus' teaching, framed in a lively and realistic narrative and separated one from another by clearly identifiable seams.[12] It can be demonstrated that several 'modal' characteristics of these Gospels are especially illustrative of their concern for realistic history.[13] One such modal factor (SM-6) is the almost awkward concern of the editors to identify the historical audience to which any particular saying of Jesus was directed.[14] This occurs in 94% of the λόγια.[15] A further example is the liveliness and realistic quality of the narrative context (SM-8), one of the unique characteristics of the Synoptics, giving the distinct impression that the author is describing what he believes to be genuine events of history. This becomes especially interesting when one compares the quality of this 'narrative modality' in the Synoptics (SM-6, SM-8, 78.3%) with the same factors in other non-canonical Christian, Greek

---

10. See J.A. Baird, *Rediscovering the Power of the Gospels: Jesus' Theology of the Kingdom* (Wooster, OH: Iona Press, 1982).
11. See J.A. Baird, *Audience Criticism and the Historical Jesus* (Philadelphia: Westminster Press, 1969), pp. 65, 187-99.
12. Baird, *Comparative Analysis*, pp. 30-40.
13. Baird, *Comparative Analysis*, p. 38.
14. Baird, *Comparative Analysis*, p. 37.
15. Baird, *Audience Criticism*, p. 49.

and Jewish literature of antiquity. The closest is Lucian's *Demonax*, with a narrative modality of 60.4%.[16]

The Synoptics as Biographical Apophthegms

The close relation between audience and λόγιον also gives us another unique feature of the Synoptic mode. There is an historical realism to this λόγιον–audience relationship which points to its narrative orientation,[17] strongly supported by the many patterns of correlation between saying and audience. This modal factor is highest in the various apophthegms (96.9%),[18] whose very nature depends on this λόγιον–context relationship. It is highly relevant to our study that a detailed audience-critical analysis of the Synoptics shows the apophthegm having the highest percentage of these nine modal factors. This identifies the apophthegm (paradigm) as the most 'characteristic' form within these Gospels.[19] Although such categorization is ultimately inadequate, it is probably more accurate to describe the Synoptics not simply as biographies, but as extended 'biographical apophthegms' where the content of the sayings of Jesus and the narrative of his life, death and resurrection are intimately interrelated, but where the focus is ultimately upon the Word.[20]

If this is correct, then such an apophthegm model gives us the strongest evidence for the importance of the narrative in the Synoptic Gospels, as in the rest of the New Testament and the early Church in general. What this also says is that, in the Synoptic material, the Word and the narrative must not be separated. The birth narratives with their stress on Jesus' relation to God, the passion narratives with their emphasis on the love and ultimate victory of God, are both necessary to the understanding of the Word. In terms of the current discussion, this suggests that to understand fully the jewel of the Holy Word, one must not only concentrate on the teachings of Jesus, but also fully appreciate the nature and function of their narrative setting.

16. Baird, *Comparative Analysis*, p. 66. It is noted that the *Gospel of Peter* comes up with an 85.8%, but the increase in the legendary quality of this material puts it out of the Synoptic 'Hebrew Mode' into the 'Greek Mode', where narrative becomes legend; cf. *Comparative Analysis*, p. 142.
17. Baird, *Comparative Analysis*, pp. 38-40.
18. Baird, *Comparative Analysis*, p. 56.
19. Baird, *Audience Criticism*, pp. 63-64; *idem*, *Comparative Analysis*, p. 57.
20. Baird, *Comparative Analysis*, p. 131.

3. *The Context of the Word*

The Separation of the λόγια *and the Narrative*

Once this has been said, however, we must go on to recognize the 'discontinuity' in the Synoptics between the narratives about Jesus, and the various reproductions of his Holy Word. This is one thing Bultmann was never able to do because of the built-in assumptions within classic form criticism that it was all a product of the *Urkirche*. I first came across this phenomenon in my audience-critical study of the Synoptics where it appeared there was a clear difference between these two blocks of material in a number of ways: in vocabulary, in the Aramaic flavor of the λόγια, in the references to the audience, and in the theology itself. The editorial stratum simply does not look the same as that of the λόγια.[21]

This factor was further born out by the comparative genre study where the independent character of the Synoptic units, separated by clearly apparent 'seams', as the form critics have been pointing out for years, brings us to a quite un-Bultmannian conclusion. The λόγια stand out as a solid body of Jesus material which antedated the narrative, but to which clung tenaciously the various narrative indications necessary for the clarity of the teachings. This is especially apparent with the apophthegm form, and in the widespread concern to identify the audience, pointing to the close interrelation of audience and Word.[22] One is reminded that the three Synoptic Evangelists did not finally edit their Gospels, and so provide the narrative whose style shows definite redactional characteristics,[23] until late in the first century. The λόγια on the other hand give all the appearance of having been preserved in small and then gradually enlarging collections of independent sayings which antedated the final compositions, and contained a quite different set of intrinsic patterns. Another way to put this is to observe that the bulk of patterns in the various editorial narratives run vertically down through a particular source or redactor. The patterns within the λόγια, however, tend to run horizontally across the three Gospels and their sources. In the λόγια and narratives, we are talking about two different bodies of material: different in origin, different in time, and different in character.

---

21. Baird, *Audience Criticism*, p. 38.
22. Baird, *Comparative Analysis*, p. 51.
23. Baird, *Audience Criticism*, pp. 142-45.

The Subordinate Character of the Narrative

This insight points then to another. If, as we have begun to demonstrate in the previous chapter, and will continue to do in the chapters to come, the Holy Word of Jesus was that which the early Church considered to be the primary data of its general consensus and self-understanding, then the narrative of his life within the Synoptics must be seen as secondary to the Word. This would explain why there is least agreement and the fewest details preserved about Jesus' life story. As Dodd, Meagher and others have pointed out,[24] there is a sketchy outline of Jesus' life emerging from the sermons in Acts, from Paul and the later New Testament. And as I have elsewhere demonstrated,[25] the 'Hebrew mode' with its concern for realistic historical narrative continues in a few of the non-canonical gospels. The overwhelming concern of the early Church from Paul through the Fathers to Eusebius, however, was for the theology of and about Jesus, and this orientation to 'the Word' was the basis of its identity and mission. The narratives of Jesus' death and resurrection are in a special category and actually illustrate this point. They were preserved as passion narrative with a particular theological purpose, important for their own intrinsic truth and value, but mostly important as an extension and support of the Holy Word, what Jesus said about God, about sin and salvation, and about himself.[26]

In the Synoptics there are two types of material in constant interrelation: a lively and realistic narrative about Jesus' life, death and resurrection on the one hand, and a solid body of teachings on the other. But the emphasis is clearly on the 'Word'. This is seen in several ways:

(1) In a very superficial way, if one thumbs through the Synoptics, it becomes obvious that Matthew and Luke begin and end with two and then three chapters each, which are mostly narrative; but between these narrative sections, the vast bulk of the material is the sayings of Jesus.

(2) In Mark this is less clear, because of the abundance of miracle stories; but even here Jesus' healing ministry is secondary to his teaching. As he insists to his disciples who remind him that people are searching for him in order to be healed: 'Let us go on to the next towns,

---

24. C.H. Dodd, *The Apostolic Preaching and Its Developments* (New York: Harper & Row, 1936); J. Meagher, *The Way of the Word: The Beginning and the Establishing of Christian Understanding* (New York: Seabury Press, 1975).

25. Baird, *Comparative Analysis*, p. 128.

26. Baird, *Rediscovering the Power of the Gospels*, pp. 117-50.

3. The Context of the Word

that I may preach there also; *for that is why I came out'* (Mk 1.38; my emphasis). The way Mark begins his Gospel without a birth narrative, and by introducing Jesus immediately as the one proclaiming the Kingdom of God, would seem to underscore for him the priority of the Word.

Geza Vermes in his book *Jesus the Jew*[27] attempts to identify Jesus as a charismatic Jewish rabbi, like Hanina ben Dosa, one of whose chief functions was that of a healer and miracle worker, a 'man of deeds'. But his emphasis is entirely on the narrative. The evidence of great crowds coming to him for healing, and the concern of the disciples that he do this, support Vermes's description of Galilee as a place where charismatic rabbis were wont to practice the healing arts. But Vermes misses the point. There were indeed many healing incidents referred to, especially by Mark; but the point of this Gospel seems to be that these were done reluctantly and out of compassion, and Jesus actually tried to avoid being identified in this role. A more complete reading of the Synoptics shows Jesus focusing on the Holy Word of the Kingdom and avoiding this popular Jewish image. The Jewish crowds misunderstood him then as they continue to do today. If one denies to Jesus any deeper significance than that of a typical Jewish charismatic, which is Vermes's basic assumption, then of course what is left is another charismatic Jew, although one who strangely avoids this traditional role and prefers to focus on more theological matters. This kind of circular logic begs the essential question. The fact that many in the early Church looked constantly for 'signs' is a further indication of the Jewish expectations of Jesus' audiences, which again he rejected: 'An evil...generation seeks for a sign' (Mt. 12.39). This is all a reflection of the understanding of religion in terms of signs, morals, good deeds and the 'traditions of the elders' which Jesus soundly rejected (Mk 7.1-23; Mt. 23.23). The highly innocuous image which Vermes presents is of a Jesus who would never have been crucified.

(3) If one compares the number of separate narrative and teaching units, this fact is even more dramatically revealed. There are in these three Gospels 56 different narrative units (miracle stories, legends) compared with 306 separate teaching units (parables, sayings, apophthegms). The narrative material, although of immense value in its

---

27. G. Vermes, *Jesus the Jew: A Historian's Reading of the Gospels* (London: Collins; Philadelphia: Fortress Press, 1973).

own right, is ultimately most significant as a setting for the Word of Jesus.[28]

(4) The main evidence for the centrality of the Word and the supportive function of the narrative, however, is the entire thrust of this book, as we shall see in Christian literature from the first to the fourth century: not only the importance of Jesus' death and resurrection, but the consistent centrality of his Word in the life and thought of the early Church.

The Changing Character of the Narrative

We have already observed the movement within the early Church in its use of the Holy Word, from 'the words of Jesus', presented in direct discourse and with an apparent concern to reproduce the actual historical sayings of Jesus, to the Word as 'gospel', which, as we shall see in the next chapter, was the Church's theological understanding about Jesus and his teachings. The movement was from what Bultmann called *Historie* to *Geschichte*, as the Church appropriated the teachings of Jesus and applied them more and more to their own needs and circumstances. The same thing seems to have happened with the narrative.

a. *The Narrative in the Synoptics*
In the Synoptics, the narrative served three main functions, and in these we can see the beginning of this theological metamorphosis. (1) The first was simply to tell the story; and Luke gives his opinion that this was done as accurately as possible in order that they might know the truth of what had transpired among them (1.1-4). This focused on the life of Jesus the man, and helped to answer the common question, 'Is not this Joseph's son?' (Lk. 4.22).

(2) In its second function, operating at the most primitive level, the narrative material provided the setting for Jesus' teachings, often being just a word or phrase identifying the audience, or the briefest of introductions to some apophthegm. This would be typical of the double tradition, and similar to what we find in the Jesus sayings in the *Gospel of Thomas*.[29] It is instructive to observe just such fragmentary narrative clinging to λόγια as reported in many alternate readings in the New

---

28. Baird, *Rediscovering the Power of the Gospels*, pp. 28-29.
29. Baird, *Comparative Analysis*, pp. 107-108.

Testament textual apparatus.³⁰ Longer narratives would be needed for introducing other λόγια, for example that surrounding the Zacchaeus incident (Lk. 19.1-10) or the brilliant reply to the Syro-Phoenician woman (Mk 7.27).

(3) Along with this, we see a third purpose dealing more with longer narratives designed not only to tell the story, but to explain it. They would include the events in the period of preparation leading up to Jesus' active ministry, like his baptism by John, the temptation in the wilderness and the rejection at Nazareth. Here we can see the narrative, in its location and arrangement, acting not only in an historical fashion, but in a subtle theological capacity, answering the question as to his identity and sense of mission. One such observable pattern comes in the transition from Jesus' popularity in the Galilean period to the increasing opposition, beginning at Mk 7.1, when the Pharisees and scribes came to Galilee from Jerusalem to test him. From there on, the opposition mounts until the climax of the cross and resurrection. Editorial purpose is indeed observable in the narrative, although some would argue that this seems as much derived from the artistic logic of telling the story as from any more apparent theological motivation.

This, of course, is a highly debated matter, and redaction critics have expended great effort in recent years trying to discover the theological motives of the redactors. It is, I think, quite apparent that in the arrangement of the narrative and λόγια material we can see the mind of the redactor; and there are certainly patterns of vocabulary and theology observable within individual sources or Gospels.³¹ Throughout the ministry, whether it be in his preaching, healing or debate with his opponents, whether in his birth, his miracles or his death and resurrection, the narrative is a 'support' to the Holy Word of Jesus, and this can be expected to have some influence on the way in which the narrative is set up. My own research, however, has found so many 'horizontal' patterns of theology, praxis and word usage cutting across all sources and Gospels that I find such redactional activity at a minimum, rather obvious and theologically innocuous.³² As we shall see, the test operating within the early Church was whether or not it was true to the Holy Word itself.

---

30. Baird, *Audience Criticism*, pp. 72-73.
31. Baird, *Audience Criticism*, pp. 142-45.
32. Baird, *Audience Criticism*, pp. 139-42.

But within this narrative attention to *Historie*, there are indeed legendary elements which reflect a degree of theological concern sufficient to identify at those points some movement toward *Geschichte* or interpreted history. The most prominent is of course the infancy narratives, filled as they are with Old Testament references, and all designed to show Jesus' fulfillment of prophecy and his direct and intimate relation to God. Other stories like Jesus' baptism, the descent of the Spirit, and the transfiguration, raise similar questions. For our purposes, there is no need here to examine each of these in critical detail. I do note, however, that in a modal study of the Synoptics, the material identified in the form of 'legend' has a lower rating than the apophthegm in terms of the modal factors most characteristic of these Gospels.[33] The legends would therefore seem to reflect a greater distance from the most primitive Jesus material.[34]

It is interesting to see the strong agreement among the four Gospels, and especially the three Synoptics, on the details of the passion. This story has a lively and credible quality quite different from the more formal and stylized character of the infancy narratives. There are, however, patterns within the resurrection narrative showing theological concern, like not recognizing and then recognizing Jesus, or doubting the resurrection (Lk. 24.16, 37; Mt. 28.17; Mk 16.11). This comes to special focus in John with the dialogue between Jesus and Thomas: 'do not be faithless, but believing' (20.27). So, there is *Geschichte* within the Synoptic Gospels; but this is in tension with the more dominant *Historie* as the narrative operates in this triple capacity: to tie the life and teachings of Jesus to actual historical events in space and time, to provide a setting for the Words of Jesus, and to give enough interpretation to promote the understanding of those words and events. This, I take it, is not a sinister development, but a very natural and inevitable response to the nature of the material and the needs of the Church.

b. *The Narrative in John*
When we come to John, we make a shift from what I have called the 'Hebrew mode' of the Synoptics, to the 'Greek mode' where there is an escalation of the attempts to explain the course of theological history.[35]

33. Baird, *Comparative Analysis*, pp. 56-57.
34. Baird, *Comparative Analysis*, p. 138.
35. Baird, *Comparative Analysis*, pp. 23-26.

3. *The Context of the Word* 75

Here *Historie* becomes *Geschichte* in the conviction that interpreted history is both valid and necessary in our understanding of the Jesus story. This is seen clearly in John in the movement away from the Synoptic mode: in the long narratives, often containing no λόγια whatever, in the lessening concern for the audience, in the long, difficult speeches, in the escalation of the 'oracular mood', and in the absence of those seams which reflect the independent character of the Synoptic units. John bears the stamp of a single editorial mind. The theological escalation is visible not only in the prologue, but more subtly in such things as the increase in 'I sayings', the expanded editorial comment and legend, and the drop in the apophthegm form with its necessary historical framework.[36] John maintains the Synoptic concern for the narrative, but the mode has shifted from Hebrew to Greek, from *Historie* to *Geschichte* and the purpose reflects the needs of the later Church: 'These are written that you may believe that Jesus is the Christ...and that believing you may have life in his name' (20.31). In this sense, John illustrates the transition from the Word *of* Jesus to the Gospel *about* Jesus and his Word.

c. *The Narrative in Acts*
The book of Acts describes this transition in process, beginning with the experience of the risen Jesus and his proclamation of the Kingdom, and moving to the preaching of the Church about this Jesus, about the Kingdom and about his resurrection. Luke conveniently summarizes the two poles of Paul's preaching: 'the Kingdom of God', that is, the Holy Word, and his 'teaching *about* the Lord Jesus Christ' (my emphasis), clearly a reference to the Gospel (Acts 28.31; cf. 28.23). As Acts proceeds, one becomes immediately aware that one large element of Luke's Gospel has dropped out, and that is the narrative about Jesus' life. It has been replaced by the proclamation of the Word as 'gospel', within which the narrative has been reduced to an interest in his death and resurrection. There are some fragmentary references, like that summary of the Church's preaching in Peter's sermon to Cornelius (Acts 10.34-43); but this is actually a case in point. It begins with the primary stress on 'the word which was proclaimed through all Judea', but ends with a second point of stress, the death and resurrection of Jesus and the forgiveness available through belief in him, with a very brief summary of his life in between: 'the baptism...he went about doing

36. Baird, *Comparative Analysis*, pp. 101-105.

good and healing...we are witnesses to all that he did both in the country of the Jews and in Jerusalem'. The teachings of Jesus as 'the Word', and the Church's gospel of the cross and resurrection, have all but swamped the Jesus narrative. Beyond a very few brief references to 'the time that the Lord Jesus went in and out among us' (Act 1.21; cf. 1.24; 4.13, 27, 30), all references in Acts to Jesus the man are to his death and resurrection.[37] Along with a continuing concern for the 'words' of Jesus, in Acts we see a clear movement away from the narrative about Jesus to what one might call the 'narrative theology' of the atonement, with its stress on the passion and resurrection of Christ, and the benefits of belief in him for men and women of faith, that is, to the gospel.

d. *The Narrative in Paul*
With Paul, we see this process continuing with no direct references to the life of Jesus, except in terms of his death and resurrection, beautifully summarized in 1 Cor. 15.3-8: 'For I delivered to you as of first importance...he was buried...raised...appeared to Cephas...' The gospel of the Word has obliterated the importance of the narrative except for the passion and resurrection. Narrative *Historie* has become narrative *Geschichte*; and this is perfectly consistent with what we have already described as the transition from the concern for the λόγος as the actual 'words... word... WORD' of Jesus, to the λόγος as the Word about Jesus, which they called the gospel. In the Church's narrative theology, narrative and gospel have become the same thing. I have no doubt that even as the direct words of Jesus continued to inform and control Paul's gospel, so also the historical narratives underlay Paul's preaching of the Word. But in the recorded epistles, all but the passion/resurrection narratives have ceased to be theologically important.

e. *The Narrative in the Rest of the New Testament*
This is also true with the rest of the New Testament, seen in the way the passion theology dominates the epistle to the Hebrews.[38] The process we are describing is clearly visible in the following chart detailing the occurrence within the New Testament of five key words. Note that the use of βασιλεία, the signature term of the historical Jesus, drops radically after the Synoptics, but persists throughout the New Testament. The reference to Ἰησοῦς continues strongly in John and Acts, but drops

37. Acts 1.16, 22; 3.1; 4.29-30, 33; 17.3, 18; 25.19.
38. Heb. 2.9; 4.14; 10.16; 12.2; 13.12; etc.

significantly in its relation to the use of Χριστός in Paul and the later New Testament. The use of θεός continues strongly throughout, with particular strength in Paul, while the λόγος persists in all the New Testament as a controlling term about as it does in the Synoptics.

	Ἰησοῦς	Χριστός	βασιλεία	θεός	λόγος
Synoptics	353	31	114	23	54
John	248	18	4	62	22
Paul	32	216	13	534	55
Acts	50	14	8	166	47
Later NT	21	27	11	180	42

In the above, the figures are important as they show the relative occurrence of these terms within a particular section or between the various sections of the New Testament. The movement vis-a-vis the historical narrative is seen particularly in the occurrence of βασιλεία and Ἰησοῦς, where the historical figure and most characteristic word of Jesus move from their strength in the Synoptics to a position of lesser strength in Paul's 'gospel of Christ', 'gospel of God'. To this must be added the observation that a new set of terms becomes increasingly apparent with Paul and others, notably the author of Hebrews: such terms as ἀνάστασις, θάνατος, σταυρός, and αἷμα emerge as a sacrificial, substitutionary doctrine of the atonement begins to assert itself. Whether or not this is true to the Holy Word of Jesus is a moot point, but one thing is clear: in the later New Testament, the theological interpretation of the passion/resurrection has almost completely taken over the Gospel narrative.

f. *The Narrative in the Later Writings*
Beyond the New Testament, the Christian literature of the first four centuries exhibits three major tendencies with regard to the narrative: (1) either the narrative drops out partially or completely, as it does in many of the Fathers and Eusebius; (2) or it continues in strength with a few of the Fathers, as in the extensive use made of written Gospels in Justin's *Dialogue with Trypho*, but with the teachings of Jesus remaining central; (3) or it remains and is even enhanced, but modified by dogmatic considerations, as in the apocryphal New Testament. The later Christian literature does then include narrative about Jesus' life, especially stressing the passion and resurrection, but the major concern for 'remembering' still seems to focus on the Words of Jesus (Lk. 22.61;

Jn 15.20). As Justin put it, 'I would wish that all...do not keep themselves away from the words of the savior' (*1 Apology* 14).

This is illustrated graphically in a genre comparison of the Synoptics with other Jewish, Christian and pagan literature of antiquity. In a literary analysis of the Synoptics, we find a fair balance between their stress on the narrative, what I call 'narrative modality' (78.3%) on the one hand,[39] and a slightly stronger stress on the Word, what I call 'Word modality', on the other (84.9%).[40] Using this as a standard of measurement, one can show the movement away from the characteristic literary mode of the Synoptics in the Hebrew, Greco-Roman and Christian literature to which they are compared. Some Christian literature moves away from the Synoptic norm by dropping out the references to the narratives of Jesus' life, and the narrative modality decreases significantly, for example, in the *Gospel of Thomas*, the papyrus fragments, the apophthegmata of the Desert Fathers, etc.[41] Other Christian literature maintains a fairly strong attention to the narrative, but the credibility of that narrative is severely strained. As the Word modality increases, theological factors take over and create, for example in the *Infancy Story of Thomas*, a Jesus who is an infant prodigy, stretching boards or killing his playmates with a wave of his hand.[42] As Maurer put it with regard to the *Gospel of Peter,* the narratives of Jesus 'are loosened out of the soil of real history and transferred to the realm of legend and myth'.[43]

g. *Summary of the Historical Shift*
In our examination of λόγος, we have observed a shift in emphasis, orientation and vocabulary in the Church's handling of the teachings of Jesus from the words and theology of Jesus to the Word and theology of

---

39. Clear audience identification (SM-6), and lively and convincing historical narrative (SM-8).

40. Direct discourse (SM-3), easily remembered (SM-4), oracular quality (SM-5), significant interrelation between λόγιον and audience (SM-7).

41. Baird, *Comparative Analysis*, p. 128.

42. Baird, *Comparative Analysis*, p. 109.

43. E. Hennecke and W. Schneemelcher (eds.), *New Testament Apocrypha* (2 vols.; Philadelphia: Westminster Press, 1963), I, p. 181; cf. Baird, *Comparative Analysis*, pp. 134-35. [See also J.H. Charlesworth and C.A. Evans, 'Jesus in the Agrapha and Apocryphal Gospels', in B. Chilton and C.A. Evans (eds.), *Studying the Historical Jesus: Evaluations of the State of Current Research* (NTTS, 19; Leiden: E.J. Brill, 1994), pp. 479-533.—Eds.]

the Church about Jesus. Now we are in a position to summarize a similar phenomenon in the Church's perception and use of the narrative of Jesus' life. As we move from the Synoptic Gospels to Paul and John and the later New Testament, and then into the Church of the first three centuries, we can see four major changes: (1) In the first place, we have observed a change from the Synoptic importance of the narrative life of Jesus to an increasing lack of attention to that narrative, except for Jesus' death and resurrection. (2) We have seen a development from the realistic historical narrative, typical of the most primitive portions of the Synoptics, to the more stylized theological narratives of Jesus' infancy and the narrative theology of the Gospel of John, to the much more radically legendized narratives of the apocryphal New Testament. (3) In the Synoptics, the Holy Word of Jesus and the narrative are clearly separate, although closely interrelated. In the rest of the New Testament, the Holy Word and the narrative have merged, and so the Kingdom of God becomes the Kingdom of Christ, the words of Jesus become the Word about Jesus, and the historical narrative becomes narrative theology. In Bultmannian terms, *Historie* has become *Geschichte*. Bultmann, then, was partly right on this point, but he failed to understand the controlling function of the Holy Word and put the shift to *Geschichte* too early in the Synoptics. It came later, and in a much more 'natural' and innocuous way. (4) In the Synoptics, the narratives of Jesus' life act as the framework for his teachings about the Kingdom of God. In the rest of the New Testament, the narrative of the death and resurrection has replaced the narrative of his life and shifted the emphasis from Jesus' proclamation of the Kingdom to God's atoning grace in and through the cross and resurrection.

In essence, it was the teachings of Jesus plus his death and resurrection which formed the substructure of the theology of the early Church, and acted as the normative basis of its life. This is seen as much in the changing character of the narrative as in the constant attention to this most basic biographical apophthegm: the Holy Word surrounded by the narrative of his passion and victory.

The Holy Narrative

As a postscript, it is worth noting that the narrative of Jesus' life is never called 'holy' in the New Testament. The holiness of the narrative emerges in and through the theological re-statement of the gospel. Even the birth narratives, certainly holy tales, do not seem to be part of the earliest written or oral material, and drop out of the teaching of the early Church as we find it in the New Testament. This accords well with the secondary character of the narrative as we have observed it. Not until the narrative and teaching are united in the narrative theology of the early Church, does the narrative become theologically important, and there, as we have said, the stress is almost exclusively on Jesus' death and resurrection. The theological importance of the birth narratives would seem to have been a phenomenon that developed late and selectively within the early Church. The holiness of the narratives of infancy, death and resurrection escalated sometimes to bizarre extremes in the apocryphal Christian writings; but the New Testament shows a noticeable restraint at this point. The holiness of the narrative as it has manifested itself in the Church would seem therefore to have been a derived holiness, the product of several important factors within that early situation: (1) First and foremost was its function as the framework for 'the Holy Word'. (2) It was also most likely a reflection of the effect of Jesus on peoples' lives which led them to call him 'The Holy One'. (3) This, in turn, I have argued elsewhere, was a product of his own self-conscious oneness with God which consumed all that he said and did, and caused him to talk to and about God in ways that his opponents, correctly from their point of view, called 'blasphemy'.[44] (4) It seems also to have been the result of the tremendous impact of his death and resurrection on the lives of his disciples and the church. (5) Finally, it would appear to have been a testimony to the effect of the Holy Spirit within the Church, and to the conviction that in the Spirit his living presence was still available to them.

---

44. J.A. Baird, *The Justice of God in the Teaching of Jesus* (London: SCM Press; Philadelphia: Westminster Press, 1963), pp. 237-53; *idem, Rediscovering the Power of the Gospels*, p. 150; *idem, Comparative Analysis*, pp. 42-47.

Chapter 4

HOLY GOSPEL:
THE THEOLOGICAL INTERPRETATION OF THE WORD

The immediate question facing Jesus' hearers was, what does it all mean, his life, his teachings, his death and resurrection? The interpretation began immediately, as his disciples heard and saw and tried to understand. Imbedded in their reporting, therefore, was inevitably an element of interpretation. But the needs of the Church demanded more than the limited interpretive element within the first Gospel collections. This was supplied by a number of early preacher-teachers, whom we today would no doubt call theologians, most notably Paul, John, Peter, the author of the book of Hebrews, and the John of the Apocalypse. Out of this growing company there quickly, naturally and inescapably emerged a body of theological substance which Paul and others called 'gospel'. This nourished the Church, and represented their attempts to understand the Word and the narrative, and to relate them to the general intellectual and spiritual needs of the community.

This seems to have been a distinctive body of theologically oriented stuff having a widely recognized and accepted identity which distinguished it clearly from what they called the 'traditions' of the Church, even as the two were closely interrelated. In the words of C.H. Dodd, this was material dealing with specifically religious themes in the reflective manner constituting theology as distinct from that consisting mainly of ethical precepts and admonitions.[1] This stratum of primarily oral data comes to light with particular clarity in the examination of a

---

1. C.H. Dodd, *Gospel and Law: The Relation of Faith and Ethics in Early Christianity* (New York: Columbia University Press, 1951), p. 5. John Meagher (*The Way of the Word: The Beginning and the Establishing of Christian Understanding* [New York: Seabury Press, 1975], pp. 1-5) makes a similar distinction between 'positive law', the explicitly regulating word, and 'common law', authoritative habit and custom.

large number of terms used for it with varying consistency through the centuries, but with special clarity in the New Testament.

The Substance of the Gospel: εὐαγγέλιον/εὐαγγελίζομαι

The most obvious place to begin is with the word 'gospel', which was peculiar to the Christian Church in its description of that widely accepted fund of the Church's understanding about Jesus, both oral and written. What is not so clear is the origin of this term as used within the Church. The noun εὐαγγέλιον has antecedents in both the Hebrew and the Greek backgrounds of Christianity, and there has been considerable debate as to its rootage. Following Gerhard Friedrich, most recently Peter Stuhlmacher has stressed the Hebrew background,[2] while Hennecke–Schneemelcher insist that its lineage is more exactly Greek, stemming from its usage in connection with the imperial cult. The problem is that the noun εὐαγγέλιον (*besrah*) does not occur in the Old Testament or the LXX in a religious sense; but it does so occur many times in Greek literature as far back as Homer (cf. *Od.* 14.152-153), as good news that is a gift of the gods for which sacrifice is to be made. In the imperial cult,[3] the emperor is the savior figure. He proclaims εὐαγγέλια. His birth, coming of age, accession to the throne, are all 'good news'. The further problem, however, is that the verb εὐαγγελίζομαι (*bissar*) does have significant religious usage in Deutero-Isaiah (57.7; 61.1) in passages that have long been considered messianic (Lk. 4.18), and is so used in the New Testament.[4] Stuhlmacher points out that it is the LXX that translates the root *bissar* as εὐαγγελίζομαι to refer to 'the *heilsgeschichtliche* medium for the prophetic word of God in which the word stem is imbedded'.[5]

When the Christian mission approached the heathen world to proclaim the Old Testament word of God, it used the LXX term εὐαγγελίζομαι. Stuhlmacher points to Rev. 14.6 and Mt. 11.2-6 (Lk. 7.18-23) as representing an early Jewish Christian use of εὐαγγελίζομαι which

2. P. Stuhlmacher, *Das paulinische Evangelium*. I. *Vorgeschichte* (Göttingen: Vandenhoeck & Ruprecht, 1968), p. 153; cf. G. Friedrich, 'εὐαγγέλιον', *TDNT*, II, p. 726.
3. E. Hennecke and W. Schneemelcher (eds.), *New Testament Apocrypha* (2 vols.; Philadelphia: Westminster Press, 1963), I, p. 73.
4. Mt. 11.5; Lk. 7.22; 4.18; Acts 13.32; Rom. 10.15.
5. Stuhlmacher, *Das paulinische Evangelium*, p. 179.

4. The Theological Interpretation of the Word 83

refers to God coming to judge and to heal. Since Jesus is seldom if ever recorded using the noun, there is a question as to whether or not the early Church derived its usage from him. The religious coinage of this concept may certainly have come into the Hebrew language from Greek influence; but the evidence seems to point to its more immediate entrance into the Christian vocabulary via its Jewish, Rabbinic and Old Testament background. Whether or not the actual terminology comes out of the Jewish-Christian Palestinian community or from the Christian-Hellenistic mission, as Stuhlmacher insists, is a question beyond the scope of this study.[6]

In its early New Testament occurrence, εὐαγγέλιον is always singular, always oral and refers in varying ways to the heart of Christian belief, concerning what Jesus said and did, what the Church was saying about him and what men and women could become through him.

In the Synoptics, the noun appears on nine different occasions; but there are patterns raising questions with regard to its authenticity as a word of Jesus. Although Luke uses the verb frequently in his Gospel and Acts, the noun is entirely omitted by him, as well as by John. The noun does occur twice in Mark along with its parallels in Matthew (Mk 13.10; 14.9), but five times it appears in Mark where Matthew omits it,[7] and twice in Matthew where Mark omits it.[8] Six of these occurrences are within sayings of Jesus, but three are Markan additions.[9] On the other hand all of Jesus' λόγια containing εὐαγγέλιον are to a disciple audience, which is where Jesus gives his most typical teaching.[10] What all this suggests is that although Jesus certainly may have used the term, the Evangelists Matthew and Mark seem especially prone to employ the noun wherever they can, and probably on occasions where it did not originally belong.

With regard to its content, εὐαγγέλιον shows its general summarizing character in a unique pattern by occurring several times in connection with various phrases referring to the extent of the proclamation: 'about all Galilee' (Mt. 4.23; Mk 1.14), 'all cities and villages' (Mt. 9.35), 'all nations' (Mk 13.10), 'the whole world' (Mt. 24.14; Mk 14.9; 16.15). It

6. Stuhlmacher, *Das paulinische Evangelium*, p. 244.
7. Mk 1.1, 14; 8.35; 10.29; 16.15.
8. Mt. 4.23; 9.35; cf. Stuhlmacher, *Das paulinische Evangelium*, pp. 56-63.
9. Mk 8.35; 10.29; 16.15.
10. J.A. Baird, *Audience Criticism and the Historical Jesus* (Philadelphia: Westminster Press, 1967), esp. p. 78, chart XVII.

describes the teaching of Jesus and the apostles concerning the Kingdom of God and the fulfillment of God's καιρός in him (Mk 1.14, 15). The εὐαγγέλιον is thus an authoritative statement concerning the sum and substance of the Christian proclamation: what Jesus said, what he did, what the early Church believed about him, and what was proclaimed to the world.

The word εὐαγγέλιον, however, is chiefly a Pauline term to describe what he calls 'my gospel',[11] which is the 'gospel of God'[12] or 'the gospel of Christ'.[13] He uses these terms interchangeably, as in the phrase 'the gospel of God concerning his son', showing how thoroughly for Paul this concept is based both on the life and on the teaching of Jesus about the Kingdom of God.[14] For Paul, the gospel was a summary statement of Christian belief about Jesus' life, death and resurrection (1 Cor. 15), and the substance of what he preached. There is a very clear pattern in the Synoptics, Acts and Paul showing the close connection between the verbs κηρύσσω and εὐαγγελίζομαι and the noun εὐαγγέλιον.[15] Paul saw this gospel as the true word about Christ,[16] which was at times disputed (Gal. 1.6, 7, 11), and which he was on occasion forced to defend (Phil. 1.16). It was a theological scheme of salvation (Rom. 10.16) regarding God's revelation in Jesus Christ which the Jews vigorously rejected (Rom. 11.28). As such, this gospel was a demanding thing (Phil. 1.27), a command to be obeyed (2 Cor. 9.13), a cause to be served (Phil. 2.22). At the same time it was also the vehicle

11. Rom. 2.16; 16.25; cf. 2 Tim. 2.8. I see no distinction between the usage in the literature which is clearly Pauline and that sometimes described as 'pseudo-Pauline'. H. Koester would seem to agree. He gives a word study of εὐαγγέλιον from the Synoptics through Justin Martyr, and sees this as originally a Pauline term, used in missionary activity to describe the content of the Christian message. See H. Koester, 'From the Kerygma Gospel to the Written Gospel', *NTS* 35 (1989), p. 361.

12. Rom. 15.16; 1 Thess. 2.2; 1 Tim. 1.11; etc.

13. 1 Cor. 9.12; 2 Cor. 2.12; 4.4; 9.13; 10.14; etc.

14. Rom. 1.1, 9; cf. 15.16, 19; etc. The one pattern I see here is that of frequency. Paul is recorded as using 'gospel of God' six times (Rom. 15.16; 1 Thess. 2.2, 8, 9; Rom. 1.9; 1 Tim. 1.11) and 'the gospel of Christ' thirteen times, all at various points in his career (1 Cor. 9.12, 18; 2 Cor. 2.12; 4.4; 9.13; 10.14; Rom. 1.16; 15.19; Gal. 1.7; Phil. 1.27; 1 Thess. 3.2; 2 Thess. 1.8). There seems to be a growing emphasis here on Christ, which is the same pattern observed in connection with the terms κηρύσσω/κήρυγμα (see the chart below).

15. Cf. Rom. 16.25; 1 Cor. 9.12; 9.18; 2 Cor. 4.3, 4; Col. 1.23; 2.2, 4; Acts 8.12; 15.7; 20.24; Lk. 7.22; 4.18; etc.

16. Gal. 2.2, 5, 7, 14; Eph. 1.13; 1 Thess. 3.2.

through which came the call and the promises of God (Eph. 3.6), a word of power (1 Thess. 1.5) and a generating source for the establishment of faith (1 Thess. 3.2; 1 Cor. 4.15). The gospel then for Paul was both an intellectual body of doctrine and also a channel for the living power of God.[17]

The noun εὐαγγέλιον occurs only twice in Acts. It is a summary of that which was preached by Peter and Paul, the word of the Kingdom from Jesus himself (Acts 15.7; 20.24).

The Apostolic Fathers similarly use εὐαγγέλιον at least sixteen times in the singular in a preponderantly oral sense. Basically this is a reference to the good news of the Kingdom commands of Jesus (*1 Clem.* 2.1) to 'pray as the lord commanded in his gospel' (*Did.* 8.2), and to act 'according to the ordinance of the gospel' (*Did.* 11.3). It refers to Jesus' instruction regarding traveling Evangelists, or for dealing with offenses within the early Church.[18] Thus in the *Didache* especially, what we will later call παράδοσις is here called gospel, and shows the concern, as Ignatius described it, 'to do nothing but after the teaching of Christ' (χριστομαθίαν; *Phld.* 8.2).

More characteristically, εὐαγγέλιον describes the message of Christ in a more general way, the gospel the apostles were to preach (*Barn.* 5.9; 8.3), 'the gospel of the common hope' (Ignatius, *Phld.* 5.2), which was the Church's theology about Jesus, and which stressed his cross, death and resurrection, and the Church's faith in him (Ignatius, *Phld.* 7.2; 8.2; cf. *Mart. Pol.* 1.1). At this level there are some possible references to Gospel in a written sense,[19] but mostly we are dealing with the oral form as a general re-statement, interpretation and extension of the theology and praxis of Jesus. Polycarp gives us an interesting

17. Martin Buber was, I think, clearly wrong in seeing Paul's concept of *emunah* in a strictly intellectual light. See M. Buber, *Two Types of Faith* (New York: Harper Torch, 1951).

18. Cf. *2 Clem.* 8.5, where what 'the Lord says in the Gospel' parallels very closely Lk. 16.10-12, and may be a reference to a written Gospel, or, as Koester insists, to the oral gospel. Cf. H. Koester, *Synoptische Überlieferung bei den Apostolischen Vätern* (TU, 65; Berlin: Akademie-Verlag, 1957), pp. 10-11; cf. also *idem*, 'From the Kerygma Gospel to the Written Gospel', p. 371.

19. *Did.* 15.3-4; 8.2; *2 Clem.* 8.5; *Mart. Pol.* 4.1; cf. J.A. Baird, *A Comparative Analysis of the Gospel Genre: The Synoptic Mode and Its Uniqueness* (Lewiston: Edwin Mellen Press, 1991), p. 50 n. 23. Koester insists the first use of εὐαγγέλιον to designate a writing appears in *The Treatise on the Resurrection* (48.8), late second century. Koester, 'From the Kerygma Gospel to the Written Gospel', p. 373.

transitional statement where gospel refers both to what Jesus said and what the apostles were saying about him: 'as he himself commanded us, and as did the apostles who brought us the Gospel' (*Phil.* 6.3).

The Ante-Nicene Fathers represent an intermediate stage between the oral gospel and the common reference to the Gospels as written documents. I find at least four references to εὐαγγέλιον as oral data, describing what Origen called 'the gospel of God' (*Contra Celsus* 6.6), and Clement of Alexandria the gospel which 'Peter publicly preached...at Rome' (*Frag.* 1). It is not unsymptomatic to find Irenaeus distinguishing between the oral gospel and the Gospels as written documents (*Adv. Haer.* 3.11.7). Primarily, however, εὐαγγέλιον is used to refer to the written Gospel. There is considerable reference to written Gospels in the plural[20] with some direct quotation and naming of a specific canonical Gospel; but at this level we find an even stronger reference to the written gospel in the singular, what Irenaeus called 'the gospel in which is recorded the doctrine regarding God' (*Adv. Haer.* 2.4.1).

This is what Justin Martyr identified as 'the so-called gospel' which he has read, reflecting that point at which, at least for him, the use of this term to describe a written collection of 'precepts', that are 'so wonderful that no one can keep them', is a new phenomenon. This written gospel is described as a 'voice' that 'teaches more urgently',[21] a 'book' containing the gospel preached by Paul[22] but which is mainly 'the doctrine regarding God',[23] written by the apostles and based on the teachings of Jesus as found in the Synoptics[24] and John.[25] By the time of Origen, there was already a concern that the followers of Marcion, Valentinus, Lucian and others had 'altered this gospel';[26] and Clement of Alexandria was able to refer to 'the gospel of the Lord', quoting Jn 21.4, 5, as 'Scripture' (γραφή), using the same term he used to describe the Old Testament.[27]

---

20. Irenaeus, *Adv. Haer.* 2.22.2; 11.7, 9; Clement of Alexandria, *Instructor* 5; Tertullian, *Against Marcion* 4.3, 5; Novatian, *On the Trinity*; Hippolytus, *Refutation*; cf. Baird, *Comparative Analysis*, ad. loc.

21. Theophilus of Antioch 3.14.

22. Irenaeus, *Adv. Haer.* 3.1.

23. Irenaeus, *Adv. Haer.* 3.2.9; cf. Tertullian, *Against Marcion* 4.3.

24. Justin, *Trypho* 100; Theophilus of Antioch 3.14; Novatian, *On the Trinity*.

25. Hippolytus, *Refutation*; cf. also Irenaeus, *Adv. Haer.* 3.4.1.

26. *Contra Celsus* 27; cf. Tertullian, *Against Marcion* 4.3.

27. Clement of Alexandria, *Instructor* 2, 3, 5.

4. *The Theological Interpretation of the Word* 87

By the time of Eusebius, 'the holy tetrad of the Gospels' (*Hist. Eccl.* 3.25.1) are almost always referred to as written documents, in either the singular[28] or the plural,[29] and sometimes by name, as 'Luke's Gospel' (3.4.7), or 'the Gospel according to the Hebrews' (4.22.8). At this late period in ecclesiastical history, I find the oral sense only once as Paul's 'preaching the gospel of Christ' (*Hist. Eccl.* 3.4.3).

The verb εὐαγγελίζομαι is interesting because of some rather dramatic patterns showing its specialized usage within the New Testament. Occurring briefly in Revelation, 1 Peter and Hebrews, the verb is more prominent in the Pauline and pseudo-Pauline literature. In Paul, one finds Old Testament rootage where εὐαγγελίζομαι reiterates the LXX proclamation of God's sovereignty (Isa. 52.7). It is even clearer in 1 Peter where it is the message of God's word in Jesus Christ (1.25; cf. Isa. 40.6-9). Mostly Paul uses εὐαγγελίζομαι to describe his preaching about Christ which centers upon 'the word of the cross'[30] and which came to him from two avowed sources: what he had 'received' from the Church concerning the life and teachings of Jesus (1 Cor. 15.1), which certainly, despite his disclaimers, must have included the apostles; and then from what he called 'a revelation of Jesus Christ' (Gal. 1.11, 12, 18). The occurrence of the verb stresses the activity of preaching the gospel; but Paul's use of the verb with the noun (1 Cor. 9.18; Gal. 1.11), and then his more abundant use of the noun, puts his emphasis clearly on the gospel as content rather than activity.

Luke, on the other hand, does just the reverse. His reluctance to employ the noun in his Gospel and Acts is dramatically countered by the abundant occurrence of the verb, stressing the gospel as activity, as the preaching of the word of the Lord, the good news about the Kingdom of God. It is interesting to note that Luke's use of εὐαγγελίζομαι in Acts follows Paul in identifying the gospel as the fulfillment of the Old Testament promise (13.32). It is the preaching of the apostles, especially Paul, 'about' Jesus;[31] but he is much more vigorous in stressing this as the word 'of' Jesus about the Kingdom of God.[32] This, then, comes to special focus in his Gospel, where not only is the Old Testament rootage

---

28. *Hist. Eccl.* 1.8.3; 1.10.6; 3.4.7; 4.22.8.
29. *Hist. Eccl.* 1.11.1; 1.12.1; 3.25.1; 3.37.2; 7.15.4; 7.18.1; etc.
30. 1 Cor. 1.17; cf. 9.16; 15.1, 2; Rom. 1.15; 15.20; etc.
31. Acts 8.35; 11.20; 14.7, 21; 16.10.
32. Acts 5.42; 8.4, 12, 25; 10.36; 15.36.

of this concept prominent,[33] but where it regularly describes the preaching of this good news in a clear progression from that prophesied in the Old Testament to the gospel pre-figured by angels (1.19; 2.10) and John the Baptist (3.18), and then proclaimed in all its fullness by Jesus[34] and the disciples (9.6; 16.16). There is a noticeable pattern in this material in the conjunction of βασιλεία τοῦ θεοῦ and εὐαγγελίζομαι, showing the centrality of Jesus' teaching *about* the Kingdom in Luke's use of the gospel verb. So, even as Luke stresses the activity of preaching the gospel, ultimately, for him as for Paul, it is the content that is the focus. The difference is that in his use of εὐαγγέλιον/ εὐαγγελίζομαι Luke stresses the Kingdom teaching of Jesus, whereas Paul stresses the cross, death, and resurrection, and the life of faith that stems from it.

In summary, we can see two types of development in the use of εὐαγγέλιον/εὐαγγελίζομαι over the first four centuries. The one is theological, and the other is literary. Both types show the Church's awareness of a solid core of belief commonly understood and widely proclaimed. The theological line follows a more logical rather than chronological development, beginning with the use of these terms in Luke–Acts to summarize Jesus' teaching about the Kingdom, either in his own words, or those of the narrator, and then moving on to describe what Paul and others were proclaiming about him, as they reiterated his teachings, or developed the theological meaning of his life, death and resurrection. In all, Jesus' teachings about the Kingdom are central; but there is a clear movement, beginning it would seem with Paul, away from the teachings 'of' Jesus to the theology 'about' Jesus. This was a transition from the theology of the Kingdom of God to a theology focused upon the advent, the death and the resurrection of Jesus the Christ. One word-study cannot establish this large theological development; but it has alerted us to it, and we can watch for its occurrence in other such probes throughout this book.

The second type of development is more literary. This shows a clear transition from the earliest use of εὐαγγέλιον/εὐαγγελίζομαι in Paul and the Synoptics as a reference to a singular, oral concept, summarizing a solid body of belief as described above, to its occurrence in the Apostolic Fathers where this same oral, kerygmatic sense prevails, but where in the *Didache*, *2 Clement*, and Polycarp we see the beginnings of

33. Lk. 7.22; 4.18; 16.16.
34. Lk. 4.43; 8.1; 20.1.

4. *The Theological Interpretation of the Word* 89

their reference to written documents, but still in the singular. Then in the Ante Nicene Fathers, where gospel describes mostly written material, we find an increasing use of the plural noun to describe individual Gospels, and in Eusebius this plural sense almost takes over to describe individual Gospels that are sacred, authoritative and widely known.[35] Throughout these four hundred years of changing usage, however, one fact is clear. Behind the individual written Gospels, and undergirding the oral gospel of the Church, lay a stable enduring understanding of Jesus Christ, what he said about God and his Kingdom, what this meant to the faith of the Church, and how men and women should act within that context.

The Gospel as Preaching: κηρύσσω/κήρυγμα

The proclamation of the gospel was more commonly described in the New Testament in terms of the verb κηρύσσω, mostly in the Synoptics (23 times), then in the Pauline literature (18 times), and in Acts (7 times). The first thing that appears in this study is a strong correlation between κηρύσσω and εὐαγγέλιον/εὐαγγελίζομαι in all three collections.[36] It was the 'gospel' which was being preached by Jesus (Mt. 4.23; Mk 1.14; Lk. 4.18; etc.), his disciples (Mk 16.15), Philip (Acts 8.12), Peter (Acts 10.37) and Paul (Gal. 2.2; Col. 1.23; etc.). The controlling element in this preaching throughout the entire New Testament, whether to describe the preaching of Jesus or of these others, was the 'gospel of the Kingdom of God', what Mark and Paul called 'the gospel of God' (Mk 1.14; 1 Thess. 2.9). The word βασιλεία occurs seventeen times in correlation with the verb κηρύσσω in the Synoptics, Acts, and the Pauline literature, and seven times in phrases like 'the gospel of the Kingdom', where βασιλεία and εὐαγγέλιον are closely linked.[37] The subject of this preaching was also characterized as λόγος[38] and as the gospel of Christ.[39] Other major preaching themes included the death and

---

35. I find one reference in *Hist. Eccl.* 3.4.3 to the oral gospel as the preaching of Paul along with seven to written Gospels: 1.8.3; 1.11.1; 1.12.1; 3.4.7; 3.25.1; 3.37.2; 4.22.8.
36. Synoptics 10 times, Acts 2 times and Paul 5 times.
37. Mt. 4.23; 9.35; 24.14; Mk 1.14; Lk. 4.43; 8.1; Acts 8.12; 1 Thess. 2.9.
38. Mk 1.45; Lk. 4.32; Acts 10.37; 20.32; 2 Tim. 4.2; Rom. 10.8.
39. Acts 8.12; 2 Cor. 4.5; etc.

resurrection of Christ,[40] faith, salvation, repentance and the forgiveness of sins.[41]

One of the clearest patterns in this study is the transition from the teaching of Jesus about the Kingdom, strongest in the Synoptics, but continuing strongly in Acts and Paul, to the teaching about Christ, his death and resurrection, and the salvation, forgiveness and new life that is available in him. This was strongest in Paul, and represents the movement from the gospel 'of' Jesus to the gospel 'about' Jesus, from Kingdom theology to narrative-based theology, from a theology centered upon God to one centered upon Christ and his atonement.

This development, which I have portrayed in the chart below, comes to special focus in the various summaries of gospel preaching found throughout the New Testament. Mark 1.14 epitomizes the preaching of Jesus in Kingdom terms: 'the time is fulfilled, and the Kingdom of God is at hand; repent and believe in the Gospel'. In Acts and Paul, we find several transition digests, showing movement from the gospel of the Kingdom to the gospel about the Kingdom. For example, Philip is described as preaching 'good news about the Kingdom of God and the name of Jesus Christ' (Acts 8.12), and Paul as 'preaching the Kingdom of God and teaching about the Lord Jesus Christ' (Acts 28.31). The recapitulation of Peter's preaching shows a complete shift away from Jesus' theology of the Kingdom to an atonement theology about Jesus: 'the good news of peace by Jesus Christ (he is lord of all), the word... how God anointed Jesus of Nazareth with the Holy Spirit... went about doing good... God was with him... they put him to death... but God raised him on the third day... commanded us to preach... that he is the one ordained by God to be judge of the living and the dead... that every one who believes in him receives forgiveness of sins through his name' (Acts 10.36-43).

The Pauline synopsis in Rom. 10.8-13 follows the same line: 'the word of faith which we preach... if you confess with your lips that Jesus is Lord and believe in your heart that God raised him from the dead, you will be saved...' This atonement, resurrection-oriented theology as a description of early Christian 'preaching' occupies a considerable portion of Acts and the Pauline literature, as the following chart makes clear. It raises a serious question as to whether or not Paul and the early Church changed the original gospel 'of' Jesus, in their preaching 'about' Jesus.

---

40. Acts 10.37-38; Rom. 10.14; etc.
41. Acts 10.43; Rom. 10.8-9; Mk 6.12; etc.

4. *The Theological Interpretation of the Word* 91

Here we should note one fact. In correlation with the verb κηρύσσω at least, the New Testament refers to this Christ, passion, faith, repentance-oriented preaching on 21 occasions in Acts, Paul and that late editorial summary in Lk. 24.46-47. The reference to preaching the gospel *of* the Kingdom of God, on the other hand, occurs on 27 different occasions. The Kingdom theme continues unabated; but the observable pattern is the escalation of Christ and atonement-oriented preaching in Acts and Paul.

Themes or Terms Co-Related with κηρύσσω	Synoptics	Acts	Paul
	(Number of Occurrences)		
βασιλεία	4	3	3
εὐαγγέλιον/εὐαγγελίζομαι	4	2	4
Gospel of the Kingdom	6	0	1
λόγος	2	2	2
Christ	1	4	7
Death and Resurrection	1	4	1
Faith/Salvation	0	1	2
Repentance/Forgiveness	5	0	3
Ethical Application	0	0	3

Occurrences of κηρύσσω with Related Themes

The innovation of παράδοσις-centered preaching in Paul[42] would seem to represent another of those later developments, where the teachings of Jesus have moved from εὐαγγέλιον as the understanding of the Church about his life and teachings, to παράδοσις, which is their application of that gospel to the practical needs of the Church (see Chapter 4). There is even some suggestion that the early Paul as pictured in Thessalonians (1 Thess. 2.9) and Acts (20.25) preached a more Kingdom-centered theology while his later preaching reflected in Romans (10.8-13) was more oriented to the passion of Christ and the concerns of faith and praxis.[43] Paul seems to have been having difficulty with many in the Church regarding his gospel (Gal. 2.2; 2 Cor. 11.4), and any radical shift from the 'gospel of God' to the 'gospel of Christ' could account for that. At this point, however, the continuation in the

---

42. Rom. 2.21; 1 Cor. 9.27; Gal. 5.11.
43. This is a difficult technical question, and cannot be dealt with here. See Chapter 10.

Pauline literature of the emphasis on the βασιλεία, and his continued use of both 'the gospel of God' and 'the gospel of Christ', would weaken this suggestion. It also underscores my major observation that although the emphasis shifted in moving from the Synoptics to Acts and Paul, the controlling element throughout, which made this a less radical shift, was the continued dedication to the teaching of Jesus about the Kingdom of God.

Whereas the verb κηρύσσω describing the activity of preaching occurs often in the New Testament, the noun κήρυγμα identifying the substance of that preaching occurs only six times. The Church obviously had other nouns it considered more important. Except for one instance where his κήρυγμα was described as 'the demonstration of the Spirit and power' (1 Cor. 2.4), Paul and then his students use this term to summarize the intellectual content of their preaching, including a strong emphasis on the resurrection (1 Cor. 15.14), and in parallel conjunction with other more prominent terms such as εὐαγγέλιον (Rom. 16.25) and λόγος (1 Cor. 2.4; Tit. 1.3). In another of those summary statements so peculiar to the Pauline material, we find λόγος, ἀλήθεια, and κήρυγμα interwoven as a description of Paul's preaching: 'their knowledge of the *truth*... manifested in his *word* through the *preaching* with which I have been entrusted' (Tit. 1.1, 3; my emphasis).

The Gospel as Word: λόγος

The next common locus for this concept surrounds the use of the word λόγος to encompass the totality of what the early Church was saying about Jesus, his life, his teachings, and what men and women could become through him.[44] This is 'the ministry of the word', 'the word of the gospel' (Acts 15.7) to which the apostles were dedicated (Acts 6.4) as they 'went about preaching the word (λόγος)...good news about the Kingdom of God and the name of Jesus Christ'.[45] Paul identifies his gospel as 'the word of the cross' (1 Cor. 1.18), 'the word (λόγος) of reconciliation' (2 Cor. 5.19), the 'gospel' by which the Corinthians were

---

44. εὐαγγέλιον/εὐαγγελίζομαι occur 107 times in the New Testament compared to 62 occurrences of λόγος in this 'gospel' sense (#4). For further details, see Chapter 2.

45. Acts 8.4, 12; cf. Acts 19.10.

to be saved.⁴⁶ Here is the 'word of truth' (Eph. 1.13), 'the word of life' (1 Jn 1.1), 'the word of Christ' (Heb. 6.1); and its use to summarize the gospel covers every facet of Christian theology in the New Testament as in the early Fathers. What we are saying is that 'word' was used by the early Church in a self-consciously technical way to describe what was also called 'gospel' (cf. Chapter 2).

The Gospel as Teaching: διδαχή

Closely allied with λόγος is the term διδαχή. In the Synoptics, it refers exclusively to the teachings of Jesus; and each time it occurs in the context of a general disciple audience.⁴⁷ This is consistent with a strong pattern in the Synoptics showing Jesus reserving his most characteristic teaching for the disciple audience.⁴⁸ It is also consistent with what we have been discovering about the use of διδαχή in the early Church to refer to an objective body of instruction by Jesus or by the apostles about Jesus, the basis of which was the teaching of Jesus. In the later New Testament, διδαχή and λόγος are parallel terms to describe the apostolic preaching (2 Tim. 4.2) and teaching (Acts 2.42) to which the early Church was committed. It was this which evoked such opposition from the high priest in Jerusalem (Acts 5.28) and astonishment from the proconsul in Cyprus (Acts 13.12).⁴⁹ This is the 'standard of teaching' (τύπον διδαχήν) to which the Roman church was committed (Rom. 6.17), and one of the formal elements of worship to which Paul ascribes an almost scriptural function: 'When you come together, each one has a hymn, a lesson (διδαχή), a revelation, a tongue or an interpretation...'

---

46. RSV: 'in what terms', τίνι λόγῳ (1 Cor. 15.2). Here, as elsewhere, the RSV obscures this meaning of λόγος in a curious bias against this translation.

47. Mk 1.22; 4.2; 11.18; 12.38; Mt. 16.12; 22.33.

48. Baird, *Audience Criticism*, p. 125.

49. There is some suggestion of a distinction between Peter's preaching (κήρυγμα) of the message of the passion and resurrection that brought these 3000 to repentance in Acts 2.42, and the διδαχὴ τῶν ἀποστόλων, the follow up instruction, which would be principally their personal recollections of Jesus' life and teachings. C.H. Dodd (*The Apostolic Preaching and Its Developments* [New York: Harper & Row, 1936], p. 7) notes that 'the New Testament writers draw a clear distinction between preaching and teaching'. There is some support for this in the reluctance of the Synoptics to show Jesus commending the preaching role to any but the twelve disciples. See J.A. Baird, *Rediscovering the Power of the Gospels: Jesus' Theology of the Kingdom* (Wooster, OH: Iona Press, 1982), p. 156.

(1 Cor. 14.26; cf. 14.6). Paul's sermon on Mars Hill is called a 'new teaching' (διδαχή), which was his restatement of the revelation of God and his judgment in Jesus Christ, stressing the resurrection as the 'assurance' of that fact (Acts 17.19, 31).

At times διδαχή appears as a collective reference to the apostolic teaching about Jesus as what Ignatius called 'the example and lesson of immortality' (*Mag.* 6.2); what is 'the way of the teaching (τῆς ὁδοῦ τῆς διδαχῆς)...the whole yoke of the Lord' in the *Didache* (6.1). In 2 John, the 'doctrine of Christ' (διδαχὴ τοῦ Χριστοῦ) comes as a summary of 'the truth' of 'the coming of Jesus Christ in the flesh' which is sufficiently identifiable to act as the test for those who do or do not have 'both the father and the son'. Behind this, however, lie the commandments which they have 'heard from the beginning' that we 'love one another' (2 Jn 6, 5), a direct reference to the words of Jesus in John's Gospel (13.34; 15.17). Thus, although this 'doctrine of Christ' is probably, as Amos Wilder and many others insist, an objective genitive, it still has about it the sense of the subjective genitive where the teaching 'about' Jesus includes at the same time the teaching 'of' Jesus.[50] This is especially true in the *Didache,* where 'the teaching of these words', the 'commandment of the teaching' (1.3; 2.1), or, in *Barnabas*, 'the gift of his teaching' (9.9; cf. 16.9), refer clearly to the sayings of Jesus.

The Gospel as Truth: ἀλήθεια

Continuing this more intellectual line, the general consensus of the early Church was described in the New Testament as 'truth' in a series of ways that cover most of the uses of εὐαγγέλιον, λόγος, and διδαχή, and finds an especially strong occurrence in Paul and John. In the Synoptics it functions as a description by a Pharisee and then a scribe of the teachings of Jesus, who teaches 'the way of God truthfully', or, more accurately, 'in truth' (ἐν ἀληθείᾳ; Mk 12.14; cf. 12.32), giving the noun its full force. This is the way we might expect these more pedagogically oriented Jews to understand Jesus' teaching.

The Gospel of John reflects this same orientation when it records Jesus summarizing his 'word' as the truth that will 'make you free', which he has 'heard from God' (8.32, 40; 18.37, 38). By far the most

---

50. See A.N. Wilder, 'The First, Second, and Third Epistles of John', in G.A. Buttrick *et al.* (eds.), *The Interpreter's Bible* (12 vols.; New York and Nashville: Abingdon Press, 1955), XII, p. 306.

4. The Theological Interpretation of the Word 95

abundant use of this term is to summarize the gospel about Jesus; not just as something that is 'true', using ἀλήθεια as an adjective, but to describe a body of theological truth which had definite parameters and was widely understood and accepted.[51] Truth for John stood in contrast to the Torah, as that which came through Jesus Christ (1.17). It was the content of Christian worship (4.23), and John the Baptist's testimony to the incarnation (5.33).

For Paul 'the truth in Christ' was a summary of his message (Rom. 9.1), the truth about the sacrifice of Christ (1 Cor. 5.8), a description of God's word which is the gospel of the glory of Christ (2 Cor. 4.2). The 'word of truth' (ἐν λόγῳ ἀληθείας; 2 Cor. 6.7) is the gospel of God which Paul is preaching (2 Cor. 11). For him this is 'our gospel' which is different from the 'traditions' (παραδόσεις; 2 Thess. 2.15), and is the essence of his Gospel of justification by faith (Gal. 2.5, 14).

This same message continues in the Pastorals and later epistles where ἀλήθεια is summarized as one God, one mediator, Jesus Christ (1 Tim. 2.4), the 'bulwark' of the Church (1 Tim. 3.15). It is based on 'the sound words of our Lord Jesus Christ (ὑγιαίνουσιν λόγοις) and the teaching (διδασκαλία) which accords with godliness' (1 Tim. 6.3; cf. 2 Tim. 2.15; 3.7, 8; Tit. 1.1, 14; etc.). This 'truth' is an intellectual word about Jesus Christ, 'the perfect law' (Jas 1.18, 21, 22), the 'wisdom from above' (Jas 3.14). It is the 'living and abiding word of God' (1 Pet. 1.22-23), and is what Timothy is most urged to be; 'a workman...rightly handling the word of truth' (τοῦ λόγος τῆς ἀληθείας; 2 Tim. 2.15). It is symptomatic of the widespread theological consensus within the early Church to see in the New Testament the interweaving of εὐαγγέλιον, λόγος, διδαχή, and ἀλήθεια, all describing essentially the same gospel phenomenon, and coming out in various phrases where the words are combined. In 2 John, the 'truth (ἀλήθεια) which abides in us' is the 'doctrine (διδαχή) of Christ' (2 Jn 1, 9). Paul, in 2 Corinthians, calls this 'the word of truth' (ἐν λόγῳ ἀληθείας; 6.7). The author of Ephesians nicely summarizes Paul's testimony to this phenomenon when he writes of 'the word (λόγος) of truth (ἀλήθεια), the gospel' (εὐαγγέλιον; 1.13; cf. 6.14; Col. 1.15).

---

51. Again, the RSV weakens the force of this point by translating this noun as an adjective or adverb, thus missing the nominative sense of an objective body of data. In 2 Cor. 6.7 ἐν λόγῳ ἀληθείας is rendered 'truthful speech', and in 2 Cor. 7.14 the substance of what Paul was saying, ἐν ἀληθείᾳ is translated 'true' rather than 'truth'. It does make a difference to the exegesis.

Following the course of this term throughout its use in the early Church reveals several typical things in that community's understanding of the gospel. For one thing, we can see the linkage with the Old Testament, and especially its concept of God in the fifteen times ἀλήθεια occurs in Paul, the Johannine literature and James, to describe 'what can be known about God' (Rom. 1.18). This is generally a reference to his judgment (Rom. 1.25; cf. Rom. 2.2; 3.7), his word (Jn 2.22; 17.17), the 'perfect law' (Jas 1.18, 21, 22), his promise to the patriarchs (Rom. 15.8), and, in a more existential fashion, to God's truth which abides within us (2 Jn 1; 1 Jn 1.6, 8). This more personal, spiritual connotation comes out in Ephesians (4.15) where 'speaking the truth in love' becomes an aspect of Christian growth toward maturity. It is especially strong in these places where ἀλήθεια refers to an experience of the power and presence of God, the counselor, 'the spirit of truth' (Jn 14.17; 15.26; 16.13), which is the power of God in Christ working within Paul (2 Cor. 13.8). As usual, the author of 1 John puts it succinctly: 'the Spirit is truth' (5.7; cf. 3.19; 4.6).

Two other uses of ἀλήθεια must be mentioned. The one is a reference to truth as something one 'does' as proof that 'his deeds have been wrought in God' (Jn 3.21), that men and women are 'children of light' (Eph. 5.9). The other is of course the application of this concept to Jesus Christ as the word become flesh, 'full of grace and truth' (Jn 1.14). In all of this, we have a term used to describe the gospel which shows a clear and typical development, from truth as a description of the teaching of Jesus, to its main use to describe the Church's theology about Jesus, and then the Christian personal experience of that living word, the ethical application of it, and finally the Christological reflection on Jesus himself as the incarnation of that truth. This is the same 'trajectory of the word' which we have seen evident in the study of λόγος.

The Gospel as Wisdom: σοφία

This theme continues with a thoroughly intellectual term which, when used to describe the gospel, becomes also very spiritual.[52] The Old Testament rootage is there in Paul's description of the 'mind of the

---

52. For a discussion of the Jewish rootage of this term, see M.J. Suggs, *Wisdom, Christology and Law in Matthew's Gospel* (Cambridge, MA: Harvard University Press, 1970).

4. The Theological Interpretation of the Word

Lord' (God) as σοφία (Rom. 11.34, 33; cf. 1 Cor. 1.21). It can describe 'the word of Christ', and 'the Kingdom of his son', with which they are to 'teach and admonish one another in all wisdom' (Col. 1.9; 3.16; cf. Acts 20.31). It is the 'mystery' the 'gospel' of which Paul was made a minister (Eph. 3.9, 7; cf. Col. 2.3). 'Wisdom' therefore has a thoroughly theological base, founded on the teaching of Jesus. But we are then immediately aware of the interplay in the mind of Paul and his students between the intellectual content of the wisdom of God as words and secrets which are revealed, and the spiritual content of those truths which is radically different from the 'wisdom of men' with their 'lofty words'. It rather consists of the demonstration of the Spirit and power of God.[53] σοφία as the word of Christ consists not only of words by and about Jesus, but also of the experience of the Word which is the power and wisdom of God himself who is incarnate in Christ.[54]

Bringing all this together in characteristic fashion, Ephesians in a masterful summary of Paul's gospel interweaves the terms mystery, word, truth, gospel, Spirit, wisdom (Eph. 1.9, 13, 17). It shows σοφία as a blend of the intellectual and the spiritual, of theology and experience, of the teachings of Jesus and the faith of the Church, of the mind of God and the minds of men and women, all typical of the Church's gospel. Wisdom is the stance (ἐν σοφίᾳ) in which the Word of Christ is proclaimed. It refers to the condition of mind and heart ('having the eyes of the heart enlightened') in which the word is proclaimed. There is a possible distinction between σοφία as the pre-condition and λόγος as the content of this experience; but any rigid distinction is difficult because they interweave. Here is the same intellectual-spiritual interrelation we have seen throughout the study of the Pauline corpus, as in other portions of the New Testament.

This comes to special focus in Paul's concept of 'the mind of Christ'. It is almost exclusively a Pauline idiom (except possibly for 1 Pet. 3.8), and represents a highly spiritualized description of the gospel. In its classic expression in 1 Cor. 2.1-16 there are several parallel ideas giving us something of the range of meaning for Paul: the secret wisdom of God, spiritual truths, the gifts of the Spirit, the mysteries of God, the Kingdom of God (4.20), the power of God. Here is the word of Christ

---

53. 1 Cor. 1.17–2.16; cf. Eph. 1.9; Col. 1.9; 2.3.
54. 1 Cor. 1.24, 30. This same phenomenon occurs in Jesus' parable of the sower (Mk 4.1-2), where the seed which is the word becomes the power of God active within the soil of men's souls; cf. Baird, *Rediscovering the Power of the Gospels*, p. 98.

and the word of God as a living presence coming together in a brilliant theological summation so typical of Paul's ability.

When referring to men and women, the νοῦς Χριστοῦ (1 Cor. 2.16; Phil. 4.7) idiom is Paul's way of describing the love and peace found in Christ Jesus, which come from holding fast 'the word of life'.[55] When referring to God, it is a description of the will and nature of him 'who searches the hearts of men' (Rom. 8.27; 11.34). When referring to the 'mind of Christ', it describes what Jesus said about the Kingdom, and what he represented in terms of the incursion of the βασιλεία, the μυστήριον, the δύναμις of God into the hearts of those 'who possess the Spirit' (1 Cor. 2.13). As Meagher correctly puts it, 'to have the Spirit is to have the mind of Christ'.[56] I would only add that behind this spiritual experience of wisdom lies the even more prominent intellectual apprehension of Jesus' word of the Kingdom. Both the intellectual and the spiritual experience of this wisdom, this truth, this word, form together the gospel nexus which is so much a part of the Church's inheritance from Jesus as from its Old Testament background. The life and teachings of Jesus are there, but they are buried deeply in the experience of the wisdom which is the living Christ within them.

The Gospel as Knowledge: γνῶσις

Occurring twice in Luke, γνῶσις refers to Zechariah's prophecy concerning John (1.77), and in a λόγιον of Jesus describes the knowledge of God in his Kingdom (11.52). Mostly it is found in Paul and the later New Testament. Like these other terms, it has some Old Testament rootage in referring to the judgments of God (Rom. 11.33), but mostly it is reserved for the Christian gospel in its more rational sense. Paul summarizes the gospel which they were 'taught' as 'the knowledge of God's mystery, of Christ in whom are hid all the treasures of wisdom…'[57] In doing so, he parallels γνῶσις with a number of other terms denoting the gospel, like λόγος (2 Cor. 2.14; 8.7; Rom. 15.14), σοφία (Rom. 11.33), μυστήριον (1 Cor. 13.2), διδαχή (1 Cor. 14.6), and εὐαγγέλιον (2 Cor. 4.6). Such rational knowledge sometimes describes the ethical rules of the Church, like those concerning food offered to idols (1 Cor. 8.1), and Paul is afraid that this kind of γνῶσις

---

55. Phil. 2.16; Rom. 8.6; 12.16; 15.6.
56. Meagher, *The Way of the Word*.
57. Col. 2.3, 2, 7; cf. 2 Cor. 10.5; 1 Cor. 14.6; etc.

might lead to intellectual and moral pride and stand in the way of love (1 Cor. 8.1-2; 13.2-4; 1 Tim. 6.20). Mostly it describes the more theological substance of the gospel.

Knowledge then was primarily a description of the gospel as a body of theological and ethical data, based on the word (2 Cor. 8.7), on the apostolic preaching about Jesus (2 Cor. 11.6), and on the glory of God as found in the face of Jesus (2 Cor. 4.6). It was also used to refer to the more existential and personal aspect of the 'knowledge of God' in Jesus Christ and the power of his resurrection which is gained through faith (2 Cor. 4.6; Phil. 3.8). In its over-all occurrence, the rational meaning was predominant, describing the gospel as a body of 'knowledge' that formed the basis of their Christian instruction.

The Gospel as Mystery: μυστήριον

Jesus summarized his message to the apostles as the 'mystery of the kingdom of God' (Mk 4.10-12), and dramatized this concept with the parable of the sower (Mk 4.1-9) where the mystery of the Kingdom is described as the seed of the λόγος of God cast into the soil of the soul.[58] This brings together three closely related terms: βασιλεία, μυστήριον, λόγος. Paul also characterizes his own message as a μυστήριον, and parallels this term with many others describing the gospel: εὐαγγέλιον (Rom. 6.25; Eph. 3.3, 4, 9; 6.19), λόγος (1 Cor. 4.3), σοφία (Rom. 11.25; Eph. 1.9; Col. 1.26-27; 2.2), Χριστός (Col. 4.3; 2.2), πίστις (Rom. 16.26; Col. 2.2), and νοῦς κυρίου (Rom. 11.34). In Jesus' parables as well as the Pauline literature, there is a tension between the mystery as a rational word of theology, and the mystery as the presence of God working within one's life. In the parable of the sower, the word of God is cast like a seed into the soil of the soul, a description of what Jesus is doing in his teaching.[59] But then this intellectual word germinates within that soil and the presence of God who 'is' the Word transforms the dead seed into the living plant of the new Kingdom life.[60] The 'mystery' is both the rational-theological word about God, and the dynamic, spiritual Word, which is God himself as βασιλεία working

---

58. J.A. Baird, *The Justice of God in the Teaching of Jesus* (Philadelphia: Westminster Press, 1963), p. 177.
59. Baird, *The Justice of God in the Teaching of Jesus*, p. 177.
60. Baird, *The Justice of God in the Teaching of Jesus*, p. 177; *idem*, *Rediscovering the Power of the Gospels*, pp. 111-15.

within peoples' lives. This is what it means to 'see', an intellectual exercise, and also 'perceive', a thoroughly spiritual experience, to 'hear' and also to 'understand'.[61] As Paul put it, 'the mind of Christ' is 'spiritually discerned' (1 Cor. 2.14-16). The selective character of this discernment is for Jesus a description of the Kingdom crisis,[62] and for Paul one of the 'unsearchable judgments of God' (Rom. 11.33).

The tension between the rational and existential character of this mystery within the Christian literature is thoroughly Hebraic and illustrates the Old Testament use of *sodh* to describe both the knowledge about the judgment of God and the experience of his presence. This comes out clearly in the Pauline material where the μυστήριον is the 'mind... wisdom... knowledge... unsearchable... inscrutable' judgments of God (Rom. 11.25, 33-34; cf. Eph. 6.19), all referring to theological content. It is also 'Christ in you the hope of glory' (Col. 1.26-27): a thoroughly existential experience. At times Paul stresses the one side of this equation, and at times the other, but mostly he brings them together in his description of the person who is 'mature in Christ' (Col. 1.28; cf. Eph. 1.9; 3.3-4, 9; 5.32). This is beautifully summarized in Col. 2.1-5, as the following re-arrangement will show:

> 'I strive...
> > that their hearts be encouraged
> > knit together in love
> > > SPIRITUAL
> > the firmness of your faith in Christ
> > assured understanding
> > knowledge of God's mystery
> > > INTELLECTUAL
> > all the treasures of wisdom and knowledge'

The mystery of the Gospel is a description for both Paul and Jesus of the interplay of theological understanding and spiritual discernment, of both 'seeing' and 'perceiving', and at this point there is a clear consistency between Paul and the Jesus of the Synoptics. The difference comes at the point where Paul then goes on to describe the μυστήριον as the 'mystery of Christ', where the term Χριστός becomes his replacement for Jesus' term, βασιλεία (Col. 4.3). This is a significant development.

---

61. Mk 4.10-12; cf. Baird, *Rediscovering the Power of the Gospels*, Chapters 7, 8.
62. Baird, *The Justice of God in the Teaching of Jesus*, p. 177.

4. *The Theological Interpretation of the Word*

The Gospel as Faith: πίστις/πιστεύω

At this point we must identify the role of πίστις/πιστεύω in this gospel stratum. By all counts this is the most prominent concept to describe what was going on within the early Church. The noun occurs 230 times and the verb 225 within all areas of the New Testament. The Gospel of John uses only the verb, but this, I take it, is an editorial rather than a substantive difference. In the Synoptics, πίστις regularly refers to a condition of belief and trust in Jesus' ability which leads to a miracle of healing (Mk 2.5; Mt. 9.29; etc.). This seems to be a more primitive usage. Throughout the rest of the New Testament, both noun and verb refer primarily to the spiritual condition which undergirds theological and ethical instruction, and identifies the work of the risen Christ, the Holy Spirit, within the lives of the early community.

For Paul this is described in terms of his signature concept of justification by faith; and on at least one occasion he is said to distinguish πίστις from instruction: 'in wisdom and...in the knowledge of him...that you may know...' (Eph. 1.18). Here, πίστις is the initial experience of Christ needing further theological substance which could be called gospel (cf. Acts 24.24; Col. 2.7). This does, however, occur more often in the use of the verb where 'those who heard the word (λόγος) believed' (Acts 4.4; cf. 8.12; 14.1; etc.). Paul in Romans seems to be using the term in both a spiritual and a theological sense when he speaks of the gospel as 'the power of God for salvation', ἐκ πίστεως εἰς πίστιν (Rom. 1.16). His purpose in preaching the gospel is to lead persons from a spiritual experience of the power of God to a theological understanding of what God was doing in and through Jesus Christ. This is what he stresses in this great theological statement. The same dual usage occurs in a classic epistemological section in Romans (10.1-17) where Paul brings together three gospel terms, ῥῆμα, πίστις, and κηρύσσω, to describe 'the word of faith' which is both something you are to 'confess with your lips', that is, ἐπι-στόμα, an intellectual confession, and 'believe in your heart', a thoroughly existential experience.[63]

The Gospel of John makes particularly abundant use of the verb πιστεύω to describe all three of the major connotations of this noun-verb complex. At a superficial level, belief is associated with hearing Jesus' word, often connected with signs (2.11; 3.2), but without confession (12.42). It is belief in Jesus' ability to do mighty works (2.11,

---

63. See Baird, *The Justice of God in the Teaching of Jesus*, p. 161.

23; 3.2; 4.39; etc.). But Jesus urged people to go further, beyond this shallow faith (2.23; 10.37-38; 14.7-11; etc.).

A second level is the intellectual belief that Jesus is the son of God (11.25), the Christ (20.31), that he is in the father and the father in him (14.1). All of these are descriptions of an emerging gospel theology. Behind this clearly lies the teachings of Jesus as 'the words' which God gave to Jesus, enabling them to 'know in truth' and 'believe' that he came from God (17.8). Throughout the entire usage of πιστεύω in John runs this sense of the Holy Word of Jesus as the ultimate basis of belief.

The third level of John's usage is a more existential belief where men and women obey the son and receive power to become children of God (3.36; 12.47; 1.12) and find eternal life (3.16). It is this third level of belief toward which the Gospel of John is pressing. Nicodemus is a classic case of one who holds to the theological form of belief, but denies its spiritual power (Jn 3.7, 12; cf. 1 Cor. 2.5), which is to believe in the heart (12.36), to eat of the living bread (6.29), to belong to his sheep (10.25).[64]

Instruction in the Gospel: κατηχέω/παραλαμβάνω

The strength and variety of the Church's understanding of gospel as a consistent body of theological content is further illustrated by two less frequently used, yet important, terms. The first is the verb κατηχέω giving the sense of disciplined instruction in Torah, which was Paul's own background (Rom. 2.18; cf. Acts 21.21). Gerhardsson insists this was parallel in the Church to what happened in the rabbinical schools. The theological character of this material is obvious as 'the word' (Gal. 6.6), the 'way of the Lord' (Acts 18.25) which is taught to the mind (Gal. 6.6; 1 Cor. 14.19). In another of those summarizing statements, we find Luke prefiguring his Gospel by bringing together two of these gospel terms: 'that you may know the truth concerning the things (λόγον) of which you have been instructed' (κατηχήθης; 1.1-4).

The term, παραλαμβάνω, was a favorite of Paul in describing what he had 'received from the Lord' (1 Cor. 11.23). Basically, for him, this described the teachings of Jesus (Col. 2.6); but it could also refer to the passion story (1 Cor. 15.1, 3), the revelation of Christ's resurrection

---

64. B. Gerhardsson, *Memory and Manuscript: Oral Tradition and Written Transmission in Rabbinic Judaism and Early Christianity* (Lund: C.W.K. Gleerup; Copenhagen: Munksgaard, 1961).

4. The Theological Interpretation of the Word 103

(Gal. 1.12), Paul's own gospel (Gal. 1.9), his moral instructions (Phil. 4.9), and the παράδοσις in general (2 Thess. 3.6). The extremely broad reference of this verb suggests not only that it was not widely used in a technical sense, but also that we are dealing with a live, oral situation where rigid literary distinctions were not being made. What we have seen above is that there is much overlapping in the usage of these gospel terms, inevitable in such a living situation. What one looks for is patterns of predominant emphasis showing what 'usually' occurs; and in that sense there is a clear cluster of terms identifying the gospel as a stable body of theological material, widely understood and consistently accepted.

The Guardians of the Gospel: ἀπόστολοι

In all this gospel layer, it is the apostles who constantly emerge as the origin, focus or transmitters of this theological interpretation of the Holy Word. We will be pointing in the next chapter to the distinction between apostles and prophets within the growing Church. The Pauline school is especially concerned to make this distinction by placing the apostles as the 'first' (1 Cor. 12.28; Eph. 2.20), the 'holy' ones (Eph. 3.5), to whose διδαχή the early converts 'devoted themselves' (Acts 2.42; cf. 5.28). The evidence of Chapter 5, revealing the doctrinal authority of these apostles and their central role in the transmission of the Jesus tradition, is congenial with the study of this cluster of terms describing the gospel. They are not the only ones to preach and teach this λόγος (cf. Acts 8.11, 20; Col. 1.7; etc.), but they are the ones to whom this message has been chiefly entrusted, and this awareness continues throughout the ante-Nicene period.

The didactic climate of the apostolic schools which we will be describing in Chapter 6 is the logical outgrowth of the strong emphasis within the early Church on the gospel as theological content. This is a further extension of the same orientation within the Synoptics toward the teachings of Jesus which I have described elsewhere.[65] These apostles seem to have been both teachers and preachers, but the preponderant reference to the gospel as διδαχή, ἀλήθεια, λόγος, σοφία, and γνῶσις as compared to its more homiletic and spiritual designation as κήρυγμα and μυστήριον points to the fact that they were primarily teachers: 'First apostles, second prophets, third teachers...' (1 Cor. 12.28). This is

65. Baird, *Rediscovering the Power of the Gospels*, pp. 32-33.

not to minimize their function as preachers, as our study of κηρύσσω, μυστήριον and πίστις has shown; nor does it downgrade their activity in worship, as the spiritual, existential connotation of these gospel terms would demonstrate; but it does point to the theological and didactic orientation of the gospel within the early Church.

Summary and Conclusions

It is now possible in the fourteen terms we have examined to document with a fair degree of confidence the existence of a layer of Christian consensus having a clear identity and a widespread occurrence. The phenomenon of the interweaving and interchangeable usage of these terms shows rather dramatically their existence as a 'complex' of ideas having a common coherence. When someone spoke or wrote of the gospel, whichever term was used, the early Church would know what was being talked about.

The substance of this gospel consensus emerging from these separate studies has taken the form of seven major patterns cutting across the entire New Testament.

(1) Underlying all of these terms, but more prominent in some than in others, lie the teachings of Jesus about the Kingdom of God.

(2) Parallel to his teachings are the references to the life of Jesus, which in this gospel stratum are sketchy at best, and which stress his death and resurrection.

(3) The most prominent pattern shows these fourteen parallel and often interchangeable terms describing the Church's teaching about Jesus, as they interpreted his message of the Kingdom, and tried to understand the meaning of his death and resurrection, especially as it applied to their own life of faith.

(4) A strong pattern moving through all the New Testament, but more concentrated in ἀλήθεια, σοφία, γνῶσις, κηρύσσω, πιστεύω and μυστήριον, deals with the Church's spiritual experience of the risen Christ and the God of the Kingdom.

(5) Another pattern shows the Church at work applying the teachings of Jesus to their own practical situations in faith and worship. Ethical concerns do appear in connection with these gospel terms, especially εὐαγγέλιον, ἀλήθεια, and παραλαμβάνω, but they are completely secondary to the more theological orientation of this gospel complex.

(6) Running throughout the New Testament occurrence of all these gospel terms is a clear tension between a stress on the theological content of the gospel, and that on the spiritual-existential apprehension of the Word. Some terms, like εὐαγγέλιον/εὐαγγελίζομαι, διδαχή, σοφία, γνῶσις, κήρυγμα and κατηχέω, stress the more intellectual-theological aspects of the gospel, while others like μυστήριον, πίστις, πιστεύω, κηρύσσω, stress the more spiritual-existential experience of the gospel. The tension comes out perhaps most clearly in those terms where the dual emphasis is particularly strong, like λόγος, ἀλήθεια and μυστήριον. Some New Testament books stress one side of this equation more than the other, but I see no clear pattern. What I do see is the continuity of the teachings of Jesus in the Synoptic Gospels with the rest of the New Testament on this dual aspect of the Kingdom. The gospel, the word, the truth, the wisdom, the knowledge, the mystery, the faith is not only something to be understood and taught. It is also something or someone to be accepted and experienced.

(7) One of the most troublesome patterns showing up in such a study is that which reflects a development in the substance of the gospel within the early Church from the teachings of Jesus about the Kingdom of God, to the theology of the Church about Jesus and the Kingdom. There seems to be a noticeable shift from the gospel of the Kingdom to the gospel of Christ, the one centered upon God, the other upon the death, resurrection and atoning power of Jesus. This is an extension of the same pattern observed in our study of λόγος.

At every point in this study, the teachings of Jesus have been the basic substance of the gospel. Contrary to John Meagher's conclusion, I would have to say that the teachings of Jesus are indeed normative for what he calls 'the way of the word', but which more exactly should be called the 'gospel'.[66] Which of the major elements within this gospel can be said to be 'the' most important in constituting and describing the early Christian consensus is highly controversial. The two major candidates seem to be the teachings of Jesus or the activity of the Holy Spirit. David Dungan has pointed to the one and Meagher to the other.[67] My research says they are both there in strength; but the teachings of Jesus would seem to be the most normative. One must remember, however, that one of the most important aspects of Jesus' teaching was the spiritual reality of the

---

66. Meagher, *The Way of the Word*, p. 197.
67. D. Dungan, *The Sayings of Jesus in the Churches of Paul* (Philadelphia: Fortress Press, 1971); cf. Meagher, *The Way of the Word*.

Kingdom as God's redeeming presence. The two are not to be separated. The Kingdom was not just the seed of a word to be seen and heard; it was also the power of God to be accepted, 'perceived' and 'understood'. This has been clearly seen in the way in which both the theological and the spiritual aspects of the gospel have converged in the occurrence of one after another of these gospel terms.

In essence, the gospel was the developing theological restatement of the Holy Word of Jesus to which was added the meaning of his life, death and resurrection and the experience of the living presence of that word, of Christ, of the Kingdom of God within the life of the Church.

Chapter 5

HOLY TRADITION:
THE APPLICATION OF THE WORD

Parallel to the development of the gospel and a further extension of the Word was the growing body of 'tradition' which applied the Word to the increasingly complex ethical, liturgical and ecclesiastical life of the Church. This was a collection of individual insights which began as an outgrowth of the Holy Word. It was quickly distinguished as the word of the Church rather than the word of Jesus. It was also differentiated from the gospel as the practical application rather than the theological interpretation of the word. Within the first three hundred years there were many terms used for this aspect of the Christian witness, originally oral, and eventually written.

The Substance of Tradition. παράδοσις

The most widely pervasive seems to have been the noun παράδοσις which itself was used in at least five distinct ways. (1) Normally it referred to oral data as distinct from written. Ignatius, for example, urged the Church to cling closely to the tradition of the apostles, which, since his martyrdom was at hand, should for safety's sake be given a fixed form in writing (*Hist. Eccl.* 3.36.4). For Irenaeus, this was 'the tradition of truth' (*Adv. Haer.* 3.4) lodged in the catholic bank, originating with the apostles (3.2.1) and handed down by them to the churches in oral form before being written (3.4.1).[1]

---

1. This same distinction was preserved by the Council of Trent when it taught that the truth of Christ is contained partly in the Bible and partly in unwritten tradition received by the apostles from Christ or from the Holy Ghost. The Council of Trent, Sess. IV: *De Canon Script*; cf. W.E. Addis and T. Arnold (eds.), *A Catholic Dictionary* (rev. with additions by T.B. Scannel; London: Kegan Paul, 9th edn, 1917), pp. 813-14, s.v. 'tradition'. For bibliography on 'tradition', see B. Gerhardsson,

The background to this Christian usage seems to have been the Hebrew distinction between oral and written Torah. As is well known, tradition for the Jew was a distinct and technical activity with certain special words referring to it (halakah, haggadah, Mishnah, midrash, maʿaseh, etc.), and a rather elaborate scheme for its preservation. This manifested itself as 'oral Torah' in clear distinction from the 'written Torah' of the Old Testament, and was clearly in a position of lesser authority, man-made as distinct from divinely given. Although eventually, as with the Mishnah, the oral Torah became written, still this distinction was maintained and formed the basis of Old Testament canonization at the end of the first century.

This was reflected in the Christian documents where Paul for example describes his early condition as 'extremely zealous...for the tradition (παράδοσις) of my fathers' (Gal. 1.14). He later came to see this as 'human tradition' (Col. 2.8), and actually a source of death (Rom. 7.9) before Christ liberated him. Jesus in the Synoptics often speaks disparagingly of the 'tradition (παράδοσις) of the elders' which are man-made rules, often luring men away from the 'commandment of God' (Mk 7.3-4; Mt. 15.3, 6). The extent to which Christian tradition was also considered of lesser authority in the life of the early Church is an important matter, and will emerge as we proceed. It would seem that

Memory and Manuscript: Oral Tradition and Written Transmission in Rabbinic Judaism and Early Christianity (Lund: C.W.K. Gleerup; Copenhagen: Munksgaard, 1961), p. 203 n. 5. For his discussion of Christian παράδοσις, see pp. 71-72, 290-91. See also R.M. Grant, 'Holy Law in Paul and Ignatius', in D.E. Groh and R. Jewett (eds.), *The Living Text: Essays in Honor of Ernest W. Saunders* (New York and London: University Press of America, 1985), pp. 65-71. He points to Käsemann's study, 'Sentences of Holy Law in the New Testament', in E. Käsemann, *New Testament Questions for Today* (Philadelphia: Fortress Press, 1969), p. 65. R.P.C. Hanson (*Origen's Doctrine of Tradition* [London: SPCK, 1954], p. 34) makes a similar point regarding the distinction I am making between tradition and doctrine: 'Chrysostom confined tradition to practical matters such as actions, not doctrine'. For a good statement of the importance of this dimension in understanding early Christianity, see W.A. Meeks, 'Understanding Early Christian Ethics', *JBL* 105 (1986), pp. 3-11. See also Grant, 'Holy Law in Paul and Ignatius', p. 65; J.F. Bethune-Baker, *Introduction to the History of Christian Doctrine* (London: Methuen, 1933). See also H. Schürmann, *Traditionsgeschichtliche Untersuchungen zu den Synoptischen Evangelien* (Düsseldorf: Patmos, 1967). More recently, M.E. Boring (*Sayings of the Risen Jesus* [SNTSMS, 46; Cambridge: Cambridge University Press, 1982]) has identified five types of material characteristic of prophetic speech within early Christianity, one of which he calls 'concrete directions for church life'.

by the time of Eusebius, 'unwritten' could on occasion have the connotation of spurious, less authentic or mythical (*Hist. Eccl.* 3.39.7-8).

(2) By all odds, the most important and characteristic use of παράδοσις within the Christian Church was as a rule of practice, augmenting faith, and applying the gospel. In this sense, it was especially comparable to the Hebrew Mishnah, and was more widely used as such in the earlier period. Eusebius points to a 'tradition of great antiquity' concerning the rules of the Church for observing 'the festival of the Savior's Pascha' (*Hist. Eccl.* 5.23.1). These practical, liturgical, ethical 'traditions' were gathered into teaching manuals in the early Church, containing detailed instruction in such matters as holding grudges, magic and sorcery and the use of water in baptism. 'If you do not have running water, baptize in some other. If you cannot in cold, then in warm' (*Did.* 7.3). The *Doctrina*, the *Didache*, the *Epistle of Barnabas*, and the early second-century sermon, *2 Clement*, are all illustrations of this concern to pull together these oral traditions of the early Church into written collections.[2]

In the New Testament, it was Paul who made the most use of the noun παράδοσις to refer to this escalating body of Christian practical and ethical belief. He commanded the Corinthians to 'maintain the traditions, even as I have delivered them to you', and then went on to instruct them in the relation of women to their husbands (1 Cor. 11.2). The παράδοσις particularly appropriate to the Thessalonians dealt with the importance of working and paying for their food, even in the face of the impending eschaton (2 Thess. 3.6). In more detail, these 'traditions' dealt with the authentication of Scripture, certain 'forms of sound words', afterwards digested into liturgies, rules celebrating the Lord's supper and administering baptism, the Christian passover and the weekly Lord's day, the Jewish sabbath and ordinances, the kiss of charity, the ἀγάπη rules concerning widows, and rules dealing with public worship.[3]

C.H. Dodd is the one who has most forcefully brought to the attention of the scholarly world this distinction, between Gospel and Law. He

---

2. See E.L. Long, Jr, *A Survey of Christian Ethics* (Oxford and New York: Oxford University Press, 1967), pp. 89-91. See also P.L. Lehmann, *Ethics in a Christian Context* (London: SCM Press; New York: Harper & Row, 1963), pp. 32-33. He points to the *Didache*, the *Shepherd of Hermas*, Tertullian, Basil of Caesarea, and Ambrose of Milan.

3. 2 Tim. 1.13, 14; 2.2; 1 Cor. 11.2; 5.8; 16.2; 2 Thess. 2.15; 3.6. See A. Roberts and J. Donaldson (eds.), *The Ante-Nicene Fathers* (10 vols.; Edinburgh: T. & T. Clark, 1898; repr. Grand Rapids: Eerdmans, 1989), II, p. 343.

found two types of literature in the New Testament—that dealing with specifically religious themes in the reflective manner which constitutes theology, and that consisting mainly of ethical precepts and admonitions. The one he identified as κήρυγμα, the other as διδαχή.[4] Dodd pointed to the 'orders' (παραγγελίας; see below) that Paul gave to Timothy (1 Thess. 4.2) as belonging to the regular course of ethical instruction for converts.[5] According to Dodd, by Paul's time there was already a traditional body of ethical teaching given to converts from paganism, and Paul could safely assume that such teaching was presented in churches outside his own sphere of influence. This was the 'pattern of teaching' which the Romans had already received (Rom. 6.17-18), and is found in various locations in the New Testament (1 Thess. 5.14-18; Heb. 13.1-3; 1 Pet. 3.8-9). All of this went back to a very early period, and represented what John Meagher has called the community's own 'sense of comportment'.[6]

The question of the source of this material is an interesting one, and there is some disagreement. Meagher, for example, talks about this as a secondary 'common law', an 'independently received' sense of comportment rooted in a 'particularly Christian renovation of understanding' based on Christian experience whose authority all Christians would recognize. Dodd on the other hand relates it to the general movement in Graeco-Roman society towards the improvement of public morals undertaken by many agencies, which Christians adopted, but which was ultimately based on the ethical instruction within the teachings of Jesus. More recently, David Aune has identified another source, the 'sacred law pronouncements' of early Christian prophets, and we shall say more about this shortly.[7] As we shall see more clearly later in the Church's use of other terms parallel to παράδοσις, the

---

4. I shall show later that although in my opinion Dodd was correct in this insight, the term διδαχή is more accurately identified with the more theological *kerygma*, while παράδοσις, διδασκαλία, πιστὸς ὁ λόγος, and παραγγελία are more properly seen as references to this Christian Mishnaic material.

5. C.H. Dodd, *Gospel and Law: The Relation of Faith and Ethics in Early Christianity* (New York: Columbia University Press, 1951). See also *idem*, 'The Primitive Catechism and the Sayings of Jesus', in A.J.B. Higgins (ed.), *New Testament Essays* (Manchester: Manchester University Press, 1959), p. 107.

6. J.C. Meagher, *The Way of the Word: The Beginning and the Establishing of Christian Understanding* (New York: Seabury Press, 1975), p. 141.

7. Meagher, *The Way of the Lord*, pp. 30, 141-42; D.E. Aune, *Prophecy in Early Christianity and the Ancient Mediterranean World* (Grand Rapids: Eerdmans, 1983).

5. *The Application of the Word* 111

teachings of Jesus do indeed always stand behind such 'tradition' within the early Church. I would guess that Dodd, Meagher and Aune are all right in terms of the many sources of these traditions. As the Christian faith rolled through those early centuries, it picked up an enormous amount of material from its experience and environment which was gradually built into its traditions. One of the very important tasks facing New Testament study at the present stage of the discussion is to separate out from Christian theology and praxis this great abundance of acquired secondary material, identifying its sources, and testing it against the primary substance of the gospel in the Holy Word of Jesus.

(3) In its later development within the Christian faith, παράδοσις generally came to designate an authoritative theological consensus, or 'rule of faith' as Tertullian called it (*Against Heresies* 28), as presented by the teaching and preaching of the apostles, what Eusebius called the 'sound faith derived from the apostolic tradition' (*Hist. Eccl.* 4.21). For Irenaeus, this 'tradition which originates from the apostles and is preserved by means of the succession of Presbyters in the churches', was the chief bulwark against heresy. Tradition was distinct from 'Scripture' (γραφή), either Jewish or Christian (Irenaeus, *Adv. Haer.* 3.5.1), and was the 'tradition of truth' (3.4.1) which at this late period represented the substance of Christian doctrine and manner of life. It was a living word, 'preserved continuously...by men who exist everywhere' (3.3.1-2). This παράδοσις was probably what Clement of Alexandria referred to as the 'ancestral seeds derived directly from the holy apostles...'[8] In this sense, παράδοσις was very broadly used and included not only the teachings of Jesus, but also their interpretation and application.[9]

(4) At times in the later period, παράδοσις referred specifically to the teachings of Jesus,[10] what Clement called 'the tradition of the Lord...the divine words...the teaching of our Lord...' (*Strom.* 7.17); but this was exceptional. Mostly it was reserved for the teachings of the apostles. This possible confusion was perhaps the necessity behind Irenaeus's reference

---

8. *Strom.* 1.1; cf. 5.10; 6.16. See Hanson, *Origen's Doctrine of Tradition*, Chapter 2.

9. In the New Testament, this use of παράδοσις to refer to the substance of faith finds very little coinage, unless one might cite Paul's reference to 'the traditions which you were taught by us, either by word of mouth or by letter'. This passage is ambiguous, however, and probably not to be taken as normative (2 Thess. 2.15).

10. See Papias, in Eusebius, *Hist. Eccl.* 3.39.14.

to what seems to be παράδοσις as 'the secondary constitutions of the apostles' (*Frag.* 37). So we have a primary tradition of the words of Jesus and a secondary one of the words of the apostles. This is reflected in the *Epistle of Diognetus* which distinguishes rather neatly between 'the faith of the Gospels' and the 'tradition of the apostles'. Gerhardsson points out that the decision of the Jerusalem council in Acts 15 is evidence of the sharp distinction the early Church drew between what was 'heard' as a saying of Jesus, and what the Church itself formulated.[11] Paul was also concerned to distinguish clearly between his own halakah and the commands of Christ (1 Cor. 7.10-12, 25-26), or to make it known when his teaching did indeed carry the authority of 'the mind of Christ' (1 Cor. 2.16). This is clearly similar to the Hebrew distinction between the 'written' and the 'oral' Torah.

(5) παράδοσις also came to describe the generally accepted history of the apostles and their successors, including the history of the origin of the Gospels. For Eusebius, it was in 'tradition' that he found the story of Thomas being allocated the region of Parthia (*Hist. Eccl.* 3.1.1), or that Philip lived at Hierapolis with his daughter (*Hist. Eccl.* 3.39.7-8), or that 'the savior ordered his apostles not to leave Jerusalem for twelve years' (*Hist. Eccl.* 5.18.14). The 'traditions' were the things Polycarp learned from the apostles, and 'which alone are true' (*Hist. Eccl.* 4.14.3). It was 'the tradition of the church' which Eusebius cited as the source of 'those writings which...are true, genuine and recognized' (*Hist. Eccl.* 3.25.6). This is probably why his sources for the origins of the Gospels all essentially agree.[12]

In summarizing the Church's use of the term παράδοσις, we have found a large stratum of Christian belief used primarily to identify and regulate the ecclesiastical, liturgical and ethical praxis of the Church, what Meagher calls its 'ortho praxis'. In its broadest sense, 'tradition' represented the Church's understanding of itself, its theology, its history, its life and institutions. It was clearly distinct from the gospel, yet it was based upon it and an extension of it, and the teachings of Jesus operated subtly at its heart. It was in this sense secondary to the 'primary constitutions' of the Church. In the use of this particular term, tradition was a consensus that developed out of the wide-ranging experience of

---

11. Gerhardsson, *Memory and Manuscript*, p. 261. See E. Hennecke and W. Schneemelcher (eds.), *New Testament Apocrypha* (2 vols.; Philadelphia: Westminster Press, 1963), II, p. 28, where παράδοσις seems to be a transition to gnostic heresy.

12. *Hist. Eccl.* 3.39.14; 5.8.1; 6.14.5-7; cf. also 3.37.4.

the post-primitive community, and in a loose and informal way is comparable to the Hebrew oral tradition which eventually was formalized in Christian Mishnaic-like literature, both within the New Testament and outside it.

The Teaching of Tradition: διδασκαλία

A second noun used to describe this early stream of consensus was διδασκαλία, a general term referring to the teaching of the apostles, given verbally to their disciples and then written down by them. In the New Testament, we find a vigorous and precise use of διδασκαλία to refer to the same body of oral data identified by παράδοσις as the ethical instruction of the early Church. This is what the author of 1 Timothy called the 'teaching (διδασκαλία) which accords with godliness', 'the sure word as taught' (διδαχὴν πιστοῦ λόγου; Tit. 1.9), what Paul called the 'rule' (κανών) according to which men are to walk (Gal. 6.16; cf. Phil. 3.16; 2 Cor. 10.13, 15). These were the 'duties' (μελέτα) which were to be taught and practiced (1 Tim. 4.15; 6.2; Tit. 2.1, 7, 10), and which the authors of the later New Testament were concerned to spell out in detail (1 Tim. 5.17-18). Such were to be in accordance with 'the glorious gospel' (1 Tim. 1.11) and the 'sound word of the Lord Jesus Christ' (1 Tim. 6.3). They were called 'sound doctrine' (ὑγιαινούσῃ διδασκαλίᾳ; 1 Tim. 1.10; cf. 2 Tim. 4.3; Tit. 1.9; 2.1), clearly distinguished from certain heretical διδασκαλία circulating within the early Church which urged such things as the forbidding of marriage, abstinence form certain foods, and doctrines of demons (1 Tim. 4.1, 6, 13, 16; cf. Col. 2.22). In this pastoral literature there was a strikingly clear distinction between 'the sound words of the Lord Jesus Christ', that is, 'the words of faith', or the 'glorious gospel', on the one hand, and 'good doctrine' (διδασκαλία), 'the teaching that accords with godliness', on the other (1 Tim. 1.10; 4.1, 6, 13, 16; 5.1, 17; 6.3).

Those who were particularly responsible for instruction in παράδοσις seem to have been 'worthy of double honor' and constituted a loosely defined office in the early Church (1 Tim. 5.17). One passage is especially interesting because it is often obscured by bad translation, where the author of 1 Timothy (5.17) makes a nice distinction between those who labor in what the RSV translates 'preaching', but which more properly should be translated 'in the word' (ἐν λόγῳ), and those who labor 'in teaching' (ἐν διδασκαλίᾳ). As we proceed, we shall see more clearly the importance of this distinction which the author of the Pastorals was concerned to make. This situation, where there were specific teachers of ethical duties within the Church, seems to have been a later one, more common to the time of the Pastorals and the so-called 'pseudo-Pauline literature' than to the earlier period of Paul's ministry.

This same usage persisted at least until Eusebius who pictured Mark being enjoined by other 'hearers' of Peter to leave them a written statement of the heretofore 'unwritten teaching' (διδασκαλία). In the case of Mark, this would have become his Gospel, so it would have included the teachings of Jesus and narratives about him as reported by Peter (*Hist. Eccl.* 2.15.1). With Eusebius, it is synonymous with παράδοσις in its larger sense. At points he uses the two terms interchangeably, as with the expression 'the true tradition of the blessed teaching', which was the 'ancestral seeds' come down from the apostles.[13] Perhaps the most important thing to observe with regard to Eusebius is the distinction he makes between the teachings of Jesus, 'the divine Word', and the 'unwritten teaching' of the 'divine message' (*Hist. Eccl.* 2.15.1) which would be the apostolic teaching about Jesus.[14] Here was clearly a broad stratum of ethical 'tradition' flowing through the early Church, which was one of its chief sources of strength in distinguishing and protecting itself from the many heretical tendencies surrounding it. The key to this was whether or not these διδασκαλίαι were true to the teachings of Jesus and were nourished on the gospel, 'the words of faith'.

The Clear and Certain Word: πιστὸς ὁ λόγος

The widespread character of this early oral tradition is seen in the variety and number of terms used to describe it. A third formula, repeated six times and only in the Pastoral Epistles, is πιστὸς ὁ λόγος, used interchangeably with διδασκαλία (1 Tim. 4.6, 9; Tit. 1.9) and in connection with the adjective ὑγιαίνουσα (Tit. 2.1). In 1 Tim. 1.15, an ethical λόγιον of Jesus, 'I have come not to call the righteous, but sinners to repentance', is paraphrased (Lk. 5.32; cf. Jn 12.47) and called πιστὸς ὁ λόγος, translated by the RSV as 'the word that is faithful and

---

13. *Hist. Eccl.* 5.11.5; cf. 3.37.4: τῆς ἀποστολικῆς διδασκαλίας ἡ παράδοσις.

14. Hanson, quoting Prestige, interprets διδασκαλία in the Fathers as an 'accretion or enlargement or confirmation of the faith' (*Origen's Doctrine of Tradition*, pp. 32-33). At best, in Eusebius the term is general and rather ambiguous.

worthy of full acceptance'. In a larger context, but still retaining its Jesus orientation, διδαχὴν πιστοῦ λόγου becomes in Tit. 1.9 the 'sure word as taught', to which a bishop must hold firm if he is to 'be able to give instruction in sound doctrine' (διδασκαλία). This would seem to refer to the teaching of Paul which had been the basis of Titus's own Christian education. In this same Epistle πιστὸς ὁ λόγος concludes and refers back to a creedal statement dealing with the work of Christ, and in 2 Tim. 2.11 introduces an early hymn, doctrinal statement or creedal formula.[15]

Most characteristically, however, this phrase describes the traditions of the early Church dealing with 'how one ought to behave in the household of God' (1 Tim. 3.1). This involves liturgical practices (1 Tim. 4.11-16), but primarily refers to ethical instruction in such matters as being sober, submissive to rulers, obedient, ready for honest work, gentle, courteous, avoiding quarreling and speaking evil of no one (Tit. 3.1-11; cf. 1 Tim. 4.9). This comes to focus in the παράδοσις describing the exemplary life of the bishop: 'the saying is sure (πιστὸς ὁ λόγος), if anyone aspires to the office of bishop, he desires a noble task'. We note in the limited use of this phrase the same general reference to the orthopraxis of the early Church, based on the teaching of Jesus, but mainly describing the Church's traditions regulating the life of the Christian community.

There are other terms employed to describe this developing body of tradition, like παραγγελία, which is often used by Paul and the author of the Pastorals to identify the ethical and liturgical instruction of the Church in its rules for observing the Lord's Supper, the behavior of widows, how traveling missionaries should comport themselves and instruction regarding monogamy (cf. 1 Cor. 11.17; 2 Thess. 3.4, 6, 10; 1 Tim. 4.11; 5.7; 6.17; etc.). This in turn seems to be an extension of Jesus' commands to his disciples for their evangelistic mission to 'preach' and 'testify' (Acts 10.42), and to begin with the 'lost sheep of the house of Israel' (Mt. 10.5; Mk 6.8).

---

15. See G.W. Knight, *The Faithful Sayings in the Pastoral Letters* (Kampen: Kok, 1968), p. 3: 'With these sayings we have come to the self-conscious creedal-liturgical expressions of the early church of its faith and life'. For C.F.D. Moule (*The Birth of the New Testament* [London: A. & C. Black, 1981], p. 222), these are 'collections of Christian maxims analogous to the words of Jesus...'

The Catholic Epistles use a different terminology like 'prophetic word' (2 Pet. 1.19), 'commandment' (ἐντολή),[16] 'truth' and διδαχή, variously translated as 'doctrine' (2 Jn 9, 10), 'instruction' (Heb. 6.2) and 'teaching' (Heb. 13.9). But in all this broad stratum of tradition we are dealing with the same phenomenon, the Church's self-conscious application of the gospel and the teachings of Jesus to its later ecclesiastical, ethical and liturgical situation.

The Mediators of Tradition: προφήτης

The distinction between gospel and tradition, between theological understanding and ethical-liturgical-ecclesiastical application, continues in the differing functions of the apostles and prophets. Even as the apostles were 'first' before the prophets, so was the theological knowledge of the gospel prior to the practical 'revelation' of the traditions of the Church. Christian prophet studies represent a newly emerging discipline within current New Testament scholarship.[17] The role of the post-Easter

---

16. 21 times in Hebrews, 2 Peter, 1–2 John, and Revelation.

17. Aune, *Prophecy in Early Christianity*, p. 215. See also D.E. Aune, 'Christian Prophecy and the Sayings of Jesus', in G.W. MacRae (ed.), *Society of Biblical Literature 1975 Seminar Papers* (2 vols.; SBLSP, 14; Missoula, MT: Scholars Press, 1975), I, pp. 131-42. For a different assessment of this situation, see Boring, *Sayings of the Risen Jesus*. Boring gives a good overview of the materials characteristic of Christian prophetic speech: eschatological paranesis, historical prediction, concrete directions for life, revelatory material and wisdom motifs. He sees these prophets present in the early Church prior to the writing of the Gospels who delivered utterances that were heard and transmitted as sayings of the risen Jesus. These were mixed with other sayings purporting to be from the pre-Easter Jesus. He thus obscures the distinction between the Holy Word of Jesus and the παράδοσις of the prophets and others as I have outlined it above. The problem with this helpful study is his own recognition of what he calls the 'stalemate on the question of the pre-Easter character of the teachings of Jesus' (p. 230). Despite his desire to go beyond Bultmann on this issue (p. 13), his historical skepticism is pretty much a classic extension of the form-critical argument from 'development', and thereby contains so many critical and historiographic problems that it would not be useful to review them here. See J.A. Baird, *The Justice of God in the Teaching of Jesus* (Philadelphia: Westminster Press, 1963), p. 26; *idem, Rediscovering the Power of the Gospels: Jesus' Theology of the Kingdom* (Wooster, OH: Iona Press, 1982), chap. 1; *idem, Audience Criticism and the Historical Jesus* (Philadelphia: Westminster Press, 1967), chap. 1; *idem, A Comparative Analysis of the Gospel Genre: The Synoptic Mode and Its Uniqueness* (Lewiston: Edwin Mellen Press, 1991). What he does is to leap over the historical question and assume that the Synoptics are filled with post-Easter

Christian prophet has become the most recent focal point for separating primary (pre-Easter) from secondary (post-Easter) elements in the tradition of Jesus' words.

The evidence has been pointing to the existence of what Aune and others have called a school or order within the Church,[18] charged with generating and passing on this growing body of tradition. In the more ecclesiastically amorphous character of the most primitive period, one must be especially careful about identifying any clearly and consistently defined 'offices' in the Church, with perhaps the exception of the apostolate, for which the term 'office' (διακονία) is used (Rom. 11.13). Perhaps the term πρᾶξις (Rom. 12.4) is more accurate because it gives a more functional designation. Nevertheless, in an incipient and no doubt undeveloped way, one can detect an emerging position dealing especially with this aspect of the early Church's escalating fund of practical instruction.

This comes to peculiar focus in the person of the 'prophet'. These were the chief non-apostolic leaders of the Church, men and women especially sensitive to the Holy Spirit, who had special insight into the interpretation and application of the Word: 'moved by the Holy Spirit who spoke from God' (2 Pet. 1.19; cf. Acts 21.9; 1 Cor. 12.28). Their 'revelations' (1 Cor. 14.30) were deemed valid if they spoke this 'prophetic word' (1 Pet. 1.19) 'in the name of the Lord' (Jas 5.10), and at his command (1 Cor. 14.37). In this way their interpretations were subject to the correction of the Holy Word. They functioned in various

---

sayings generated by Christian prophets. His rejection of Taylor, Riesenfeld and Gerhardsson is not on critical textual grounds, but purely polemical ones based on classic form-critical assumptions. He by-passes the Synoptics and goes to 'sources beyond the Synoptic material' for his evidence, since the Synoptics are 'too controversial'. This is hardly acceptable methodology. If current research on the historical Jesus is any indication, this is still an open question, and lest we beg that question we must continue to re-examine the primary Synoptic data as well as our own critical presuppositions. See also M.E. Boring, 'Christian Prophecy and the Sayings of Jesus: The State of the Question', *NTS* 29 (1983), p. 108. For a similar view, see R.J. Miller, 'The Rejection of the Prophets in Q', *JBL* 107 (1988), p. 240. For a different view, see T.W. Gillespie, 'The Pattern of Prophetic Speech in 1 Corinthians', *JBL* 97 (1978), pp. 74-95. David Hill (*New Testament Prophecy* [Atlanta: John Knox Press, 1979]) gives a good description of the characteristics of the Christian prophets, but needs to include one of their chief functions which was to apply the teachings of Jesus to the life of the early Church as we have detailed above.

18. Aune, *Prophecy in Early Christianity*, p. 198.

other important capacities, such as the laying on of hands (Acts 13.1-3), preaching (Acts 15.32), and predicting the future (Acts 11.27). In all this they held a recognized position second only to the apostles. Aune gives a picture of early Christianity as small communities with both resident and traveling prophets dotted about Syria-Palestine, and spreading out from there. The author of Ephesians gives a nice summary of this situation by describing the 'household of God, built upon the foundation of the apostles and prophets, Christ Jesus himself being the chief cornerstone' (2.20). The 'mystery' of God's revelation in Christ was revealed 'to his holy apostles and prophets by the Spirit', and Paul gives us the recognized order of priority: 'first apostles, second prophets, third teachers...' (1 Cor. 12.28).[19]

Even as the apostles had a special function within the early Church as the guardians of the Holy Word and the source and focus of its interpretation which they called gospel, so the prophets had this special and distinct function of generating and transmitting its ethical-liturgical-ecclesiastical traditions. These were what Käsemann called 'apodictic divine law' originating in Christian prophetic pronouncements. These 'prescriptive oracles', enjoining a particular type of action, were based upon what Aune describes as 'established kerygmatic norms',[20] accompanied by tests of authenticity, 'the most important of which was agreement with kerygmatic tradition', what I have called 'the Holy Word'. It would seem that here we have come to the creative origin and center of the Church's παράδοσις/διδασκαλία/πιστὸς ὁ λόγος in the revelation of Christian prophets who interpreted and applied the Word of the Lord which was delivered to them by the apostles and impressed upon them by the Holy Spirit, so that they 'may learn and be encouraged' (1 Cor. 14.3). These are the 'prophetic utterances' which were commended to Timothy to 'inspire' him to 'hold faith and a good conscience' (1 Tim. 1.19), and are descriptions of the πιστὸς ὁ λόγος (1.15), which we have seen can describe the substance both of faith and

19. See T. Boman, *Die Jesus Überlieferung im Lichte der neueren Volkskunde* (Göttingen: Vandenhoeck & Ruprecht, 1967). Boman argues that the kerygmatic tradition proclaimed by the apostles was quite separate from the gospel traditions which were recounted by a special group of narrators subject to the apostles and prophets. Boman's recognition of the oral 'offices' within the Church seems to be in the right direction; but his failure to distinguish more carefully between gospel and παράδοσις, as between apostle and prophet, confuses matters. See J.W. Bowman, *The Religion of Maturity* (New York: Abingdon-Cokesbury, 1948), p. 21.

20. Aune, *Prophecy in Early Christianity*, pp. 235, 338.

of ethics, but, represents primarily the ethical, practical, liturgical application of the Holy Word.

Who were these prophets? The Apocalypse makes numerous references to them (Rev. 11.18; 16.6; 18.20, 24; 22.6, 9), including John himself, possibly the 'angels' of the seven churches, and one Jezebel of Thyatira who was teaching immorality and false doctrine (Rev. 2.20-22). John the Baptist is sometimes listed in this category. Others who exhibit these characteristics in the New Testament are Judas and Silas (Acts 15.32), Agabus (Acts 21.10), Barnabas, Simeon who was called Niger, Lucius of Cyrene, Manaen, a member of the court of Herod the tetrarch, Saul (Acts 13.1), Philip the Evangelist and Philip's daughters 'who prophesied' (Acts 21.9).

In the *Didache*, the prophet occupies a position of great honor (13.3), and Lucian, the reputed author, can probably be called a 'prophet'. The *Shepherd of Hermas* (*Mand.* 11.9) gives a description of a prophet acting within worship, and distinguishes between false and true prophets. Still other candidates could be Polycarp of Smyrna, Melito of Sardis, Ammia of Philadelphia, Quadratus, Cerinthus, and a list of gnostics like Marcus, Philumene of Appelles, Barsabbas and others. Aune compares them to the Athenian χρησμολόγοι, who collected oracles and applied them to current situations, and could perhaps be seen as the pagan precursors of Christian prophets who both collected and collated their own prophecies.[21]

In all of this we are seeing the development from the earliest times of a growing body of tradition which applied the Holy Word to the practical life of the Church, was the special function of Christian prophets, and formed an important, continuing and enlarging deposit of Christian instruction.

---

21. Aune, *Prophecy in Early Christianity*, p. 243.

Chapter 6

HOLY APOSTLES:
THE CUSTODIANS OF THE WORD

'You are fellow citizens with the saints and members of the household of God, built upon the foundation of the apostles and prophets, Christ Jesus himself being the chief cornerstone' (Eph. 2.19-20).

Holy Word, holy narrative, holy gospel, holy traditions. The story of New Testament formation is primarily the story of the working out of this theological-historical paradigm. It is this paradigm which arose naturally out of the practical exigencies of Christian history and provided the guiding principle for the eventual canonization of the New Testament and the survival of the Christian Church. The apostles were the key actors in this drama. They functioned as the repository and principle line of transmission for the Holy Word. They were the chief original sources of its gospel interpretation, the central focus of the consensus and life of the Church. After the time of Jesus, it was to the apostles that the Church turned, and the unanimous testimony of the available literature points to their enormous influence.

The Origin of ἀπόστολος

Before proceeding, we must face the critical question of the origin and early use of the term ἀπόστολος. Schneemelcher, for example, has recently challenged Rengstorf's view that the Hebrew institution of the שליח stood behind the New Testament usage, thus calling into question the primitive use of this term by either Jesus or his immediate disciples. He calls the concept of apostolic authority 'a dogmatic abstraction' according to which what was 'apostolic' became the guarantee of the

6. *The Custodians of the Word*

genuine tradition.[1] The evolution of the use of this term to refer to the authoritative inner circle is clear when one notes that although it does

---

1. E. Hennecke and W. Schneemelcher (eds.), *New Testament Apocrypha* (2 vols.; Philadelphia: Westminster Press, 1963), II, pp. 27, 31. It is Walter Schmithals (*The Office of Apostle in the Early Church* [Nashville: Abingdon Press, 1969]), however, who has most exhaustively called the traditional conception of apostleship into question. He bases his reconstruction of the apostolic office entirely on Paul, and from this he derives eighteen characteristics of apostleship as Paul saw them. He points out that Paul uses the term widely to refer to many others besides the original twelve, including himself, and the image is mainly a missionary one. Schmithals then goes on to demonstrate that within early gnosticism, the term apostle is used in strikingly abundant and similar ways. He then concludes that the primitive Christian apostolate was not derived from Jesus, but was an appropriation of the missionary office of Jewish or Jewish-Christian gnosticism as found in first-century Syria (p. 229). The failure of the gnostic conception then led later in the early second century to the super-imposition back upon the Gospels and the entrance into the Church, of the formula, apostle equals the twelve plus Paul, and the conception of apostleship in the less missionary, more administrative sense of the Hebrew שליח.

Schmithals has done a service to the understanding of this question by bringing a new dimension to our knowledge of the similarity between Paul's concept of apostleship and that of primitive gnosticism. He has also clearly shown the differences between Paul's more missionary use of ἀπόστολος in the sense of the Christian prophet, and the more administrative conception which dominates the Synoptics and the early Church and is contained in the Hebrew שליח. Beyond that, one would have to take considerable exception to this brilliant illustration of German *Grundlichkeit*. There is only need for one major criticism, for it is central, and decisive for Schmithals's thesis. He begs the entire question at the outset and throughout, by his critical historical skepticism regarding the Synoptic Gospels, what he calls 'the erroneous idea that the twelve had been considered apostles already in the first period of primitive Christianity' (p. 241; cf. pp. 108-109). 'There is no passage in the New Testament which makes it plain that the twelve played any special role either in Jerusalem or later on' (p. 70). These statements are based not on any new evidence, but on his fundamental rejection of the historical authenticity of the Synoptic material, and on his insistence that they are very late, reflecting the mind-set of the second century. This leads him to base his entire thesis on the Pauline concept of apostleship, with hardly any mention of the material in Matthew and Mark, and only a few references to Luke. His insistence that 'there are no generally recognized principles for the evaluation of the Synoptic tradition' (p. 71) is made on the basis of a deeply imbedded set of assumptions which are taken as axiomatic, and which simply ignore an abundance of Synoptic evidence that would strongly alter his thesis. This has produced a strange, distorted, arbitrary patchwork of ideas, based on several premises which I would call 'patently false'. See J.A. Baird, *Audience Criticism and the Historical Jesus* (Philadelphia: Westminster Press, 1967), Chapter 1; *idem*, *The*

occur in all three of the Synoptics, and at least once in the double tradition, its occurrence in Lk. 11.49 (Mt. 18.34) may well not be a reference to the Christian apostles.[2] In all the other Synoptic references, either one or another Gospel parallel omits the term (Mt. 10.2; Mk 6.30; Lk. 17.5; 22.14; 24.10) or the text is in serious question (Mk 3.14). Luke regularly seems to add it to what is otherwise double or triple tradition. This fact, coupled with the abundant occurrence in Acts and the letters of Paul, suggests that the earliest usage of the term came through Luke and out of the experience of the apostle Paul. John never employs this title except in the general sense of an 'emissary' (13.16). It is also possible to see a subtle shift at Acts 14.14 where ἀπόστολος, up to then used to refer to the twelve disciples, suddenly begins to take on a larger reference to Paul and Barnabas; and then in Rom. 16.7 and 1 Thess. 2.6 it identifies both Paul and his disciples, Andronicus, Junias, Sylvanus and Timothy. Never on the other hand is Jesus said to have uttered this word (שליח). All in all it would seem wise with Schmithals to question its use by the Christian community earlier than Paul or Luke.

This, however, does not deny the reality of the institution to which ἀπόστολος refers. For our purposes the exact derivation of the term is beside the point. The important matter is that this title is used to set the twelve apart from the rest of the disciples in their relation to Jesus and also to the early Church, and this unique status can be documented as a primitive datum of history, not only in the early Fathers, but in all the sub-sources of the Synoptics. I have demonstrated in my study on audience criticism[3] that one of the best-attested facts about the Synoptics is that they concur to a high degree not only in distinguishing regularly between the twelve and the crowd of disciples, but in revealing Jesus in his λόγια regularly changing his message, vocabulary and praxis as he moves from the twelve audience (D) to the larger group of disciples (DG). The twelve were a select group, specially called, instructed and used by Jesus. Their unique identity in Jesus' mind is evident in the nineteen terms the Synoptics show him reserving exclusively for them,

---

Justice of God in the Teaching of Jesus (London: SCM Press; Philadelphia: Westminster Press, 1963), Chapter 1.

2. See M.J. Suggs, *Wisdom, Christology and Law in Matthew's Gospel* (Cambridge, MA: Harvard University Press, 1970), p. 23.

3. Baird, *Audience Criticism*.

especially δοῦλος, μικρός, and μαθητής.⁴ So we would conclude that although the term ἀπόστολος is probably a later designation, reflecting the growing ecclesiasticism of the early Church, and heavily influenced by Pauline usage, it is based on an historical reality that has its justification in the most primitive Jesus account.

The Sanctity of the Apostles

There is a longstanding and universal testimony from Eusebius back to the earliest Gospel sources that the twelve apostles were the principal 'pipeline' of the gospel. Their centrality is apparent in Eusebius who writes the history of the early Church primarily in terms of the apostles. These, along with other disciples, remained in Jerusalem for 40 years (*Hist. Eccl.* 3.7.8), provided the earliest bishops of the Church, were dispersed along with the rest of the Jews in AD 70 (*Hist. Eccl.* 3.11.1) and survived that holocaust along with Jesus' relatives (*Hist. Eccl.* 3.10.11). The apocryphal New Testament is written chiefly in the name of the apostles, generally like the *Didache*, or individually like the *Gospel of Peter*.

The Ante-Nicene Fathers were accustomed to begin their thinking about the Gospels with what Tertullian called the 'sacred deposit' of the apostles (*Against Marcion* 4.5). Hippolytus reflects this apostolic centrality in his two books, *On The Twelve Apostles*, and *On The Seventy Apostles*, where he gives the final history of each of the twelve and then the seventy, most of whom were said to have become bishops of the Church. The Apostolic Fathers merely reflect the fact, so apparent in the New Testament, that it is the acts, the epistles and the testimony of the apostles that are the principal telescope through which we see Jesus. There is a positive fixation upon the apostles that is characteristic of the early Christian Church. The dominant impression one receives from all this literature is that of 'holy apostles' (Eph. 3.5) from whom is directly derived the 'tradition of the blessed doctrine' (Clement of Alexandria, *Strom.* 1).⁵

---

4. J.A. Baird, *Rediscovering the Power of the Gospels: Jesus' Theology of the Kingdom* (Wooster, OH: Iona Press, 1982), p. 154; *idem*, *Audience Criticism*, pp. 33-36.

5. For abundant documentation of this apostolic sanctity in the Fathers, see Hennecke and Schneemelcher (eds.), *New Testament Apocrypha*, II, p. 40.

There is however one level, outside that of later heretics, on which I find the sanctity of the apostles questioned. That is in the Synoptic teachings of Jesus. The λόγια are noteworthy for their almost complete absence of praise for the twelve, and for the intense criticism of these whom Jesus called 'men of little faith, foolish and slow of heart to believe' (Lk. 12.47-48; 18.1-8; 22.31-34; 24.13-53).[6] Beyond the Gospel level, however, we find a positive escalation of apostolic sanctity, perhaps epitomized by Irenaeus, for whom they were 'truly perfect', authoritative because they were kept from error by the Holy Spirit (*Adv. Haer.* 3.11.9).

Ecclesiastical Authority

One aspect of this apostolic sanctity was the ecclesiastical authority ascribed to them by the tradition. Eusebius describes 'the pious disciples of great men' who built in every place 'on the foundations of the churches laid by the apostles' (*Hist. Eccl.* 3.37.1). For Tertullian it was they who gave authority to the so-called 'apostolic churches' (*Against Marcion* 4.4). Hegesippus writes of the descendants of Jude, the brother of Jesus, that 'they ruled every church' (*Hist. Eccl.* 3.32.3-4). This apostolic authority more broadly defined was well established by Paul's day, for whom ἀπόστολος was the title of an office to which he was 'appointed', whether by God (Gal. 1.1) or by men (1 Tim. 1.1; 2 Tim. 1.11) being a moot question, an office which was 'first' in the hierarchy of the Church's primitive structure (1 Cor. 12.28). It is this which Paul is constantly concerned to re-assert (Rom. 1.1; 1 Cor. 1.1; etc.), and which he defends jealously (1 Cor. 9.1-2) as the source and 'seal' of his authority. Luke shows us the same apostolic authority over ecclesiastical matters throughout Acts as Barnabas sells his field and lays it 'at the apostles' feet' (4.37). He underscores it with the curious tale of Ananias and Sapphira who are so terrified by their disobedience of the apostles, and so of God, that they fall down dead. The theme continues with the necessity for the laying of the apostles' hands on each new convert. It is seen in the regular distinction Luke makes in Acts between the apostles and the other 'brethren' (11.1), and in the ordination of the first deacons (6.6), and comes to a climax with the Jerusalem conference where 'the apostles and the elders were gathered together'. Even the independent Paul, despite his blustering denial in Gal. 1.19-20, feels it necessary after

6. Baird, *Audience Criticism*, p. 123.

his conversion to check with Cephas and James (Gal. 1.18-19), and possibly other 'pillars' of the Church.[7]

In the Synoptic material we find a 'tension' between the giving of authority to the twelve (Mt. 16.17-19; 18.18-19; 19.27-28; Lk. 22.28-30; etc.) and the denying of it (Mt. 20.24-28; 23.8-12; Mk 10.42-43; etc.). Jesus seems to have given them authority, but to have warned against the authoritarianism which emerged, and which was reflected in the question of the sons of Zebedee.[8] The ecclesiastical thrust behind this question runs like a swelling stream throughout the entire New Testament, and this authority was a source and an aspect of apostolic sanctity. How early we can really refer to 'holy apostles' is an important question. I find no break but only an escalation between the special status given them in the Synoptics and the authority which they have in Acts and the later New Testament, or in the writings of Irenaeus, Tertullian or Eusebius. It would seem that in the authority of the apostles we are dealing with a very primitive and abiding phenomenon.

Doctrinal Authority

Another facet of this apostolic sanctity is their authority in matters of doctrine.[9] Eusebius, drawing upon Hegesippus, points to the beginnings of heresy, 'the federation of godless error', at the time when the 'sacred band of the apostles' and those 'to whom it had been vouchsafed to hear with their own ears the divine wisdom' no longer existed (*Hist. Eccl.* 3.32.8). The apostles had been the chief defense against heresy. For Clement of Alexandria, going back to the apostles is sufficient authority for Christian doctrine. In the first book of the *Stromata* he refers to those who 'reserved the true tradition of the blessed teaching directly from Peter and James and John, the holy apostles, son receiving it from father...and by the blessing of God they came down to us to deposit those ancestral and apostolic seeds' (*Hist. Eccl.* 5.11.4-5). The basis of Tertullian's proof that the 'rule of faith' is valid is Jesus' special attention to the apostles, and the Holy Spirit making them inerrant (*Against Heresies* 22). Irenaeus attributes to the apostles 'perfect

---

7. For a study of developing clericalism within the Church, see H. Schoeps, *Paul* (Philadelphia: Westminster Press, 1961), p. 73.

8. Baird, *Audience Criticism*, pp. 199-220.

9. See Schmithals, *The Office of Apostle*, p. 40. The authority of the apostles resides in the message (κήρυγμα).

knowledge of the gospel of God' (*Adv. Haer.* 3.1): 'For the Lord of all gave to his apostles the power of the gospel, through whom also we have known the truth, that is the doctrine of the Son of God...' (Irenaeus, *Adv. Haer.* 3).

This dependence upon the apostles as doctrinal authorities is clearly reflected in Acts where the early converts 'devoted themselves to the apostles' teachings' (2.42), and their 'testimony to the resurrection' (4.33). Even Paul, who saw himself as an apostle vested with theological authority (1 Cor. 2.16; 4.15-16; 9.2), felt the necessity of laying his gospel before James, Cephas, and John, 'lest somehow I should be running or had run in vain' (Gal. 2.2). He exposed his sensitivity by pointing out that this was done 'privately', and with a bit of sarcasm about those 'pillars' who were 'reputed to be something', but to whom he, Paul, was not about to 'yield submission' (Gal. 2.1-2). Inadvertently, through this somewhat bitter denial, Paul testified to what must have been the considerable authority of the first apostles in matters of doctrine as well as ecclesiastical affairs.

Going back to the Synoptics and their sources, we do not find any direct reference to doctrinal authority, but there is much indirect evidence to that effect. Jesus was particularly concerned to instruct the twelve (Mk 8.27-33), and explain to them his parables (Mk 4.10-12).[10] A massive study of the Synoptics reveals the didactic material to be in the greatest abundance in the teachings addressed to the twelve. It is these to whom he seems to have most completely spoken his mind, balancing his teaching about the wrath of God with a strong message of love, his message about the present with that about the eschaton, his traditional Jewish vocabulary with that which was creatively new.[11]

Throughout the New Testament and the Fathers, one can trace this constant theme: the twelve apostles and then Paul and those others whose apostleship was attested by signs and wonders (Acts 5.12), who were witnesses to the resurrection (1 Cor. 9.1) and called of God by the revelation of his Holy Mystery (Eph. 3.5). These were the final arbiters of Christian doctrine. Their sanctity from the earliest times was a function of their doctrinal authority.

---

10. Baird, *Audience Criticism*, pp. 101-102.
11. Baird, *Audience Criticism*, pp. 122-23.

Pipeline for the Word

The sanctity of the apostles was finally an aspect of their central role in the transmission of the Jesus material. They had known Jesus in the flesh and had been called by him to this special ministry. By the time of Tertullian (AD 145–220), it was firmly established that the 'original sources of the faith must be reckoned for truth, as undoubtedly containing that which the said churches received from the apostles, the apostles from Christ, Christ from God' (*Against Heresies* 21; cf. *Against Marcion* 4.5). Clement of Alexandria echoes this view in more gnostic language: 'Christ himself...taught the apostles during his presence...and the gnosis itself is that which has descended by transmission to a few, having been imparted unwritten by the apostles' (*Strom.* 6.7). He gives us an even more interesting view of this process when he quotes an independent λόγιον of Jesus with the audience still attached: 'Peter said that the Lord said to the apostles: "if any one of Israel then wishes to repent and by my name to believe in God, his sins shall be forgiven him..."' (*Strom.* 6.5). Irenaeus also reflects this dominant view: 'For the Lord of all gave to his apostles the power of the gospel, through whom also we have known the truth, that is, the doctrine of the Son of God...' (*Adv. Haer.* 3 [preface]). He further pictures Clement and Polycarp being instructed by the apostles (*Adv. Haer.* 3.2.3-4).

Justin Martyr describes the gospel as that which was 'proclaimed by the apostles', a band of twelve men who 'went forth from Jerusalem' (*1 Apol.* 42, 38; cf. also *Trypho* 109); and Papias even earlier says that although he had not been a 'hearer or eyewitness of the sacred apostles', nevertheless, 'he had received the articles of faith from those who had known them' (*apud* Eusebius, *Hist. Eccl.* 3.39.2). A close parallel to Papias's quotation occurs in the *Apocryphon of James*: 'The twelve disciples (were) sitting together at the same time and remembering what the savior had said to each one of them, whether in secret or openly, and (putting it) in books'. In all of this there is a strangely uncritical and almost universal acceptance of the apostles as the direct vehicle for the life and teachings of Jesus.[12]

---

12. See H. Koester, 'From the Kerygma-Gospel to Written Gospels', *NTS* 35 (1989), pp. 361-81, esp. p. 375. This apostolic line is further echoed in Eusebius's use of the term διαδοχή: 'many others...occupying the first step in the succession (διαδοχή) from the apostles... Godly disciples of such great men, built upon the foundations of the churches...laid down by the apostles' (*Hist. Eccl.* 3.37.3; cf. 1.1).

This is pre-figured, but more subtly, in the New Testament where we find the author of 2 Peter urging his readers to 'remember...the commandment of the Lord and Savior through your apostles' (2 Pet. 3.2), and the author of Ephesians talking about the apostles and prophets as the 'foundation' of the household of God (2 Pet. 2.20), those to whom God has revealed the 'mystery of Christ' (2 Pet. 3.1-4). There are some such references in Acts where the 'apostles' teaching' is the source of Christian instruction (Acts 2.42); but in this more primitive environment of Acts and especially the Synoptic Gospels, this theme of apostolic transmission becomes muted in the complexities of Gospel formation. Here we are in the well-spring of the Jesus tradition, and one does not expect a spring to comment upon itself. The closest is perhaps Luke's prologue that talks about 'those who from the beginning were eyewitnesses and ministers of the word' (1.2); then Mark's longer ending (16.20), 'And they went forth and preached everywhere, while the Lord worked with them and confirmed the message (λόγον) by the signs that attended it' (cf. Acts 5.12).[13] These, however, are both later editorial comment. Our own understanding of the formation of the Synoptics is of course far more complex and critical, but one cannot expect these early scholars and churchmen to have anticipated the insights of modern biblical criticism. The point here is that the concept of the apostolic 'pipeline' to Jesus is another aspect of the sanctity with which the apostles were held from a very early period.

Historical Implications

What does this sanctity mean to our study of gospel origins and the historical Jesus? Certainly we would not agree with Tertullian that it made the apostles inerrant. What one could argue, however, is that this apostolic sanctity was an important source of stability for the Jesus story as it passed through the early Church. It is true that there were those called heretics who claimed apostolic authority; but the literature is too

---

13. I note also Lk. 11.49: 'The Wisdom of God said, "I will send them prophets and apostles"', but I have already commented upon it as probably a non-Christian intrusion. See Suggs, *Wisdom, Christology and Law in Matthew's Gospel*, pp. 74-75, for further discussion of the centrality of the apostles in passing on the Jesus material. Schmithals (*The Office of Apostle*, p. 50) points to Paul's definition of the apostolic office in terms of special insight into the mystery of Christ, quoting G. Bornkamm, 'μυστήριον', *TDNT*, IV, p. 821.

filled with their denunciation for us to be drawn away from the fact that the Church from the earliest times claimed to know what the apostles taught, and treated this knowledge with the utmost respect. Orthodoxy meant apostolic authority; and the sanctity of the apostles from earliest times was one of the keys to orthodoxy, that is, what these early Christians believed was 'straight judgment' because it was attested by those closest to Jesus, and most conversant with his Holy Word.

Chapter 7

HOLY SCHOOLS:
THE ENVIRONMENT OF THE WORD

Our concern now is to identify the more formal environment in which this apostolic sanctity and authority expressed itself, especially with regard to the production, preservation and transmission of the Gospels. The original environment for the teaching of Jesus was that school of twelve disciples which immediately surrounded him. This became the model for the preservation, study and transmission of the Holy Word, with many of the twelve and Paul having their own schools of disciples. Generally speaking it would seem that it was the teaching situation and the school format as it was specially adapted to the needs of the Church that formed the nexus of the Gospel process.[1]

The term 'school' must be rather broadly defined if it is to be useful in this historical analysis. To cover the various relevant situations, we shall identify a school with a variety of situations: a small group, a larger 'community', a formal instructional situation, a 'church', or with a more

---

1. There is some debate over whether or not these later schools were a continuation of the school activities in the early Church. For the two sides of the question, see W. Bousset, *Judische-Christlicher Schulbetrieb in Alexandria und Rom* (FRLANT, 6; Göttingen: Vandenhoeck & Ruprecht, 1915); K.H. Rengstorf, 'διδάσκειν', *TWNT*, II, p. 162; K. Stendahl, *The School of St Matthew* (ASNU, 20; Lund: W.K.C. Gleerup; Copenhagen: Munksgaard; rev. edn Philadelphia: Fortress Press, 1969), p. 17. In one of the most recent analyses, Werner Kelber (*The Oral and the Written Gospel* [Philadelphia: Fortress Press, 1983], p. 18) rejects the notion that Jesus was the head of a school tradition. In his justifiable enthusiasm for the oral dimension of the early formation process, he undervalues the literary dimension. See below, Chapters 7 and 10. For a recent critical analysis of Kelber's work, see B. Witherington, *The Christology of Jesus* (Minneapolis: Fortress Press, 1990), pp. 17-20; [and now L. Hurtado, 'Greco-Roman Textuality and the Gospel of Mark: A Critical Assessment of Werner Kelber's *The Oral and the Written Gospel*', *BBR* 7 (1997), pp. 91-106.—Eds.]

loosely structured 'school of thought'. The signal criterion will be the pedagogical character of these situations as they define themselves in the data to follow. It was within this school environment that the Holy Word was most carefully preserved, and out of which came the written New Testament, the primary defense of the Church against the burgeoning heresy of the first century.

Jewish Schools

The background to the Christian experience is clearly that of first-century Judaism. Contemporary scholarship has pretty much abandoned the nineteenth- and early twentieth-century fixation on the Hellenistic background of the New Testament. The extent to which early Christianity rigidly followed the Judaic patterns, however, is a continuing discussion which tends to focus on the work of Birger Gerhardsson in his definitive work, *Memory and Manuscript*.[2] Gerhardsson draws many convincing parallels between the Christian community and the practices of the schools for the study of Torah. These range from the *Beth Sefer* where elementary instruction was given by *sopherim* in the written Torah, to the *Beth Hamidrash*, which covers a complex variety of schools, from the quite elementary Mishnah schools to the most highly qualified rabbinic academies (*yeshiboth*) in Palestine and Babylon.[3] These would have varied from simple instruction in written Torah in a home or outdoors in some public or private place, to more and more structured situations in their own buildings, presided over by rabbis of wide

---

2. B. Gerhardsson, *Memory and Manuscript: Oral Tradition and Written Transmission in Rabbinic Judaism and Early Christianity* (Lund: W.K.C. Gleerup; Copenhagen: Munksgaard, 1961). There has been a recent upsurge of interest in the Jewish orientation of early Christianity. The final publication of the Dead Sea Scrolls has greatly encouraged this. James Charlesworth (*Jews and Christians: Exploring the Past, Present, and Future* [New York: Crossroad, 1990]) has recently edited a collection of essays on the subject by a variety of scholars. This is a semi-popular use of New Testament and Hebrew scholarship to bring Jews and Christians closer together, which underscores the point I am making. It also gives further credence to my evidence pointing to the orientation of the Synoptics toward the 'Hebrew mode' (J.A. Baird, *A Comparative Analysis of the Gospel Genre: The Synoptic Mode and Its Uniqueness* [Lewiston: Edwin Mellen Press, 1991]). See also the Fortress Press series on 'Studies in Judaism', especially G. Boccaccini, *Middle Judaism, Jewish Thought 300 B.C.E. to 200 C.E.* (Minneapolis: Fortress Press, 1991).

3. Gerhardsson, *Memory and Manuscript*, p. 89.

reputation and dedicated to the study of oral Torah.[4] The schools of Hillel and Shammai are well documented within first-century Judaism, and reflect the nature of these more sophisticated schools as not only institutions of Torah learning, but as 'schools of thought', representing at times a radical polarity in viewpoint.

Basically, Gerhardsson's plan is to determine the transmission techniques of the later Amoraic period, and thus reach far enough back in time to make a valid comparison with the comparative phenomena in early Christianity.[5] He begins the comparison by stressing the scrupulous care with which the written Torah was copied by the *sopherim*, who were skilled Scripture specialists. All of this was part of the intense respect which the Jew had for the written Torah.[6] The provisions for accurately preserving the written Torah were built into the very structure of Hebrew society, with the use of Scripture in regular public worship and its rote memorization in public education. Not only the written Torah, but also the oral Torah, the sayings and scriptural interpretations of the rabbis, were held in high regard, and immense care was expended in their accurate preservation and transmission. It is in the nature and use of the oral Torah that Gerhardsson finds the closest parallels with the formation of the Synoptics. He points to the concern of the student to preserve the exact words of his rabbi,[7] primarily as a product of highly trained memories; but also, on occasion, both teacher and pupils made use of written notes to aid them.[8] It is in the techniques for remembering practiced by the rabbis, who expected to be remembered, and taught so as to facilitate that fact, by the Tannaim for whom remembering was a vocation, and by the students for whom mnemonic devices were essential, that Gerhardsson finds the most clues to Synoptic formation. He points to the practice of condensation, abridgment, association, grouping, signs, acrostics, repetition and other techniques for memorization that were all part of the daily process of rabbinic instruction.[9]

Besides the demands of the school, these pupils revered their masters as the chief doctrinal authorities, the bearers of the Sinai tradition.

4. Gerhardsson, *Memory and Manuscript*, pp. 89-92.
5. Gerhardsson, *Memory and Manuscript*, p. 77.
6. Gerhardsson, *Memory and Manuscript*, p. 55.
7. Gerhardsson, *Memory and Manuscript*, pp. 130-31.
8. Gerhardsson, *Memory and Manuscript*, p. 160.
9. Gerhardsson, *Memory and Manuscript*, pp. 136-37.

Consequently they were concerned to preserve their every word with a slavish attention almost incomprehensible in modern western society.[10] Often the more legal teachings (*Halakoth*) were derived from some narrative about a rabbi, and in such situations the value of the *Halakoth* was entirely dependent upon the historicity of the narrative.[11] The pattern here is a slavish attention, a devoted carefulness to the written Torah, to the oral Torah, and to the words and deeds of those rabbis who were the guardians of Torah. This is what characterized the rabbinic tradition from the days of Jesus on through later Amoraic times.

It is against such a background that Gerhardsson draws his parallel with early Christianity: 'The sources do not suggest that Jesus used any method radically different from that which was normal in his milieu'.[12] Nor did his disciples revere him whom they believed to be the Messiah any less than the disciples of the rabbis revered their masters.[13] The sources, according to Gerhardsson, reveal the apostles having a particularly authoritative place in the Church, not as individuals, however, but as a 'collegium', still in residence in Jerusalem as late as the fifties, in much the same fashion as the collegium at Qumran. The work done by this Jerusalem collegium in the Holy Scripture and the tradition from and about Christ (ὁ λόγος τοῦ κυρίου) resembled in some ways the labors of rabbinic Judaism on the Holy Scriptures and the oral Torah (דבר יהוה) and the Qumran community's work on Scripture and its own traditions, all of which were partly written and partly oral. Gerhardsson supposes that, as with the pupils of the rabbis, so with these 'ministers of the word' (ὑπηρέται), there was an intensive study of Scripture for deeper insight into the Kingdom of God and the person of Jesus. There must have been the same kinds of theological discussions in this collegium and in church congregations as in the rabbinic schools, where 'the word of the Lord' was remembered, repeated, expounded and applied. The fact that 'the Jesus tradition in the early Christian documents is isolated from the sayings of other authorities...shows that it had a distinctive position among early Christian doctrinal authorities and a peculiar dignity'.[14]

10. Gerhardsson, *Memory and Manuscript*, p. 179.
11. Gerhardsson, *Memory and Manuscript*, p. 183.
12. Gerhardsson, *Memory and Manuscript*, p. 326.
13. Gerhardsson, *Memory and Manuscript*, p. 258.
14. Gerhardsson, *Memory and Manuscript*, pp. 332-33.

As I see it, this situation converges with Christian history at many points. Paul readily identified himself as a student brought up in Jerusalem at the feet of Gamaliel (Acts 22.3). The school of Johanan ben Zakkai was well known, and may have been the training ground for the evangelist Matthew (see below). Broadly defined, the Qumran community could be called a school of Torah study, focused upon the work and influence of the 'teacher of righteousness'. The possibility of some influence of this community upon Christianity, perhaps through John the Baptist, is very real.[15] Josephus is concerned to mention other schools of this period surrounding outstanding teachers, and it is difficult to imagine this active school environment not having some influence upon the early Christian community (*War* 1.33.2 §§648-650; *Ant.* 17.6.2 §§149-154).

The formal character of these schools no doubt varied widely; but this attachment to an outstanding teacher, forming a school of thought and instruction, is part of the mentality of the ancient Mediterranean world and seems to have carried over into the Christian Church: 'I belong to Paul...I belong to Apollos' (1 Cor. 3.4). The teacher in these early centuries tended to have disciples rather than pupils. Irenaeus described himself looking for a teacher to whom he could attach himself. Justin presented himself to various teachers as a disciple (*Trypho* 38). This mentality is perhaps best preserved today in the German tradition of graduate instruction: 'I am a Bultmannian, I am a Barthian'. It was in this school tradition that we find the most natural environment for the preservation, interpretation, application and dissemination of the Holy Word as the disciples followed in the footsteps of their master.

There has been much objection to Gerhardsson's thesis, and it is possible that he has gone too far with the rabbinic analogy. Morton Smith and others have raised some important questions. Smith criticized Gerhardsson's thesis vigorously in order, as he says, to 'forestall a number of errors' likely to be occasioned by it. Smith raises essentially two types of questions.[16] The first deals with chronology, the second

---

15. F.M. Cross, Jr, *The Ancient Library of Qumran and Modern Biblical Studies* (Garden City, NY: Doubleday, 1958), pp. 151-52; see also M. Black, *The Scrolls and Christian Origins* (New York: Charles Scribner's Sons, 1961); C.T. Fritsch, *The Qumran Community* (New York: Macmillan, 1956); Gerhardsson, *Memory and Manuscript*, p. 86.

16. M. Smith, 'A Comparison of Early Christian and Early Rabbinic Tradition', *JBL* 82 (1963), pp. 169-76.

with the Synoptic–rabbinic parallels. The most telling criticism of Gerhardsson's work is Smith's objection to a possible Hebrew anachronism. Gerhardsson agrees with G.F. Moore that there was a 'normative' pharisaic or rabbinic Judaism remaining substantially the same from pre-Christian down to Mishnaic and Talmudic times.[17] He defends this by referring to the 'utterly conservative milieu' of rabbinic Judaism that would have discouraged radical changes between the first and the third centuries.[18] Smith on the other hand points to the radical changes that must have taken place in the revolutionary years between AD 65 and 140 when the small, exclusive, pharisaic party of the Temple was replaced by a developed rabbinic Judaism. He quotes G. Allon and J. Neusner for evidence of dramatic readjustments in Judaism in both Palestine and Babylonia during that time,[19] and complains that Gerhardsson is too dependent on non-Jewish scholars like Moore for his information regarding the Tannaitic period. W.D. Davies also points to the Dead Sea Scrolls as supplying added proof that Judaism before AD 70 was very different from the developed Judaism of Jamnia, and open to more outside influences than Moore admitted.[20]

This is potentially a serious argument against Gerhardsson's thesis; but before it can be decided one way or another we must have more exact data regarding the earliest Tannaitic period than either Smith or Gerhardsson is able to provide. In the absence of direct evidence of rabbinic practices in the early first century, it would seem that the only alternative to endless quotation of conflicting authorities is to do what Gerhardsson has done and compare the Synoptics with the only rabbinic Judaism we can be certain of, which is post AD 70, since there seems to have been a particularly effective obliteration of early Judaism and its records in that terrible Holocaust. Actually our best source for the Judaism of this early period is still ostensibly the Synoptics. If there are significant parallels with post-AD 70 Judaism, it would seem logical to conclude that there must have been some influence one way or another, more probably from rabbinic Judaism to Christianity than vice versa.

17. Gerhardsson, *Memory and Manuscript*, p. 111.
18. Gerhardsson, *Memory and Manuscript*, p. 77.
19. Smith, 'A Comparison', p. 170 n. 3.
20. W.D. Davies, *Christian Origins and Judaism* (Philadelphia: Westminster Press, 1962), p. 106. See also H. Koester (in J.M. Robinson and H. Koester, *Trajectories through Early Christianity* [Philadelphia: Fortress Press, 1971], p. 138 n. 65), whose opposition to Gerhardsson 'can hardly be exaggerated'.

The second form of the chronological question has to do with what Smith considers to be a radical difference between the Christianity of the earliest Jesus period and that of the Pauline period just prior to the destruction of the Temple. If we find traces of rabbinic technique in the Gospels and Paul, then we are dealing with the increase of pharisaic and Essene influence of later pre-AD 70 Judaism rather than that existing during the days of Jesus or the earliest period of Gospel formation. He insists that the Gospels and Paul are a good deal closer to rabbinic Judaism than were Jesus and his immediate followers.[21] What Smith is doing is drawing a radical distinction between Jesus and Paul and between Jesus and those who formulated the Gospels.

This is based upon such a plethora of assumptions. He points to the disappearance of the teaching of Jesus' followers, the 'false accretions' of such material as birth and nature miracle narratives, the loss in the Gospels, except for passing reference, of two or three of the resurrection appearances mentioned by Paul in 1 Cor. 15.1-8, and the 'loss of any reliable record as to Jesus' attitude towards the Law', as evidence against the early Church's concern for the preservation of primitive material. Every one of these assertions is an opinion which Smith must know is highly debatable, and which merely reflects his most basic assumptions concerning what he calls 'the mess of contradictory scraps of evidence which the Gospels preserve'.[22] Since the Gospels are not authentic, how can you take them as evidence that Jesus or his disciples used rabbinic techniques? The circularity of this logic is so apparent that it really has no place in a scientific discussion of an historiographic question. Whether or not the Gospels are authentic *is the question,* and one cannot use an apriori as evidence to prove an apriori.

The second type of question Smith raises has to do with the actual parallels which Gerhardsson draws between the Synoptics and the rabbinic tradition. His detailed objections I would find a mixture of good sense and the quibbling of a threatened apriori. (1) Smith objects to comparing the mentality of Jesus with that of the first-century rabbis, arguing that Gerhardsson has not read enough Jewish literature to see the difference.[23] To my mind, the fact that the Christian Church developed out of the synagogue and that early Christianity continued a close relationship to Judaism makes the use of rabbinic techniques for

21. Smith, 'A Comparison', p. 176.
22. Smith, 'A Comparison', p. 176.
23. Smith, 'A Comparison', p. 170.

transmission and retention natural enough. I would, however, want to urge more of an awareness of Jesus' creative divergence from his environment, and the more prophetic cast of his mind.[24]

(2) Smith insists that Jesus did not teach as the scribes. I would agree; but his use of Mt. 7.29 as evidence misses Matthew's point that it was in 'authority' that he differed—Matthew is saying nothing about method. To insist that the disciples were 'unlearned' and so could not have functioned in ways similar to the disciples of the rabbis is an old, tendentious argument that really ought to be retired. My audience studies have shown clearly that the term μαθητής covers a much wider group than merely the twelve, including men and women of wealth, position and learning, and probably some Pharisees, priests and scribes.[25] One of Gerhardsson's points is that it is memory, rather than written texts, that formed the heart of the early Gospel formation situation. The evidence of Chapter 7 below clearly supports this contention. I would want to add, however, that the transition from oral memory to written 'memoir' was probably much earlier than Gerhardsson has anticipated.

(3) Smith further objects that the Gospels diverge more freely from each other verbally and theologically than do the rabbinic materials. He admits that the halakic parallels given in E. Melamed's collection sometimes contradict each other, although they 'generally show close adherence to the same verbal formulae'.[26] This comment is based more upon his fundamental rejection of the Gospels as a contradictory 'mess' than it is on the evidence. There is no question that the Gospels do differ; but Gerhardsson has well pointed out that they are primarily not *Halakah*, but *Haggadah*, which is a more popular, informal type of saying, permitting a freer rendering. Actually, the evidence for Synoptic verbal 'patterns' indicates the survival of key verbal formulae, and a surprising stability regarding both halakic and haggadic material.[27] Memorization is one very likely source of these verbal patterns. The evidence for theological patterns of continuity further refutes Smith's

---

24. See J.A. Baird, *The Justice of God in the Teaching of Jesus* (London: SCM Press; Philadelphia: Westminster Press, 1963), p. 35; *idem*, *Comparative Analysis*, pp. 79-99.

25. See J.A. Baird, *Audience Criticism and the Historical Jesus* (Philadelphia: Westminster Press, 1967), pp. 37-43.

26. Smith, 'A Comparison', p. 173 n. 9.

27. See Baird, *Audience Criticism*, Chapter 5.

description of the Synoptics as a 'mess of contradictory scraps' (see Chapter 6).

(4) Smith argues that the Synoptics differ in that they are narrative and the rabbinic material expository; they are given for a homiletic purpose but the bulk of the rabbinic teaching has no apparent end save exposition itself, is devoted to exact determination of the sense of particular laws, deals with regular sets of questions asked in regular succession about each successive law, and deals with them in fixed, legal formulae recurring again and again. This is a good point, and warns us not to press the analogy too far; but it does not necessarily preclude analogies at certain points. Jesus was a homilete; but incidents like that at Caesarea Philippi (Mk 8.27-30), the dominance of the didactic 'sayings' form in the Synoptics,[28] and indeed the evidence of this entire book, point very clearly to the techniques and concerns of one who is predominantly a teacher.

(5) Smith sees the Gospel tradition as oriented toward Jesus the miracle worker, filled with stories which 'by the standards of common sense are incredible, for instance that he raised the dead, walked on water, himself rose from the dead and ascended into heaven'.[29] The Tannaitic material on the other hand does have some miracles, but is a tradition which did not go far beyond historical facts. One does not have to accept all the details of the nature miracles to see that Smith is here using an apriori as evidence for historical authenticity—in this case what would seem to be a general rejection of the 'transcendent' dimension in the Gospels. Thus we see that questions of faith, or non-faith, are involved in making historical judgments. As for making 'standards of common sense' the basis for rejecting the resurrection and all the records that describe it, such self-serving statements do not advance the cause of scientific research. Certainly we can agree that the Gospels and the rabbinic material differ in content; but this says nothing about Gerhardsson's thesis, which deals primarily with similarities in method.

(6) A further objection by Smith is that there is no comparison in the principles of arrangement of materials in the two collections. Rabbinic material is connected by topic or text, the Gospels by their relation to the life of Jesus. It is true that the general tenor of the Gospels differs as Smith says; and I would want to argue that the Synoptics differ from the rabbinic tradition more basically then they agree in their genre, mode

---

28. See Baird, *Audience Criticism*, p. 63.
29. Smith, 'A Comparison', p. 173.

and arrangement. But this does not say that at times they do not indeed agree, for example in the topical arrangement of many proto-collections within the Synoptics.[30] Connection with the life of Jesus is only one basis for the arrangement of Gospel material.

(7) Finally, Smith objects that the literature of the New Testament shows almost no trace of the methods of teaching and the mnemonic techniques which rabbinic literature always presupposes. Gerhardsson obviously thinks differently, and I have no intention of arguing each point here. We are all agreed that such techniques do *at times* appear in the Gospels. I would refer to the evidence for the presence of the 'Hebrew mode' in the Synoptics.[31] They are outstanding in their difference at many points from the Greek material in their Hebrew methodological modality. If they are similar to rabbinic material at times, which Smith admits, then we do have a parallel, and although perhaps not as consistent as Gerhardsson has suggested, still a closer methodological parallel than with any other type of ancient non-Christian literature. It is possible to push this parallel too far, and Smith is right in warning of this, but surely he is too doctrinaire in rejecting any parallel at all.[32]

My own evidence points to the Gospel genre as unique and *sui generis*; and, although couched in the 'Hebrew mode', it diverges significantly from rabbinic literature. In the language of my genre study,[33] the 'Synoptic mode' with its characteristics of independence (SM-1), brevity (SM-2), direct discourse (SM-3), ease of memorization (SM-4) and evidence of seams separating individual units (SM-9) clearly represents Jewish modal characteristics which Gerhardsson shows are paralleled in the rabbinic tradition.[34] So I would grant that the rabbinic

30. See Baird, *Comparative Analysis*, pp. 53-56.
31. See Baird, *Comparative Analysis*, pp. 50-51.
32. For other assessments of Gerhardsson, pro and con, see Kelber, *The Oral and the Written Gospel*, pp. 8-9; C.K. Barrett, *Jesus and the Gospel Tradition* (Philadelphia: Fortress Press, 1968); Witherington, *The Christology of Jesus*, p. 16; R. Riesner, *Jesus als Lehrer: Eine Untersuchung zum Ursprung der Evangelien-Überlieferung* (WUNT, 2.7; Tübingen: Mohr Siebeck, 1981); B. Gerhardsson, *The Origins of the Gospel Tradition* (Philadelphia: Fortress Press, 1977); P.H. Davids, 'The Gospels and Jewish Tradition: Twenty Years after Gerhardsson', in R.T. France and D. Wenham (eds.), *Studies of History and Tradition in the Four Gospels* (Gospel Perspectives, 1; Sheffield: JSOT Press, 1980), pp. 75-99.
33. Baird, *Comparative Analysis*, pp. 31-42.
34. Gerhardsson, *Memory and Manuscript*, pp. 148-49.

methods strongly influenced the Gospel writers, and probably the praxis of Jesus. Nevertheless, the Synoptics are closer to Torah, than to Mishnah, and for the early Christians Jesus was closer to God than to Moses.[35]

Despite these caveats, in general I assess Birger Gerhardsson's contribution to the question of Synoptic origins as one of the most creatively constructive in recent years. The parallels he draws between the process of presentation, fixation and transmission of the sayings of the rabbis and those of Jesus are natural and convincing at many points, and one must suppose that first-century pharisaic Judaism had significant influence on Jesus and the early Church in these matters of methodology. This all suggests that in these Jewish schools we see the principal sociological background for the Jesus community, but we must be prepared for the 'Jesus school' to go beyond this environment in its own creative ways.

The School of Jesus

According to Eusebius, there was a long experience of Christian schools in the early history of the Church, and the evidence points to Jesus as the originator of the practice. We see this in the more overt pictures of Jesus calling his disciples, living and traveling with them or going apart with them into the desert or to a mountain retreat like Caesarea Philippi to test them as to their understanding (Mk 8.22-33). We see it in more subtle ways as Jesus is pictured regularly taking his disciples to some private place to explain to them the meaning of his parables (Mk 4.10-12).[36] Even more subtly, the text reveals the ethos of the classroom where the most abundant form is that of the saying, a teaching form as distinguished from the more homiletic parable, and where the most characteristic mode is that of the apophthegm where the question and answer format reflects the activity of a teaching situation (SMU). There would seem to be more than apocryphal fiction to the observation in *The Gospel of Truth*: 'in a school he appeared, he spoke the word in the capacity of a teacher'.[37]

---

35. Gerhardsson, *Memory and Manuscript*, Chapter 9, the 'Torah Parallel'.
36. See Baird, *Audience Criticism*, pp. 102-109.
37. 'School' here could mean 'synagogue'. 'Word' is probably a reference to the word of God or the gospel. 'Teacher', literally 'scribe', 'Probably not *grammateus, sopher*, but a native Egyptian parallel to the Jewish semantic

It would seem that the school environment was the primary ethos for the retention, transmission and interpretation of the Holy Word from the very beginning because Jesus set it up that way. Later apostolic schools were merely following the basic pattern set by Jesus, the master teacher, presenting a body of instruction that was distinctive and absolutely normative, drawing together a group of student disciples in some kind of contiguity, lecturing them publicly and privately, examining them, sending them out to teach and preach, inspiring them to produce written accounts of his life and words, and attaching his name to them with such fidelity that forever after they can do nothing more than trace their spiritual and theological lineage back to him. This is exactly the pattern that holds true for apostolic schools throughout the entire range of early Christian history and there is a naturalness to this that would hardly seem to be accidental.

David Aune pictures early Christian congregations 'isolated from each other and alienated from the pagan environment, with a strong inclination to identify with other Christian congregations and conform to the "Christian" norms and values which were constantly being transmitted, inculcated and homogenized by traveling Christians'.[38] This is congenial with what I am finding in this study, and suggests not only that the Holy Word, gospel and παράδοσις were the basis of this congregational instruction, but that the schools, as we shall be describing them, probably functioned at a higher level as sources of doctrinal authority and the writing of Christian literature. The prophets were mostly lay men and women, and they were supervised by the apostles in matters of doctrine and church discipline. Aune points to much conflict among these traveling prophets, which suggests the necessity for such oversight. Whether we can talk about schools of the prophets is another question. The evidence suggests they were probably too independent for this (cf. Chapter 4). What Aune rightly does is warn us against tying the development of Christian gospel and παράδοσις too rigidly to any formal, highly structured school situation.

---

development... the coptic word also means "expert"'; see *The Gospel of Truth* (trans. K. Grobel; Nashville: Abingdon Press, 1960), pp. 19, 19-20.

38. D.E. Aune, *Prophecy in Early Christianity and the Ancient Mediterranean World* (Grand Rapids: Eerdmans, 1983), pp. 215-17.

The Apostolic College

The Fathers have in one way or another pointed to the existence in the earliest period of the apostolic 'school', or 'college', composed of the twelve, augmented by the seventy. Eusebius records that for forty years the greater number of the apostles and disciples, along with James, 'survived in this world...dwelling in Jerusalem' (*Hist. Eccl.* 3.7.8). With the destruction of the city in AD 70, they would have been scattered along with the rest of the Jews.[39] One and another has referred to the apostles as a group exercising authority in doctrine and theology, and acting as the prime channel for the transmission of the teachings of Jesus. The *Kerygma Petrou* gives a fascinating, if apocryphal, picture of James in Jerusalem supervising the training of Christian teachers (1.1-3).

Without rehearsing all the evidence, it would seem to me that both Birger Gerhardsson and Krister Stendahl have shown the logic of looking to the rabbinic school milieu as a prototype for the early Christian situation.[40] Whether this would be the formal schools of the Pharisees, or those more like the Qumran חבורה, is still an open question. The parallels are there. The school was the natural expression of apostolic authority. A group of twelve disciples invested with a very special knowledge of Jesus and the 'mystery of the gospel' (Mk 4.10-

---

39. This is a thorny question for which new evidence is needed. See S.G.F. Brandon, *The Fall of Jerusalem and the Christian Church* (London: SPCK, 2nd edn, 1952); W.D. Davies, 'Reflection On a Scandinavian Approach to the Gospel Tradition'; in A.N. Wilder *et al.* (eds.), *Neotestamentica et Patristica: Eine Freundesgabe Herrn Professor Dr. Oscar Cullmann zu seinem 60. Geburtstag überreicht* (NovTSup, 6; Leiden: E.J. Brill, 1962), pp. 14-34. Davies insists that there is no evidence in the New Testament for the importance Gerhardsson ascribes to the twelve in Jerusalem. The center of gravity for primitive Christianity was not a body of words or works but Jesus Christ. The evidence of Chapter 1 of this study would seem to negate Davies's objection. See N. Perrin, *Rediscovering the Teaching of Jesus* (New York: Harper & Row, rev. edn, 1976), p. 31. Barrett (*Jesus and the Gospel Tradition*, pp. 10-11) rejects the apostolic college thesis, primarily on his assumption that the Synoptics are written in 'the Greek epic'. My analysis of the Synoptic genre suggests that this line of argument is unfounded textually and historically. Basically *sui generis*, the Synoptics reflect both Greek and Hebrew modes, but are more oriented toward the latter. See Baird, *A Comparative Analysis*, pp. 24-26.

40. Gerhardsson, *Memory and Manuscript*; also see Stendahl, *The School of St Matthew*. For a good description of a school, see D.M. Smith, *John* (Proclamation Commentaries; Philadelphia: Fortress Press, 1976), p. 69.

12), they were looked upon as authorities in doctrine. They possessed as a result a natural leadership in transmitting the Jesus story and administering such a group. As such they could be expected to operate as an administrative and pedagogical whole (cf. Chapter 5).

The evidence of the New Testament argues in this direction, whether we are talking about the necessity of electing a Matthias to fill out the inner twelve, or the function of the apostles in ordaining deacons, disciplining miscreants, sending out missionaries, laying on of hands or convening a Jerusalem council where even the independent Paul is called to account. The evidence from source criticism further supports this logic. Two of the major sub-sources of the Synoptics, the Lukan special source (L) and the Matthean special material (M) both show a distinct orientation to Jerusalem. The M source, especially with its commonly recognized interest in Jewish concerns, suggests that it is the product of the apostolic community in Jerusalem.[41]

The exact nature of this 'college' remains in doubt. I would tend to agree with what I understand is Stendahl's reluctance to accept the more formal aspects of Gerhardsson's picture of the apostolic college. My own evidence from this study suggests that although there is a clear rabbinic parallel it was not so formally close to the highly organized rabbinic schools of the later Amoraic period. The one problem with the apostolic college concept is that there is no dominant teacher who set his stamp upon the group, and by whose name they were identified. This may be because of the 'Holy' influence of Jesus who as risen Lord continued to dominate the apostles. There is some suggestion that Peter first, then James, and even Paul tried to play this dominant role, with varying success. The absence of a living Jesus may have hastened the dissolution of the apostolic college into the many schools of the apostles.

The 'Q' Community

The existence of Q as a separate document utilized by Matthew and Luke is an hypothesis that continues to intrigue Synoptic scholarship. My own evidence repeatedly supports the existence of some such written collection, or collections, which may better be referred to as the 'double tradition' without giving it the formal character of a

---

41. Baird, *Audience Criticism*, pp. 144-77.

document.[42] What is evident is that despite considerable effort to the contrary, this hypothesis refuses to go away. Recently there has been a renaissance of Q scholarship, and considerable progress in identifying not only the so-called Q document, but, even more importantly for our purposes here, the Q community.

The current research into this question usually assumes the existence of Q as a document. John Kloppenborg's doctoral dissertation has received considerable attention. He assigns two recensions to Q, created and edited by the Q community, made up of speeches or 'sayings compositions'; first as an aid to sending missionaries into the field, and later as the product of a more sedentary community that was more 'sapientic' than prophetic.[43] Arland Jacobson, by 'peeling' back the historical onion from the text of Q, arrives at three stages, and detects evidence for a failed mission to Israel which prompted the announcement of bitter judgments against them. This assumption of Q as a document and the presumption of a Q community is based upon considerable conjecture and many redaction-critical assumptions which unfortunately are highly debatable, and weaken the hypothesis.

There is, however, other more objective evidence which helps to identify a Q community. (1) There is the Galilean provenance. B.H.

---

42. See Baird, *Audience Criticism*, pp. 61-65, for the figures on the agreement between Matthew and Luke on the hypothetical Q source. Especially instructive is the comparison of word agreement between Matthew and Luke on the double tradition (86%), and that between the three Evangelists on the Markan source (90%). If we see Markan agreement as evidence for Mark as a written source for Matthew and Luke, then we must also entertain the same possibility for the Q material. See R.A. Edwards, *A Theology of Q: Eschatology, Prophecy, and Wisdom* (Philadelphia: Fortress Press, 1976); D.E. Aune, *The New Testament in Its Literary Environment* (Philadelphia: Westminster Press, 1987), p. 409. For an excellent bibliography on Q, see F. Neirynck, 'Studies on Q since 1972', *ETL* 56 (1980), pp. 409-13. The most recent research on Q seems to take the existence of a Q community for granted, and concentrate on the history and structure of Q. See A.D. Jacobson, 'The History of the Composition of the Synoptic Sayings Source, Q', in K.H. Richards (ed.), *Society of Biblical Literature 1987 Seminar Papers* (SBLSP, 26; Atlanta: Scholars Press, 1987), pp. 285-94.

43. J. Kloppenborg, 'The Literary Genre of the Synoptic Sayings Source' (University of St Michael's College, Toronto School of Theology, 1984), revised and published as *The Formation of Q: Trajectories in Ancient Wisdom Collections* (Philadelphia: Fortress Press, 1987); *idem*, 'The Formation of Q and Antique Instructional Genres', *JBL* 105 (1986), pp. 443-62; Jacobson, 'The History of the Composition of the Synoptic Sayings Source, Q', pp. 285-94.

Streeter, who is experiencing a mild renaissance today, pointed years ago to the orientation of the Q material toward Capernaum[44] which was, according to the rabbis, for many centuries considered a great center for the 'minim' or Christians: 'It is probable that others of the twelve made that city their headquarters'.[45] Streeter referred to the Galilean flavor of Lk. 16.16, 'The law and the prophets were until John', which reflects the 'freer' atmosphere of Galilee, and referred to Lk. 7.1-10, where Jesus' praise of the centurion's faith seems to be a criticism of Israel, and again reflects a Galilean environment: 'At a time when the Judaizing section of the church wished to give the uncircumcised an inferior status, that story was in itself a charter of Gentile liberty'.[46] Capernaum is as likely a place as any, although some archaeological evidence suggests that Nazareth could also have been such a center.[47]

(2) The Q community seems to have been largely a non-apostolic, that is, a lay community. When correlated according to audience, the Jesus λόγια in the double tradition show a strong orientation toward the larger group of disciples.[48] My audience study has shown that the audience orientation of a saying as found in the Synoptics tends to reveal the types of persons either who heard the saying in the first place, or who pulled together and eventually edited the collection of sayings and events in which they were particularly interested. In the absence of evidence for apostolic leadership, we are probably talking about a lay situation. Luke gives us a clear listing of dominant laymen such as Stephen, Philip, Prochorus, Nicanor, Timon, Parmenas and Nicholas a proselyte of Antioch. At least two of these were active in this northern region. The activity in Samaria of Philip the Caesarean evangelist, one of the seven laymen chosen for the ministry of serving (Acts 6.1-6) who was preaching 'good news about the kingdom of God, and the name of Jesus Christ' (Acts 8.12), underscores the lay character of this group. Luke's description of the great persecution in Jerusalem which scattered the Church throughout Judea and Samaria, 'except the apostles', further

---

44. B.H. Streeter, *The Four Gospels: A Study of Origins* (London: Macmillan, 1951), p. 233.
45. Streeter, *The Four Gospels*, p. 233.
46. Streeter, *The Four Gospels*, p. 233.
47. The evidence for a primitive Christian synagogue beneath the Catholic Basilica of the Annunciation in Nazareth is one possible indication, although this needs further confirmation to be relied upon. See B. Bagatti, *Excavations in Nazareth. I. From the Beginning till the XII Century* (Jerusalem: Franciscan Printing Press, 1969).
48. Baird, *Audience Criticism*, pp. 54-73.

documents this (Acts 8.1). The felt need of the apostles in Jerusalem to send Peter and John to the Samaritan Christians to baptize them with the Holy Spirit (Acts 8.14) further underscores such an incipient clergy–laity distinction.[49] The report that Philip had four unmarried daughters 'who prophesied' (Acts 21.9) suggests the activity of prophets in the vicinity of Caesarea; and the record of Stephen's preaching has the distinct ring of Christian prophecy (cf. Chapter 4). Dominant lay men and women, some of whom bear the stamp of the Christian prophet, seem clearly to have played an important part in the proclamation of the Holy Word and παράδοσις in the northern area.

(3) A third subtle indication of the character of such a community comes from the hints at its didactic nature. When the λόγια of Jesus in both the Markan and Q collections are correlated according to form and audience, several interesting facts appear. For one thing, there is a particularly high verbal and audience agreement in both collections in apophthegms, parables and sayings, between 83 and 96 percent.[50] This suggests the early written character of these data. Furthermore, while the agreement between Mark, Matthew and Luke in the presumed Markan material is higher in parables and apophthegms, the so-called Q material agrees more highly in the sayings, clearly the most didactic of the three forms. The community that preserved this material seems to have been one composed largely of lay men and women, in a didactic setting, and engaged among other things in the editing and dissemination of Jesus material.

Whether or not we can refer to a Christian 'school' in Galilee or Samaria needs much more evidence. Probably we would do better not to use that term for these lay groups, whose existence seems to have been more functionally determined than were the more authoritatively constituted schools of the apostles. Because of the Galilean orientation of the Q material, it is usually assumed that this material was gathered and collated in the churches of that area. Certainly there is abundant evidence of active Christian communities in that region. If we posit a Q document, or merely a collection of individual memoirs, then we must entertain the possibility if not probability that there was a significant group there with sufficient knowledge of the primitive Jesus situation to produce such material. The important thing for our thesis is that the center of their proclamation was the person of Jesus, 'the Righteous

---

49. See Baird, *Audience Criticism*.
50. Baird, *Audience Criticism*, p. 64 chart XII.

7. The Environment of the Word

One' (Acts 7.52), and his Word about the Kingdom of God (Acts 8.12, 14, 25). The focus of Q upon the teachings of Jesus, with only a minimum of narrative, dramatically illustrates the point we have been making about the centrality of the Holy Word in the early Christian Church.[51]

Schools of the Apostles

Pushing the process forward one step, we come to the evidence depicting the immediate 'disciples' of the apostles (*Hist. Eccl.* 4.14.7). One view of this process is well described by Clement of Alexandria: 'To James the Just and John and Peter, the Lord after his resurrection imparted knowledge (τὴν γνῶσιν). These imparted it to the rest of the apostles, and the rest of the apostles to the seventy, of whom Barnabas was one.' In *Stromata* 1, he writes: 'They (Tatian, Theodotus, and Pantaenus) preserving the tradition of the blessed doctrine derived directly from the holy apostles, Peter, James, John, and Paul, the sons receiving it from the father...came by God's will to us also to deposit those ancestral and apostolic seeds'. Epiphanius in his 'Treatise on Weights and Measures' (14B–15B) refers to 'the disciples of the apostles' flourishing in Jerusalem after AD 70.[52]

Irenaeus refers to 'the elders before us, who also were disciples of the apostles...' (*Hist. Eccl.* 5.20.5; cf. also 3.37.2; *Adv. Haer.* 4.32.1; 3.15.3). Diognetus identifies himself as 'a disciple of the apostles' who is 'becoming a teacher of the heathen' (*Diogn.* 11.1). Justin Martyr in a classic quotation speaks of 'the memoirs, drawn up by his apostles and

---

51. Baird, *Audience Criticism*, pp. 64-65.
52. R.H. Smith, *The Pella of Decapolis* (2 vols.; Wooster, OH: College of Wooster, 1973), I, p. 47. See R. Scroggs, 'The Earliest Hellenistic Christianity', in J. Neusner (ed.), *Religions in Antiquity* (Leiden: E.J. Brill, 1968), pp. 176-77. Scroggs rejects the idea that Christianity was from the first led by the former disciples in Jerusalem. He argues that Acts is inaccurate at this point. It is with the Hellenistic Christians of Jerusalem that we find the beginning of the Christian mission, which then became the mother of western Christianity. His evidence concentrates on Stephen's speech in Acts and the Hellenistic Christian mission to Samaria. There is no doubt that the Hellenistic influence was strong in the early Church, but Scroggs needs to pay more attention to the rest of the New Testament and the writings of the Fathers, where the evidence for apostolic leadership is strong. See E. Hennecke and W. Schneemelcher (eds.), *New Testament Apocrypha* (2 vols.; Philadelphia: Westminster Press, 1963), II, pp. 45-46.

those who followed them' (*Trypho* 103). Papias, who made it plain 'that he had in no way been a hearer and eyewitness of the sacred apostles', taught that he had 'received the articles of faith from those who had known them who were their pupils (γνωρίμων διδάσκει)...but if ever anyone came who had followed the presbyters, I inquired into the words of the presbyters, what Andrew or Peter or Philip or Thomas or James or John or Matthew, or any other of the Lord's disciples, had said, and what Aristion and the presbyter John, the Lord's disciples, were saying' (*Hist. Eccl.* 3.39.2-3). Clearly, the closer we get to the first-century situation, the more vivid becomes the testimony to this 'apostolic pipeline', which seems to have taken the form of close pedagogical association with the apostles and their disciples.

The School of Peter

Even more specifically, there is sufficient evidence to trace the 'trajectory' of these apostolic schools through some of their dominant disciples. There is evidence for example of what can be called a 'school' of Peter, if not in the formal sense, then at least in terms of his disciples and interpreters. The classic location for such a thesis would perhaps be the *Kerygma Petrou*, a work Clement regarded as being composed by Peter, and variously dated between AD 80 and 140.[53] There he writes to James, 'the lord and bishop of the holy church', about the books of his 'preaching' which he is forwarding to them in Jerusalem, to be handed over to the 'seventy brethren that they may prepare those who are candidates for positions as teachers'. The atmosphere here is clearly a pedagogical one, not only on the part of Peter, presumably in Rome, but also in Jerusalem with James and the other disciples.

Clement of Alexandria is the most abundant source of information about a possible 'school' of Peter. He gives us a glimpse of Peter publicly preaching the word at Rome before 'many', including 'some of Caesar's equites'. Mark, 'who had followed him for a long time and remembered what had been spoken' was urged by 'the hearers of Peter...not satisfied with a single hearing or with the unwritten teaching of the divine proclamation...seeing that he was Peter's follower (ἀκόλουθον ὄντα), to leave them a written statement of the teaching (διδασκαλίας) given them verbally' (*Hist. Eccl.* 2.15.1; cf. 6.14.5-7).

53. Hennecke and Schneemelcher (eds.), *New Testament Apocrypha*, II, pp. 94-95.

He adds in the *Fragments* (1) that Peter in his preaching in Rome 'adduced many testimonies to Christ in order that thereby they might be able to commit to memory what was spoken...by Peter'. This sounds very much like a teaching situation. In his *Stromata*, Clement adds the further details that the heretic Basilides claimed his master Glaucius was 'the interpreter of Peter', while Marcion, 'who arose in the same age with them, lived as an old man with the younger (heretics) and after him Simon (Magus) heard for a little the preaching of Peter' (7.17). Clement supports the earlier statements of Papias in his famous quotation in Eusebius: 'Mark became Peter's interpreter, and wrote accurately all that he remembered...for he had not heard the Lord, nor had he followed him, but later on as I said followed Peter, who used to give teaching (διδασκαλίας) as necessity demanded, but not making as it were an arrangement of the Lord's oracles (λογίων)' (*Hist. Eccl.* 3.39.15). Here Peter is clearly cast in a teacher-preacher role, the substance of whose teaching, given to be memorized and recorded by his disciples, was the 'oracles' of Jesus. Tertullian writes that the Gospel 'which Mark published may be affirmed to be Peter's whose interpreter Mark was. For even Luke's form of the Gospel was usually ascribed to Paul. And it may well seem that the works which disciples publish belong to their masters' (*Against Marcion* 4.5).

Whether or not this evidence can refer to a 'school' of Peter is perhaps a matter of definition. Certainly many of the ingredients of a school are here. The influence of Peter in the churches of Jerusalem, Rome and Antioch, where he seems at an early period to have been considered bishop,[54] his pastoral role reflected in the Catholic Epistles, where he is recorded calling himself 'fellow elder', 'servant' and 'apostle' (1 Pet. 5.1; 2 Pet. 1.1), and the voluminous Petrine literature in the canonical and apocryphal New Testament, all point to a person and a situation that prompted scholastic and literary activity.

The School of John

One of the most clearly attested 'schools' is that of the apostle John whose line of disciples includes such names as Polycarp, Papias, Irenaeus

---

54. See, e.g., O. Cullmann, *Peter: Disciple, Apostle, Martyr* (Philadelphia: Westminster Press, 1962), p. 235.

and Hippolytus.[55] In a letter to Florinus, whom he describes as 'a man of rank in the lower hall...in Polycarp's house...endeavoring to stand well with him', Irenaeus records some childhood recollections:

> I remember the events of those days...so that I can speak even of the place in which the blessed Polycarp sat and disputed, how he came in and went out, the character of his life, the appearance of his body, the discourses which he made to the people, how he reported his intercourse with John and with the others who had seen the Lord, how he remembered their words, and what were the things concerning the Lord which he had heard from them, and about their miracles, and about their teaching, and how Polycarp had received them from the eyewitnesses of the word of life, and reported all things in agreement with the Scripture. I listened eagerly even then to these things...and made notes of them, not on paper but in my heart... (*Hist. Eccl.* 5.20.6-7; cf. 5.24.16).

In his treatise *Adversus Haereses* (*Against Heresies*), Irenaeus describes Polycarp as one 'instructed by apostles' who had 'conversed with many who had seen Christ'. He was also appointed bishop of the church in Smyrna 'by Apostles in Asia...always having taught the things which he had learned from the apostles, and which the Church has handed down, and which alone are true'. Meeting Marcion one day, Polycarp is said to have drawn back in horror, 'I do not know thee, the first born of Satan...such was the horror which the apostles and their disciples had against holding even verbal communication with any corrupters of the truth'. It was he who reported the incident of John rushing from the bath house, because 'Cerinthus, the enemy of the truth, is within' (*Adv. Haer.* 3.3.4; cf. 4.14.3-4). In the *Martyrdom of Polycarp*, the author describes Irenaeus handing on 'the ecclesiastical and catholic rule, as he had received it from the Saint' (Polycarp), and then the Christian scribe adds this illuminating note: 'Gaius copied this from the writing of Irenaeus, a disciple of Polycarp, and he lived with Irenaeus, and I, Socrates, wrote it out in Corinth, from the copies of Gaius... and I, again, Pionius, wrote it out from the former writings, after searching for it... and I gathered it together when it was almost worn out by age...' (*Mart. Pol.* 22.2-3).

Papias adds his testimony as a 'hearer of John and a friend of Polycarp' (*Hist. Eccl.* 3.39.7). Not himself an eyewitness of the holy

---

55. See Smith, *John*, p. 69; A. Culpepper, *The Johannine School* (SBLDS, 26; Missoula, MT: Scholars Press, 1975).

7. The Environment of the Word

apostles, he tells us that he 'received the things of the faith from those who were acquainted with them':

> And I shall not hesitate to append to the interpretations all that I ever learnt well from the presbyters and remembered well, for of their truth I am confident. For unlike most, I did not rejoice in them who say much, but in them who teach the truth, nor in them who recount the commandments of others, but in them who repeated those given to the faith by the Lord and derived from truth itself; but if ever anyone came who had followed the presbyters, I enquired into the words of the presbyters, what Andrew or Peter or Philip or Thomas or James or John or Matthew, or any other of the Lord's disciples had said, and what Aristion and the presbyter John, the Lord's disciples were saying. For I did not suppose that information from books would help me so much as the word of a living and surviving voice (*Hist. Eccl.* 3.39.2-4).

We note here the centrality of the teachings of Jesus, and the basically oral nature of this apostolic teaching which was given to be remembered and then passed on, certainly suggesting a pedagogical environment for the Holy Word.[56]

The school of John is clearly indicated in Clement's account in Eusebius, 'that John...conscious that the outward facts had been set forth in the Gospels, was urged on by his disciples, and divinely moved by the Spirit, composed a spiritual Gospel' (*Hist. Eccl.* 6.14.7). This is echoed in the *Muratorian Canon*: 'John...when his fellow disciples and bishops entreated him, he said, "fast...now with me for the space of three days and let us recount to each other whatever may be revealed to each of us"'. It was then revealed to Andrew that John should narrate all things in his own name 'as they called them to mind' (*Fragments of Caius* 3.1-4).[57]

This all raises again the distinct possibility that in the New Testament, the Johannine material, the Gospel, the epistles and conceivably the Apocalypse, are all products of this Johannine school, produced by various ones within the company, but all drinking deeply of the

---

56. See the *Fragments* of Papias, from *Anastasius Sinaita*: 'Taking occasion from Papias of Hierapolis, a disciple of the apostle who leaned on the bosom of Christ'.

57. See Hennecke and Schneemelcher (eds.), *New Testament Apocrypha*, II, p. 82: 'The circle in which this tradition (of John) originated and was fostered seems to have continued in the circle to which the author of the *Acta Johannis* belonged and for which he wrote'.

influence of its founder, and attaching his name to its products. There is an enticing pattern here, which needs much more work to establish.

The School of Matthew

Perhaps the most intriguing is the evidence for a school of the apostle Matthew. There is little or no reference to such a school in the Fathers and later Christian literature; but there is an abundance of subtle evidence coming from the study of the Gospels themselves. This thesis in most recent years is especially associated with the work of Krister Stendahl in his book, *The School of St Matthew*. The question as he sees it is the nature of the original *Sitz im Leben* of the Gospel. The form critics under the influence of Martin Dibelius have pointed to the influence of preaching: *Im Anfang war die Predigt*. G.D. Kilpatrick takes a different view, insisting that the liturgical use of the Scripture was the focus of the Church's use of the Gospel material.[58] In expounding the texts read in the services, the needs of the church were connected with the words recorded in the Gospel. Stendahl is critical of both of these views, and suggests rather that 'the school may be invoked as a more natural *Sitz im Leben*. The systematizing work, the adaptation towards casuistry instead of broad statements of principles, the reflection on the position of the church leaders and their duties, and many other similar features, all point to a milieu of study and instruction.'

The main line of argument used by Stendahl is that of proving the close affinity between the type of Old Testament interpretation to be found in a certain group of Matthew's quotations and the way in which the sect of Qumran treated the book of Habakkuk. As von Dobschütz has argued, Matthew was a rabbi, probably trained in the school of Jochanan ben Zakkai. When he became a Christian teacher he made use of his Jewish training in presenting his Gospel. Stendahl argues that 'If we owe the Gospel to a converted rabbi, we must suppose that he was not working entirely alone, but that he took an active part in the life of the church where he lived and served'. The particular type of Old Testament quotation and interpretation is called the 'pesher', and Matthew in his free handling of the LXX and interpreting it in the light of the Gospel of Mark represents the creative activity of the Matthean church. This pesher translation of the LXX presupposes an advanced

---

58. G.D. Kilpatrick, *The Origins of the Gospel according to St Matthew* (Oxford: Clarendon Press, 1946), p. 20.

7. *The Environment of the Word*

study of the Scriptures, and a familiarity not only with the LXX but with the Hebrew text. All of this points to the activity of a rather sophisticated school, similar in many ways to the schools of the rabbis. Stendahl is impressed with the fact that Jesus was called a 'rabbi', and clearly gathered a school about himself; and so he interprets Mt. 23.8-10 in the light of such a school environment.[59]

Of further note is the evidence of the Qumran scrolls, which point to an actual 'Jewish חבורה', a brotherhood that acted as a school, preserving and expounding the doctrines of its founder, and existing just at the time of Gospel formation. All of this suggests that 'there may be an unbroken line from the School of Jesus via the "teaching of the apostles", the "ways" of Paul, the basic teaching of Mark and other ὑπηρέται τοῦ λόγου, and the more mature School of John to the rather elaborate School of Matthew with its ingenious interpretation of the Old Testament as the crown of its scholarship'.[60] It may be this kind of Old Testament interpretation that was practiced by the later school of Polycarp, to which Irenaeus refers: 'After this fashion also did a presbyter (Polycarp?), a disciple of the apostles, reason with respect to the two testaments... then shall every word also seem consistent to him, if he for his part diligently read the Scripture in company with those who are Presbyters in the Church, among whom is the apostolic doctrine...' (*Adv. Haer.* 4.32). This is an intriguing thesis, and makes a

---

59. Stendahl, *The School of St Matthew*, pp. 29, 30, 34, 191-92, 204. More recently there has been an approach to this question from research into the activity of early itinerating Christian prophets and apostles. Aune (*Prophecy in Early Christianity*, pp. 198, 214-17), for example, sees Matthew as the representative of a Christian community located somewhere in Syria-Palestine in the last half of the first century. He presents the current picture in Synoptic circles of many congregations operating independently, yet tied together by itinerating prophets and apostles whose teaching was subject to the authority of the Christian communities. This is a creative suggestion, but I think may put too much authority in the hands of loosely defined 'communities'. The evidence points rather to specific apostles and their collective authority, to particular prophets and their inspiration, and finally to the Holy Word of Jesus as the authoritative sources of the Word, its interpretation and application. For a discussion of the 'community of Matthew', see J.D. Kingsbury, 'The Verb ἀκολυθεῖν ("To Follow") as an Index of Matthew's View of His Community', *JBL* 97 (1978), pp. 56-73.

60. This last quotation is a statement which Stendahl (*The School of St Matthew*, pp. 31, 34) in the revised edition of his book feels was a 'careless' one and needs more evidence. I think that Stendahl's original instincts were on target. The evidence presented here strengthens his case.

great deal of sense in context with the evidence already amassed for the schools of the disciples. The one major problem as I see it is the lack of reference to such a dominant school in the literature of the Fathers, although the argument from silence is most often simply a confession of the poverty of one's resources.

The School of Paul

There is abundant evidence for a school of Paul, mostly in the New Testament, but also in a few references in the Fathers. In Eusebius, Origen, discussing the epistle to the Hebrews in his *Homilies*, adds the remark that although 'the thoughts are the apostle's (Paul)...the styles and composition belong to one who called to mind the apostles' teachings and, as it were, made short notes of what his master said' (*Hist. Eccl.* 6.25.13). This is clearly a school situation. Clement of Alexandria also, in his *Stromata*, refers to the heretic Valentinus who was 'a hearer of Theudas, a pupil of Paul' (7.17). It is interesting how many so-called 'heretics' traced their lineage to one or the other of the great apostles. The evidence in the New Testament of the many churches who owed their lives to Paul, and the many disciples who traveled with him, ran his errands, kept records of his journeys and probably edited and perhaps even wrote some of his letters, is too well known to reiterate here. That the author of Luke–Acts was the same Luke who traveled with Paul has, I think, become well established, and need not be defended at this point; and here again is the same pattern wherein the school situation surrounding a dominant apostle produced epistles, at least one major Gospel, and in this case the principal history of the Pauline period. The point I would make is that Paul's immediate environment was that of a school, with documents, lectures, and a line of students, proud to bear his name, record his deeds, edit his works, and pass on the memoirs of Jesus' life and teachings which they had collected and redacted.

The School of Matthias

There is also some evidence for a school of Matthias, the disciple who was officially made an apostle in Jerusalem shortly after Pentecost (Acts 1.26). Eusebius, in describing the heresy of Nicolas, records that 'They also say that this was the teaching of Matthias, to slight the flesh and abuse it...to make the soul grow through faith and knowledge' (*Hist. Eccl.* 3.29.4). Clement also testifies to a Matthias school of thought: 'They (the Gnostics) say that Matthias also taught as follows...' (*Strom.* 3.4). The heretical trend of this apostle's thought is further reflected in a well known quotation from Hippolytus: 'Basileides and Isadorus the true son and disciple of Basileides, say that Matthias communicated to them secret discourses which being specially instructed he heard from the Savior. Let us see how clearly Basileides...and the entire band of their followers, not only tell lies about Matthias but even about the Savior himself' (7.20.1). In the most recent work on the Nag Hammadi documents, there is raised the possibility that *The Book of Thomas the Contender* was written by Matthias.[61]

Orthodox Schools

The catechetical school at Alexandria is well known.[62] Eusebius calls it ἐξ ἀρχαίου ἔθους, and Jerome dates its origin from the first planting of Christianity: 'Pantaenus had charge of the life of the faithful in Alexandria, for from ancient custom a school of sacred learning existed among them'. 'Orally and in writing (he) expounded the treasure of the divine doctrine... this school has lasted on to our time' (*Hist. Eccl.* 5.10.1). Clement of Alexandria is well known as a pupil of Pantaenus, thoroughly trained in 'the divine scriptures' (*Hist. Eccl.* 5.11.1-5), and the teacher of the famous Origen, 'men powerful in their learning and zeal for divine things' (*Hist. Eccl.* 5.10.1). Eusebius clearly locates the school of Pantaenus within the 'succession' of the apostles when he quotes Clement in what he considers to be an allusion to Pantaenus:

> This work is not a writing composed for show, but notes stored up for my old age, a remedy against forgetfulness, an image without art, and a sketch of those clear and vital words which I was privileged to hear, and of blessed and truly notable men. Of these, one, the Ionian, was in Greece, another in South Italy, a third in Coelo-Syria, another from Egypt, and there were others in the East, one of them an Assyrian, another in Palestine of Hebrew origin. But when I had met the last, and in power he was indeed the first, I

---

61. This may be Matthew or Matthias; see Robinson, *Trajectories*, p. 81 n. 28. Bruce Metzger (*The Canon of the New Testament: Its Origin, Development, and Significance* [Oxford: Clarendon Press, 1987], p. 135) has recently called attention to Clement of Alexandria's reference to the traditions of Matthias.

62. See Metzger, *Canon of the New Testament*, pp. 111, 129-30, for a recent review of the scholarly work of the Alexandrian school.

hunted him out from his concealment in Egypt and found rest. But these men preserved the true tradition of the blessed teaching directly from Peter and James and John and Paul, the holy apostles...' (*Hist. Eccl.* 5.11.2-5).

Origen, a pupil of Pantaenus, teacher at Alexandria and the catechetical school in Caesarea, continued this tradition, being the mentor of one Theotecnus whom Eusebius says 'also was of the school of Origen' (*Hist. Eccl.* 7.14.1). 'It is said that Origen, who was over sixty years of age, inasmuch as he had now acquired immense facility from long preparation, permitted shorthand-writers to take down the discourses delivered by him in public...' (*Hist. Eccl.* 6.36.1). Not only in Egypt, but closer to the cradle of Christianity, was the school established by Pamphilus in Caesarea, 'a most eloquent man and a true philosopher in his mode of life who had been deemed worthy of the presbyterate of that community' (*Hist. Eccl.* 7.32.25).[63] Tatian is said to have been a 'hearer' (ἀκροατής) of Justin in Rome; 'but after the martyrdom of Justin he left the church, being exalted by the idea of becoming a teacher and puffed up as superior to others' (*Hist. Eccl.* 4.29.3; cf. Irenaeus, *Adv. Haer.* 28).

Heretical Schools

Heresy and conflict began early in the controversy between the apostles and prophets, and between various prophets themselves. Jesus is recorded warning his disciples at an early period against 'false prophets...ravenous wolves' who call him 'Lord, Lord', but do not enter the Kingdom of heaven (Mt. 7.15-23). The author of 1 John urges the beloved to 'test the spirits to see whether they are of God, confessing that "Jesus Christ has come in the flesh"' (4.1-3), and this is echoed in Paul's identification of one of the gifts of the Spirit as 'the ability to be able to distinguish between spirits' (1 Cor. 12.10). This was a sufficient problem for Paul to urge the Corinthians to test the prophets: 'let two or three prophets speak, and let the others weigh what is said' (1 Cor. 14.29). There seem to have been many competing voices within the earliest Church situation as described in the New Testament, and this

---

63. The founder of the catechetical school in Caesarea has been a matter of doubt. Eusebius here claims it was Pamphilus. The *Encyclopedia Brittanica* says he was 'unknown'. Metzger (*Canon of the New Testament*, p. 135) identifies Origen as the founder there of 'a new biblical and theological school'.

continued in the post-apostolic Church, as seen in the *Didache* (11), the *Shepherd of Hermas* (*Mand.* 11), and the *Acts of Thomas* (79).

The school tradition found a ready clientele among the many later heretical groups. It was typical of early Christians to follow dominant teachers, become their disciples and bear their names. Eusebius lists many such: Simonians, Cleobians, Dositheans, Manichaeans, etc. (*Hist. Eccl.* 4.22.5). He calls these αἱρέσεις, 'sects', which can be translated 'schools', and these would for Eusebius have had a special connotation as schools of thought. Satorninus and Basilides 'established schools (διδασκαλεῖα) of God-hating heresies' stemming from the work of Menander, a pupil of Simon Magus (*Hist. Eccl.* 4.7.3). Apollinarius talked of the 'lying organization' (τάξις) called the 'New Prophecy... abominated in the whole of Christendom...' (*Hist. Eccl.* 5.19.2). Tertullian identified various heresies as 'schools' (*institutionem*). Justin in his dialogue with Trypho complained that 'some are called Marcions, and some Valentinians, and some Basilidians... each called after the originator of the individual opinion...' (*Trypho* 8). One of the activities of these heretical schools was the production of books. There were so many that Eusebius felt compelled to list the canonical works and distinguish them from the 'books the heretics put forward in the name of the apostles, whether as containing Gospels of Peter and Thomas and Matthias, or even of some others besides these, or as containing Acts of Andrew and John and the other apostles' (*Hist. Eccl.* 3.25.1-7). In Mesopotamia, Bardesanes, 'a most able man and skilled in Syriac, composed dialogues against the Marcionites...' (*Hist. Eccl.* 4.30.1). So prevalent were they in the second, third and fourth centuries, that one could almost equate the concept of a 'school' with heresy.[64]

Summary

By now it is possible to see the general outlines of the 'school' emerging from the evidence. The characteristics of the apostolic and heretical

64. The classic analysis of this struggle is of course still that of Walter Bauer in *Rechtglaubigkeit und Ketzerei im altesten Christentum*. This has been made available to English-speaking audiences in America in Georg Strecker's fine translation (W. Bauer, *Orthodoxy and Heresy in Earliest Christianity* [trans. G. Strecker; Philadelphia: Fortress Press, 1971], esp. p. 224). For more on this, see Aune, *The New Testament in Its Literary Environment*, pp. 218-19. For a recent review of the place of fringe groups in the development of the canon, see Metzger, *Canon of the New Testament*.

schools of the first three centuries concur in several patterns that seem to constitute the rough parameters of what one might call the Christian version of the rabbinic school.

(1) The school was presided over by a dominant teacher, whether a Polycarp, a Peter, or a Jesus.

(2) The school represented a 'school of thought' in that its life was centered on a particular doctrine or set of precepts. In the case of the apostolic college, or of the various apostolic schools, this would have been the teachings of Jesus. In the case of the heretical schools, it would have been the modification of this Word with the particular emphasis of the heretical teacher, for example the ascetic doctrines of Nicolas.

(3) The school consisted of a group of pupil-disciples who either were in residence or had at one time been in residence with the dominant teacher.

(4) Public sermons, lectures and private teaching sessions were the rule, where pupils often took notes because they were expected to remember the words of the teacher.

(5) Written documents were studied and others were produced by the teacher directly, or by his disciples, or both. This regularly consisted in accounts of the life and teachings of the Master.

(6) Pupils were examined, and when prepared, were sent out to preach and teach the words of the master, and often to duplicate and spread the books produced within the school.

(7) The disciples of the dominant teacher were concerned to identify themselves with their master, and to trace their lineage back to Jesus via the apostles.

Implication and Conclusions

The early Christian literature, from the New Testament through Eusebius, reflects a continuing high regard on the part of the Church for the 'Holy Apostles' (cf. Chapter 5). They were the prime deposit for the Holy Word of Jesus, the special choice of the master. Their authority in matters of Scripture, doctrine and Church affairs was final. The apostolic environment, from the days of Jesus through the early days of the Church and then down through the years along the line of 'apostolic succession' with disciples of disciples of the apostles, was basically a pedagogical one, and the school was the natural product and expression of this fact. We have good reason to believe that the young Church in all its enthusiasm was ordered and organized, not only in the administration of its growing mission, but also in its handling and treatment of the Holy Word of Jesus. These schools tended to be repositories, interpreters and transmitters of the sacred word, and one of their regular functions was that of the writing of books, and the preservation of sacred records. The full extent of the contribution of these schools is yet to be explored; but there is sufficient evidence to suggest that their influence was probably great. The existence of an educated clergy from the earliest period would seem to be the legacy of that influence.

One major implication of all the above is the disciplining and stabilizing of the reception, retention, interpretation, recording and transmission of the Holy Word. A natural product of the sanctity of the apostles, their college and their individual schools was to produce sources and standards of doctrine that from the beginning were used in the battle against heresy. One inevitable result of this pedagogical climate prevailing from the 'school of Jesus' would seem to have been the careful treatment of the Word, and the almost automatic production of written records, and to this we now turn.

Chapter 8

HOLY ΓΡΑΦΗ:
THE REPOSITORY OF THE WORD

From the earliest stirrings of literary activity within the oral community, to the formal γραφή so treasured by the Fathers, there would seem to be good evidence pointing to a distinct literary activity going back at least as far as Paul, and most probably to the time of Jesus himself. The purpose of the next two chapters is to trace the development of this literary process, and to show the centrality of the Holy Word and the emergence of narrative, gospel and tradition within it. In that highly literate age, writing quickly augmented memory as the means by which the Word was preserved and passed on, and it is in this growing literary deposit that we find further evidence for the preservation and transmission of this message.

Memory as a Source of Literature

The natural beginnings of this literary process lay in the inevitable dynamics of the oral situation itself. To begin with, these were Jews, and their lives were lived within the dominant rabbinic environment of first-century Judaism. To ignore this is to create an image of an early Church in the likeness of another age, another culture, usually that of ancient Greece, or of the modern western scholar. The story begins with the Jewish understanding of the difference between 'oral' and 'written' Torah. As is well known, this was a two-fold distinction: the one being a reference to the form of the material, and the other, the more important, a reference to the authority and priority possessed by that material within the religious community. The written Torah was carefully distinguished from the unwritten sayings of the rabbis; and this distinction not only was known to the early Christians, but seems to have been preserved by them in their distinction between the Holy Word

8. *The Repository of the Word* 161

of Jesus and what they called gospel and traditions, which were human interpretations and applications of the Word.

But this distinction, as I have tried to show elsewhere, however important theologically, and whatever may have been the popular prohibition against writing down the teaching of one's rabbi, in practice did not eliminate the production of written records.[1] As the inescapable exigencies of practical pedagogy and scholarship operated within the rabbinic community, inevitably there were produced larger and larger collections of written rabbinic sayings. 'Written' or 'unwritten', then, became primarily, if not exclusively, a designation of theological priority and authority.

The oral Torah of the Jew found its way into written form in the Mishnah, probably in the first century AD. Gerhardsson has clearly shown that the art of memory was highly developed within rabbinic circles, and this was the basic mechanism for the collection, preservation and transmission of the sayings of the rabbis. Within the school tradition, the rabbis and their pupils wrote notes, ὑπομνήματα, to aid their memories, and it would seem that here is the original parallel mechanism for the inception of Christian literature. Gerhardsson calls ὑπομνήματα the nearest *Gattung* to the Gospels; and although *Gattung* is perhaps too formal a term, yet the evidence of historical analysis clearly points to the interconnection of memory and written notes as the true genesis of the Synoptic Gospels.

In the New Testament, the verb μνημονεύω is used primarily in three ways: (1) Jesus shows a concern to be remembered. This occurs mostly in John, where Jesus urges the disciples to 'Remember the word that I said to you...' (15.20), or indicates his purpose in saying certain things was so 'that when their hour comes, you may remember (μνημονεύετε) that I told you of them' (16.4), or when he promises that 'the Holy Spirit will...bring to remembrance all that I have said to you' (14.26). In Mk 8.18-21, the verb refers not only to remembering, but also to understanding: 'Do you not remember...when I broke...five loaves... do you not yet understand?' This same concern of Jesus to be remembered and understood is repeated elsewhere in the Synoptics, but without the verb being used (e.g. Mk 8.27-28).

(2) A second use of this term has to do with the evidence that the disciples did indeed remember what Jesus had said: 'And Peter

---

1. J.A. Baird, *The Justice of God in the Teaching of Jesus* (London: SCM Press; Philadelphia: Westminster Press, 1963), pp. 24-25.

remembered the word of the Lord' (Lk. 22.61); '...when he was raised from the dead, the disciples remembered that he had said this' (Jn 2.22); '...when Jesus was glorified, then they (disciples) remembered that this had been written of him...' (Jn 12.16). Here is the beginning of the 'memoir', a λόγιον plus an event remembered by the apostles and recorded sometime thereafter. In Acts 11.16 there is a good illustration of the λόγιον-memory-memoir sequence when Luke describes Peter preaching: 'and I remembered the word of the Lord, how he said, "John baptized with water, but you...with...Holy Spirit"'. Here is a disciple of an apostle quoting a λόγιον of Jesus as an oral recollection of Peter and turning it into a written 'memoir'.

(3) The third use of the verb for remembering is the logical and historical outgrowth of the first two, and that is where reminding the Church of Jesus' Word and gospel has become a function of the apostles. Paul continually urges his churches to 'remember what I told you' (2 Thess. 2.5); '...remember that...you have been brought near in the blood of Christ' (Eph. 2.11-13; cf. Col. 4.18). The author of the Pastorals shows Paul urging Timothy to 'remember Jesus Christ, risen from the dead...as preached in my Gospel' (2 Tim. 2.8; cf. 2 Tim. 2.14; Tit. 3.1). The author of 2 Peter is perhaps the clearest illustration of this apostolic function: 'I intend always to remind you of these things, though you know them...to arouse you by way of reminder...and I will see to it that after my departure you may be able to recall these things...' (2 Pet. 1.12; cf. 3.1; 2 Jn 10; Jude 5, 17; Heb. 13.7). The purpose of this apostolic reminder is two-fold: to inspire the Church with the memory of Jesus, and to confirm that memory by the careful preservation of his Holy Word, and the narrative, gospel and traditions surrounding it.

This 'reminding' orientation put the stress on the historical event of Jesus, his word and his life, so that whatever present evidence there was of the work of the Spirit was conditioned, instructed, prompted, chastened and directed by the 'remembrance'. All the signs point to the determination of the members of the early Church to preserve this body of reminiscence with a zeal compounded of the traditional Jewish attention to the words of the rabbis plus their conviction that this Word of Jesus, along with his life, death and resurrection, was the fulfillment of God's design for mankind.

Remembering, accurately and completely, with understanding, would seem to have been a basic key to the 'stability' of the Synoptic Gospels.

8. *The Repository of the Word* 163

It is this which gives them their brilliance and vitality of historical detail.[2] It is this that enables them to reveal so many patterns under the penetrating scrutiny of computer analysis.[3] This memory pattern phenomenon clearly pictures the apostles, Christian scribes and Evangelists, as first of all historians of the word and life of Jesus, and then theologians, or ethicists as the case may be. There is a possibility of confusion here in stressing the role of the Evangelists as historians unless we remember that the primary data of history for them was the Holy Word of Jesus, the basic substance of theology and ethics. This is dramatically revealed in the character of the Synoptics as what I have called 'biographical apophthegmata', with the memory of what had been actually said and the historical framework within which it was said intimately related, but with the primary focus upon the Word.[4] It was not until later that John was prompted to write a theological counterpart to the Synoptic memoirs which I have called 'narrative theology;[5] and one is reminded that John was not immediately accepted by some segments of the early Church. The memoirs represent the facts of the Gospel as distinct from those works dealing with interpretation and ethical application. As Stendahl has put it, 'the facts were not proclaimed in the sermon, but rather the implications discussed of that which was well known'.[6] Surely this is one reason Paul did not rehearse the data of the life and teachings of Jesus in his letters. By this time they were well known, and his was a different task, to call them to remember and understand what they had already heard (1 Cor. 15.1-11).

Justin Martyr is especially concerned to describe the most primitive Christian literature in these terms. In his *1 Apology*, he talks about 'the memoirs...which are called "Gospels"', and composed by the apostles, being read at Christian worship along with the writings of the prophets (66). In his *Dialogue with Trypho*, he tells of Jesus keeping silence in the presence of Pilate, 'as has been declared in the memoirs of his apostles'. It is in these 'memoirs, drawn up by his apostles and those that followed them', that Justin has learned of Jesus' temptation by the Devil, his

2. J.A. Baird, *A Comparative Analysis of the Gospel Genre: The Synoptic Mode and Its Uniqueness* (Lewiston: Edwin Mellen Press, 1991), p. 38.
3. J.A. Baird, *Audience Criticism and the Historical Jesus* (Philadelphia: Westminster Press, 1967), pp. 90-135.
4. See above, also Baird, *Comparative Analysis*, pp. 56-58.
5. See above, also Baird, *Comparative Analysis*, pp. 101-105.
6. K. Stendahl, *The School of St Matthew* (ASNU, 20; Lund: W.K.C. Gleerup; Copenhagen: Munksgaard; rev. edn Philadelphia: Fortress Press, 1969), p. 18.

agony in the garden, his birth, the changing of Peter's name, the prediction of Jesus' resurrection and certain of his λόγια (*Trypho* 103, 105, 106, 107). For Justin, these memoirs, mostly found in Matthew and Luke, include both narrative and λόγια, and are the authoritative center and focus of Christian belief.

Eyewitness notes by the apostles and those who followed them, aids to memory, individual units brought together into larger collections, well known, held in high esteem, read as the center of Christian worship, the 'memoir' is the most common and most primitive description of written Gospels found in the Apostolic Fathers. This is an old Hebrew technique, and one we find reflected in Josephus who used the 'memoirs' (ὑπομνήματα) of Vespasian and Titus as sources for his history of *The Jewish War*. This also occurs in Philo who describes the founders of the Alexandrian Jewish sect of Therapeutae using the 'memorials' (μνημεία) of their founders as sources for their way of thinking (*Vit. Cont.* 25).

Clement of Alexandria defined ὑπομνήματα as well as any, describing the process by which he remembered the teachings of 'distinguished members of the apostolic succession' whom he heard:

> this work is not a writing composed for show, but notes (ὑπομνήματα) stored up for my old age, a remedy against forgetfulness, an image without art, a sketch of those clear and vital words...of blessed and truly noble men... (who) preserved the true tradition of the blessed teaching directly from Peter and James and John and Paul... they came to us to deposit those ancestral and apostolic seeds (*Hist. Eccl.* 5.11.3).

For Clement these could well have been notes taken by him on the spot. Eusebius points to this as the fundamental and most primitive source of the Jesus material from Christian prophets: 'Since we...collected in special treatises (ὑπομνήμασιν) the prophetic utterances concerning our savior Jesus Christ' (*Hist. Eccl.* 1.2.27); '...of all those who have been with the Lord, only Matthew and John have left us their recollections (ὑπομνήματα), and tradition says that they took to writing...' (*Hist. Eccl.* 3.24.5). These are the 'single points as he remembered them' (ἀπεμνημόνευσεν) of Mark, who 'became Peter's interpreter and wrote accurately all that he remembered' (ἐμνημόνευσεν). This term seems to reflect not the artful design of a literary stylist, but the act of a reporter-historian striving for accuracy of detail regarding 'individual points', although it is true that at times it can be used to describe the letters of an Ignatius or Clement (*Hist. Eccl.* 3.37.4), or the Old Testament interpretation (ἀπομνημονευμάτων) of a certain 'apostolic presbyter' (*Hist. Eccl.* 5.8.8). Primarily, however, we are talking about notes of individual details, written for memory, and/or from memory, regarding a special teacher, which were then gathered together into larger collections of one kind or another.

A further illustration comes from the Pseudo-Clementine *Recognitiones*: 'I have adopted the habit of recalling in my memory (*revocare ad memoriam*) the words of my lord which I heard from himself, and because of my longing for them I force my mind and my thoughts to be roused, so that, awaking to them, and recalling and repeating each one of them, I may keep them in memory' (2.1; *PL* I, col. 1249). Birger Gerhardsson likens this to the *Haggadah* on Rabban Johanan ben Zakkai, who, 'sitting in the pitch darkness of a Roman prison, measured the passage of time with the help of his recitation of the Mishnah'.[7] The difficulty of estimating the date and origin of this material, however, prevents us from taking it too seriously.

In fine, it would seem that the activity of remembering the life and teachings of Jesus, whether oral or written or both, was one of the central functions of Christian apostleship, scholarship, teaching and preaching. This was the heart of the life and worship of the Church from its earliest beginnings, and the situation of conception for the written Gospels.

The Transition from Oral to Written

At this point, we must face the question raised by Werner Kelber and others as to the extent to which the transition in *form* of the earliest New Testament reminiscences from oral to written, what Kelber calls 'the new technology of written text', would have compromised the oral Gospel as a transformation in *substance*.[8] Kelber's book is searching for the original form and substance of oral materials. It is concerned about the print-oriented bias of western hermeneutics that does not take into consideration the differences between spoken and written words.[9] Written Gospels subverted what he calls 'the homeostatic balance' of the

---

7. B. Gerhardsson, *Memory and Manuscript: Oral Tradition and Written Transmission in Rabbinic Judaism and Early Christianity* (Lund: W.K.C. Gleerup; Copenhagen: Munksgaard, 1961), p. 207.

8. W. Kelber, *The Oral and the Written Gospel* (Philadelphia: Fortress Press, 1983), p. 93. See W.J. Ong, *Orality and Literacy* (New York: Methuen, 1982).

9. Kelber, *The Oral and the Written Gospel*, p. 14.

oral tradition; and so the technology of the written word produced a Christology in tension with and a replacement of oral Christology.[10]

This insightful study provides a much needed revival of concern for the oral dimension of the earliest Christian reminiscences. It is really aimed at the quest for the historical Jesus, at the point of transition between the oral and the written word, and so will be dealt with at length in Chapter 10. Kelber's one historical criterion is that of environmental probability, in this case the 'tendencies' of oral folklore and its transition to literature. What is needed is a broader attention to other historical criteria, and to the evidence from the entire New Testament and early Christian literature. Kelber's work also needs more appreciation of the part played by ancient writing in the preservation of the Christian story.

My own analysis of this problem suggests that Kelber has created a psycho-philosophical dilemma which is more theoretical than realistic. Any spoken word about any subject faces the same problem; but in the practical world of men and women leading normal lives, it is possible to communicate in writing a *sufficiently* accurate account of spoken words or acted events to use as the basis for normal living. This is about all that can be expected, especially in a pre-television world, and Kelber is making an impossible demand for absolute knowledge about the Christian story that he would never make for the normal commerce of human lives, or the writing of human history.

Actually, the problem is deeper than the psychology of communication. He is begging the most basic question, and his answers are more determined by his critical Synoptic presuppositions than by any new evidence. Can we rely upon the words of Jesus as written in the Synoptics to be a viable source for our understanding of the oral Jesus? That is the crux of the matter. In Chapter 10, in a more positive assessment, I attempt to show that there are many criteria for getting at this question, and those he uses must be augmented by many others. His excellent study falters because of a poverty of historical criteria. At this point, what his study does is to warn us that to point to the early writing of Christian material is not necessarily to show fidelity to the substance of the oral originals. It only 'fixes' in time the material presented, and suggests that in the mechanics of literary composition, the substance 'may' have been distorted. This, of course, could also have happened at the oral level, if what Kelber says about oral 'tendencies' is correct. This

10. Kelber, *The Oral and the Written Gospel*, p. 93.

is a healthy caution that we cannot take early writing as the only, or even the most important, criterion for the historicity of the Jesus λόγια. But it is one criterion, and if used with caution, along with many others, can speak to this essential question.

Proto-Sources

Kelber does admit that 'the concept of a predominantly oral phase is not meant to dispense with the existence of notes and textual aids altogether', and one wonders what this says to his concept of 'homeostatic balance'. 'The Q tradition, other sayings collections, anthologies of short stories, parables, miracles and the like could well have existed in written form', and they need not have transcended an essentially 'oral state of mind'.[11] What this does is bring us back to an old thesis receiving new impetus, that there were available at the earliest period certain 'proto-sources' which by that time were in writing. In another work, I listed fourteen such 'recording units' of material in the Synoptics which hold together under one or another system of coherence.[12] This multiple source hypothesis has been presented for years, going back at least to Edward Meyer in 1921 (*Ursprung und Anfang des Christentums*), but has been submerged by the form-critical insistence on the 'strictly oral' nature of this earliest period. In 1953, W.L. Knox did perhaps as much as anyone to revive Meyer's approach, and in recent years there has been a steady line of scholars pointing to the existence of various types of written proto-sources.[13]

11. Kelber, *The Oral and the Written Gospel*, p. 23.
12. Baird, *Comparative Analysis*, p. 54.
13. W.L. Knox, *The Sources of the Synoptic Gospels* (2 vols.; Cambridge: Cambridge University Press, 1953). Other adaptations of this approach are the Proto-Luke hypothesis, as developed by Vincent Taylor, *The Formation of the Gospel Tradition* (London; Macmillan, 1949); and the *Ur-Marcus* theory of A. Wendling, *Die Enstehung des Markus-Evangelium: Philologische Untersuchungen* (Tübingen: Mohr Siebeck, 1908). See also B.P.W. Stather-Hunt, *Primitive Gospel Sources* (London: Clark-Philosophical Library, 1951); F.C. Grant, *The Gospels: Their Origin and their Growth* (New York: Harper, 1957); E. Hennecke and W. Schneemelcher (eds.), *New Testament Apocrypha* (2 vols.; Philadelphia: Westminster Press, 1963), II, p. 76; T.W. Manson, 'Studies in the Gospels and Epistles', in H.K. McArthur (ed.), *In Search of the Historical Jesus* (New York: Charles Scribner's Sons, 1969), Chapter 1; Kelber, *The Oral and the Written Gospel*, p. 23; Baird, *Audience Criticism*, ad loc.

In my own studies, various types of evidence have continued to point in this direction. For example, in the use of content analysis it was clear that certain miracle stories and legends had a much higher historical, geographical and literary agreement than did other forms.[14] This suggested a standardized proto-form whose consistent agreement in the various Gospels pointed to well rehearsed oral stories, and very possibly written proto-sources. The passion narratives and miracle tracts would be illustrations of this. It is also apparent that Mark and Luke have the largest number of suggested proto-sources, reflecting Luke's awareness that 'many have undertaken to compile a narrative...' The continuing evidence of Aramaic originals behind the Synoptic λόγια points to proto-sources that could possibly have been written.[15]

There is further evidence for written proto-sources in the existence of lacunae, for example, in the comparison of Mt. 12.41-45 with Lk. 11.31, 32, 24-26. The wording is exact, with two lacunae in Matthew (omits ἑπτά in v. 45 and τῶν ἀνδρῶν in v. 42), and two in Luke (omits σχολάζοντα in v. 25 and μετ' ἑαυτοῦ ἑπτά in v. 26), pointing to the written nature of at least some portion of the double tradition. This same suggestion of written sources behind Mark arises when one finds lacunae in Mark in what is presumably the Markan source. In the parallel between Mt. 19.4-6 and Mk 10.6-9, the two are exact in their wording with the significant omission of καὶ κολληθήσεται τῇ γυναικὶ αὐτοῦ.[16]

The suggestion of an early mutilated copy of Mark arises when in Mk 11.27-35 we find him agreeing with Matthew at points against Luke, suggesting that Matthew has both Mark and Q, but Luke has only the Q version of this material, his copy of Mark being broken at this point. There is also some possibility that the kinds of concluding statements one finds in Mt. 7.28, 11.1, 13.53, 19.1, and Lk. 9.28 reflect the editor's recognition that the group of sayings he has just concluded form a block which represents some kind of proto-collection. One of the strongest evidences comes from our survey of λόγια quotations in the Apostolic

---

14. Baird, *Audience Criticism*, p. 64.

15. See Baird, *Comparative Analysis*, pp. 53-56; *idem*, *Audience Criticism*, pp. 80-81. The classic work here is still that of Matthew Black, *An Aramaic Approach to the Gospels and Acts* (Oxford: Clarendon Press, 3rd edn, 1967).

16. See Mk 14.12-16 and parallels for the suggestion of a mutilated written copy of the passion narrative at this point. See also Mk 7.17-23; 9.37; 10.18-26; 12.44; 13.24-27; 14.3-9.

Fathers, where the total percentage agreement of the Greek with that in the Synoptics is 64%, and where some λόγια in the Fathers agree with the Synoptics more closely than one Synoptic with another (cf. Chapter 8). Much more work needs to be done on the proto-source dimension of Synoptic study before we can speak with the kind of assurance that befits historical analysis. At this point, the possibilities of early written proto-sources are clear, and the probabilities are much more numerous than they were a decade ago.[17]

Christian Scribes

What this points to is the existence within the earliest Christian community of a group of Christian scribes who, as Gerhardsson suggests, would have been the Christian counterpart to the *sopherim* within the rabbinic schools.[18] These were Scripture specialists, who at

---

17. Both Robinson and Koester (H. Koester, *Synoptische Überlieferung bei den Apostolischen Vätern* [TU, 65; Berlin: Akademie-Verlag, 1957)], pp. 4-6; J.M. Robinson and H. Koester, *Trajectories through Early Christianity* [Philadelphia: Fortress Press, 1971], p. 96) point to the existence of collections of λόγοι available to the Fathers and to Paul (Acts 20.35). I would agree; but the turning of this into a λόγοι *sophon* genre is making too much of a limited body of data. As part of the Synoptic mode, this evidence I think makes more sense (Baird, *A Comparative Analysis*, ad loc.). A. Resch (*AGRAPHA: Aussercanonische Schriftfragmente* [TU, 15. 3, 4; Leipzig: Hinrichs, 1906; repr. Darmstadt: Wissenschaftliche Buchgesellschaft, 1974], p. 28) argues that 'Paul had at his disposal some earlier documents, a collection of Jesus' sayings of which the evangelists made use...' James Stewart (*Man in Christ* [New York and London: Harper & Brothers, 1935], p. 29) says: 'This is certainly not impossible'. Kelber's assumption (*The Oral and the Written Gospel*, p. 91) that there was no significant writing before Mark needs to pay more attention to this contrary evidence. Perhaps it is a matter of defining 'significant', since he has admitted the existence of smaller segments of written material before Mark. In the real world of writing books, what is a source for one could be a source for another, however large or small.

18. Gerhardsson, *Memory and Manuscript*, pp. 28, 44, 64, 159, 195, 202, etc. See J.J. Vincent, 'Did Jesus Teach his Disciples to Learn by Heart', *SE* 3 [= TU 88] (1964), pp. 104-105. Hans Küng (*On Being a Christian* [New York: Pocket Books, 1961], p. 121) points to the memory of Jesus as that 'which holds the New Testament together'. Herder's thesis that trained Scripture specialists were proclaimers of the word has in recent years been espoused by Thorlief Boman, Albert B. Lord, and Thomas Boomershine. See J.G. Herder, *Vom Erlöser der Menschen: Nach Unsern drei ersten Evangelien* (Riga: Hartknoch, 1796; repr. in Herder's *Samtliche Werke*, XIX; ed. B. Sophan; Berlin: Wiedmann, 1880-). This suggestion supports

times functioned as teachers, but mostly confined their activities to copying the Old Testament. They were not theologians, and their status was considerably under that of the rabbis who were the teachers and doctrinal authorities. This is important to remember, since the modern redaction critic tends, wrongly I think, to turn the Evangelists, the Christian *sopherim*, into active theologians.

There are a few direct references in the New Testament to what would seem to be Christian scribes. This may be what the author of 2 Timothy is referring to when he urges that 'what you have heard from me before many witnesses entrust to faithful men who will be able to teach others also' (2.2). More certain is the evidence for scribes among the Pauline disciples, like Tertius, who claims to be the writer (ὁ γράψας) of Romans (16.22). Several times it would seem that Paul is writing his letters through an amanuensis (1 Cor. 16.21; Gal. 6.11; Col. 4.18; 2 Thess. 3.17). In Acts 13.5, John Mark is called ὑπηρέτης, the same term Luke uses to describe those who compiled narratives of the things which had been accomplished among them (1.2).[19] Luke suggests (Acts 6.7) that a 'great many of the priests were obedient to the faith', and this tallies with my suggestion that the larger group of disciples (DG) was made up of rulers of the synagogue (Lk. 8.41), Pharisees (Lk. 7.36-50; 13.31), elders of the Jews (Lk. 7.3) and a number of scribes (Lk. 20.39; Mk 9.14; 12.32-34; cf. 15.43; Mt. 8.19-20; 13.52).[20] This may well have been what Jesus was referring to in Mt. 13.52: 'Every scribe who has been trained for the kingdom of heaven is like a householder who brings out of his treasure what is new and what is old'. Stendahl suggests that this may be a veiled reference to Matthew himself, which is consistent with von Dobschütz who referred to Matthew as a converted

---

Bultmann's 'strictly oral' thesis, and is too radical to be true to the evidence for early writing developed in this chapter. I would suggest both oral and written functions for these Scripture specialists. David Aune's (*The New Testament in Its Literary Environment* [Philadelphia: Westminster Press, 1987], pp. 40-41) reference to the χρησμολόγοι as collectors and interpreters of the Mantic oracles may be a parallel in classical antiquity.

19. There are many in recent years who have pointed to Mark as the *chazzan* of the apostles. See R. Taylor, *The Groundwork of the Gospels, with Some Collected Papers* (Oxford: Basil Blackwell, 1946), pp. 21-26; Stendahl, *The School of St Matthew*, p. 33; J.W. Bowman, *Which Jesus?* (Philadelphia: Westminster Press, 1970), p. 114.

20. Baird, *Audience Criticism*, p. 37.

8. *The Repository of the Word*

rabbi.[21] This is supported by the approach of content analysis, where I find the largest number of λόγια 'word patterns' in the special Matthew material. The vocabulary of the Synoptic editors on the other hand sounds more like that of the 'opponents' in Jesus' audiences, the scribes, Pharisees, and priests.[22]

The term ὑπηρέτης raises the possibility of a special office in the early Church dealing with the written word. Stendahl, for example, compares the Christian ὑπηρέτης to the *chazzan* who took care of the scrolls in the Hebrew synagogue, or was an officer in the court (Mt. 5.25) or sanhedrin (Mt. 26.58). Actually, in the New Testament we find several uses of this term. The simplest and most basic seems to designate a minor court official who does the judge's bidding: 'Make friends quickly with your accuser...lest your accuser hand you over to the judge, and the judge to the guard (ὑπηρέτῃ)...' (Mt. 5.25). In a more specialized way, Luke identifies the *chazzan* in the Nazareth synagogue as ὑπηρέτης: 'and he closed the book, and gave it back to the attendant' (Lk. 4.20). When Peter was skulking in the courtyard, the servants of the high priest were called ὑπηρετῶν (Mk 14.54). John shows the application of this term to the apostles when he has Jesus say, in the garden of Gethsemane, 'If my kingship were of this world, my servants (ὑπηρέται) would fight' (Jn 18.36). Luke seems especially prone to use this term, and in Acts he employs the verb ὑπηρετέω three times to refer to David's service to God (13.36), the service of Paul's disciples to their master (24.23), and, in his defense before Agrippa, Paul's call to God's service (26.16). In this last case, we see the concept beginning to take on the larger connotation of service to God in the words of Jesus as a 'witness to the things in which you have seen me...' It is in this larger sense, and yet still retaining its connotation of more mundane, even literary, service that Luke uses the term to describe John Mark's assistance to Paul and Barnabas as 'they proclaimed the word of God' and 'had John to assist them' (εἶχον...ὑπηρέτην). Mark was their ὑπηρέτης. Whether this refers to his special function as historian and Gospel writer, or just to his general aid to these apostles, is an open question. Eusebius, in quoting Papias's comments on Mark, calls him

---

21. Stendahl, *The School of St Matthew*, p. 30. See also M.J. Suggs, *Wisdom, Christology and Law in Matthew's Gospel* (Cambridge, MA: Harvard University Press, 1970), p. 120.

22. See Baird, *Audience Criticism*, pp. 37-43; Stendahl, *The School of St Matthew*, p. 32.

'Peter's interpreter' (ἑρμηνευτής), who wrote accurately all he remembered...of the things said or done by the Lord', thus in effect giving him this more literary, even scholarly (ἀκριβῶς, τάξει), function (*Hist. Eccl.* 3.39.15).

The classic passage is of course that of Luke's prologue where ὑπηρέτης clearly has this dual function of being a 'minister of the word' and also producing written narratives. For Luke, ὑπηρέται τοῦ λόγου seem to fill an official function if not an office within the early Church, the special thrust of whose service was the production of Gospels. So, in the New Testament, Paul, Mark and the apostles, as well as certain 'eyewitnesses', are all called ὑπηρέται. The focus in its more sophisticated usage was a dual one: the witnessing to the divine word as seen in Jesus, and the compiling of written records of that word. This would seem to include the activity of the synagogue *chazzan* in its more literary aspects, but its broader usage goes beyond that more narrowly defined literary function. In this broader sense, ὑπηρέται τοῦ λόγου is closer to the concept of 'ministers of the word' as it is expressed in several other phrases. In Acts 6.2, 4, the apostles in making the first distinction between clergy and laity declare, 'It is not right that we should give up preaching the word of God to serve tables... we will devote ourselves to prayer, and to ministry of the word' (διακονίᾳ τοῦ λόγου). In 2 Cor. 2.17, Paul distinguishes his own ministry from those who are mere 'peddlers of God's word' (καπηλεύοντες), and in Col. 1.25 describes himself as 'a minister of the word of God' (διάκονος). The author of the Pastorals points to the elders who have double honor because they 'labor in preaching and teaching' (ἐν λόγῳ καὶ διδασκαλίᾳ; 1 Tim. 5.17), and enjoins Timothy (in 2 Tim. 2.15) in his office in the church to be 'a workman who has no need to be ashamed, rightly handling the word of truth' (τὸν λόγον τῆς ἀληθείας).

The same concept of the office of handling the word continues in Hebrews (5.12; 7.28) and Revelation (20.4), and on into the usage of the early Fathers. Ignatius refers to the 'deacons of the mysteries of Jesus Christ' as 'ministers' (διάκονοι) not 'of food and drinking, but servants' (ὑπηρέται) of the Church of God (*Trall.* 2.3; cf. Ignatius, *Pol.* 6.1). Eusebius then, as he so often did, sums up the matter by describing 'the number of those who in each generation were the ambassadors of the word of God *either by speech or pen*' (*Hist. Eccl.* 1.1.1; my emphasis). One fine example would be the catechetical school of

Pantaenus where 'there were many evangelists of the word on the apostolic model' (πλείους εὐαγγελισταὶ τοῦ λόγου; 5.10.2).

There is a long tradition of such concern for the literary heritage of the Church. Africanus writing in the mid-third century, and explaining why Herod was unable to stamp out the memory of Jesus' genealogy, even after he burned the official family registers of the Jews to obscure his own lowly birth, referred to 'a few careful people (who) had private records of their own, either having remembered the names or otherwise securing them from copies' (ἀντιγράφων; *Hist. Eccl.* 1.7.14). Along with Luke, Mark, as the disciple of Peter, is the non-apostle most often referred to as a Christian scribe. As Eusebius said, Mark 'wrote accurately...the dominical oracles...kept a single aim in view...not to omit anything of what he heard nor state anything therein falsely' (*Hist. Eccl.* 3.39.15). Eusebius saw him as something of a scholar.

Another brief glimpse of scribal activity comes in a delightful addendum to the *Martyrdom of Polycarp*, where the Christian scribes identified themselves: 'Gaius copied this from the writings of Irenaeus, a disciple of Polycarp, and he lived with Irenaeus, and I, Socrates, wrote it out in Corinth from the copies of Gaius... and I, again, Pionius, wrote it out from the former writings, after searching for it... and I gathered it together when it was almost worn out by age...' (22.2). The author of *2 Clement* enjoins 'him who is the *reader* among you' to 'pay attention to that which is written', which in this case is the commandments of Jesus (19.1 my emphasis; 17.6). Kirsopp Lake comments, 'It is probable though not quite certain that this refers to a definite order of "readers" in the church'.[23] There is also a note in Lucian's *The Passing of Peregrinus* (11) referring to Christian priests and scribes in Palestine.[24]

The apostles themselves were also described in the capacity of Christian scribes. Irenaeus asked: 'How should it be if the apostles themselves had not left us writing?' (*Adv. Haer.* 3.4.1). Justin Martyr even earlier, in commenting on his quotation of Mk 14.22-24, reflected the same view: 'For the apostles in the memoirs composed by them, which are called Gospels, thus handed down what was commanded them' (*1 Apol.* 66). More exactly, however, only certain ones of the

---

23. K. Lake (trans.), *The Apostolic Fathers* (LCL, 24-25; London: Heinemann; Cambridge, MA: Harvard University Press, 1912-13), I, p. 159.

24. H.D. Betz (*Lukian von Samosata und das Neue Testament: Religionsgeschichtliche und paränetische Parallelen* [TU, 76; Berlin: Akademie-Verlag, 1961], p. 8) cautions that Lucian did not distinguish between Christians and Jews.

apostles were said to have done any writing of Gospels. There was a tradition which Eusebius accepted that Matthew and John were the only ones of the disciples who actually wrote 'memoirs of Jesus' discourses' (*Hist. Eccl.* 3.24.6-7). Mostly, it is Matthew to whom Eusebius refers. Four times, from the works of Origen, Irenaeus and Papias, Eusebius says that Matthew composed his Gospel in the Hebrew tongue (*Hist. Eccl.* 3.39.16; 5.8.2; 5.10.3; 6.26.4). Others of the apostles are also mentioned in this role. Tatian's *Diatessaron* describes Nathanael as a scribe, a tradition which is found again in Chrysostom's exposition of the Gospel of John (*Hom.* 20) and in Augustine (*Tract.* 7.17).[25] Nicodemus is said to have written the *Acts of Pilate* (1.1-2). The *Kerygma Petrou* tells of 'books' of Peter's sermons being handed over to the teachers in training (1.1-3). In *Pistis Sophia* (42), Philip, Thomas and Matthew are the three disciples charged with recording the words and deeds of Jesus. From the evidence of the Fathers, however, it would appear that Matthew is the most likely apostolic candidate for the role of Christian scribe.[26]

It would seem from this study that there was in the Church a continuing 'ministry of the word' from the earliest times, which was considered both a special function and an office. The apostles were the models, but many disciples and evangelists took part, witnessing to the life and teaching of Jesus in both oral and written form. Among these were those whose special talents led to the expression of this ministry in literary fashion, either as copiers, like Tertius, editors, compilers and historians like Mark and Luke, original witnesses like Matthew, or an interpreter and theologian like John. All of these can be called ὑπηρέται in the broader sense, and some of them can be called 'Christian scribes'. Whether 'professional' or not, they were men with literary and scholarly interests who were called 'ministers (ὑπηρέται, διάκονοι) of the word of God'. There could have been some women among them, but there is no clear evidence for that as yet.

---

25. Hennecke and Schneemelcher (eds.), *New Testament Apocrypha*, II, p. 65.

26. E. von Dobschütz ('Matthew as Rabbi and Catechist', in G.N. Stanton [ed.], *The Interpretation of Matthew* [London: SPCK; Philadelphia: Fortress Press, 1983], pp. 85-97) suggests that Matthew intended to offer the church a manual of discipline and a catechism of Christian behavior. P. Carrington (*Primitive Christian Calendar* [Cambridge: Cambridge University Press, 1940]) compares the teachers of the Matthean school with the elders and the Tannaim of contemporary Judaism.

Luke 1.1-4

It is in such a context that we take a closer look at Luke's prologue as he described the literary situation to us. There are three natural divisions within this artfully constructed passage, hinging on the words 'many', 'those' and 'me'.

a. ἐπειδήπερ πολλοὶ ἐπεχείρησαν ἀνατάξασθαι διήγησιν περὶ τῶν πεπληροφορημένων ἐν ἡμῖν πραγμάτων...

The verb ἀνατάξασθαι suggests the work of a compiler who has many units to bring together. As far as the verb is concerned, they could be oral or written or both; but the act of 'compiling' suggests a scholarly exercise which would probably demand that the units be written first before being arranged into some kind of orderly account. Papias suggests that Mark wrote down such 'single points as he remembered them' (*Hist. Eccl.* 3.39.15). The noun διήγησις, 'orderly account', can refer either to written or oral material. The comparison Luke is making with his own 'writing' clearly points to written accounts: but given the way Luke collected his special material, it is probably both written and oral.[27] The stress in v. 1 is on the narrative (πραγμάτων); and one is reminded of Luke's special interest in narrative history. But this is more than balanced by the two references to the 'word' or the 'words' in which they had been instructed (κατηχήθης λόγων). Here Luke gives us a summary of his gospel, both narrative and word, but the stress is really on the λόγος, the only term that occurs more than once in this passage. The word πολλοί arouses our interest, and seems perfectly in keeping with the evidence we have discovered already. There seem to have been many accounts, collections, sources, proto-sources, both oral and written, prior to and parallel with the Synoptic Gospels.

---

27. J.C. Meagher (*The Way of the Word: The Beginning and the Establishing of Christian Understanding* [New York: Seabury Press, 1975], p. 207 n. 2) argues that Lk. 1.1-4 refers to both Luke and Acts. The function of memory as a source is easily documented. See Mk 5.16; 9.9; Lk. 8.39; 9.10; Acts 8.33; etc. Luke is noted for collecting eyewitness accounts, not only of the activities of Paul, but also of the early Christian community, for example the intimate recollections of the many women in the developing Church, including the mother of Jesus, which figure so strongly in the special Lukan source (L).

b. καθὼς παρέδοσαν ἡμῖν οἱ ἀπ' ἀρχῆς αὐτόπται καὶ ὑπηρέται γενόμενοι τοῦ λόγου...

The comparison implied in καθὼς παρέδοσαν ἡμῖν suggests that there is a similarity between what Luke is doing, what the 'many' who compiled narratives have done, and what those who delivered them to us from the beginning have done: that is, a written compilation. If these three sections of the prologue are parallel, and if the force of καθώς is that there is a comparison between them all, then Luke is telling us that he stands in a kind of third rank behind those who have already compiled narratives, and the 'eyewitnesses' who first delivered these things 'accomplished among us'. This would have been in written as well as oral form, if this logic is sound. The verb παρέδοσαν is used in the New Testament to refer to the handing down verbally or in written form of the gospel, the Mosaic customs or certain practical rules augmenting the gospel (cf. Chapter 4). These 'ministers of the word', ὑπηρέται, are particularly interesting, for, as I have shown, this term very probably refers to an office in the Church especially concerned with the handling in written and oral form of the 'Word', the sacred deposit of Jesus material.

c. ἔδοξε κἀμοὶ παρηκολουθηκότι ἄνωθεν πᾶσιν ἀκριβῶς καθεξῆς σοι γράψαι, κράτιστε Θεόφιλε, ἵνα ἐπιγνῷς περὶ ὧν κατηχήθης λόγων τὴν ἀσφάλειαν...

We note with interest that every word in this passage clearly reflects the 'school' environment of this Gospel and the scholarly intentions of its author: παρηκολουθηκότι is a strengthened form of the verb 'follow', with the meaning 'to investigate', or 'research'; ἄνωθεν, 'from the beginning', testifies to Luke's long research; πᾶσιν again reflects the scholar's concern to investigate 'all things'; ἀκριβῶς underscores the carefulness of his research; καθεξῆς is possibly a criticism of others, who, like Mark, according to Papias, did not write 'in order' (*Hist. Eccl.* 3.39.15); γράψαι is the activity of the literary man; ἵνα ἐπιγνῷς... ἀσφάλειαν is the concern for proof characteristic of the scholar rather than the evangelist; κατηχήθης λόγων reflects the oral instruction of the catechetical schools in which Theophilus had probably been trained. In this classic passage, we would seem to have an especially good testimony to the developing thesis of these pages that the scholarly concern of careful writing of the oral Jesus tradition was active in Luke, and, if he is any indication, in 'many' others as well.

8. The Repository of the Word

But who are these others? According to the four document hypothesis, at the least he would have known Mark and the so-called Q material, as well as his own special source (L). That Luke could have been aware of some of the apocryphal gospels is possible; but more probably he is referring to what Koester has called the 'parallel' tradition of written gospel material which is reflected in the λόγια quotations in the Apostolic Fathers. I have already referred to at least fourteen possible proto-sources in the Synoptics, including some in Luke, although special Luke and the double tradition seem to have the lowest number of hypothetical sources, suggesting they are the most independent of the major Synoptic blocks.[28]

Romans 16.25-27

The doxology in Paul's epistle to the Romans offers us another possible reference to early Christian writing:

> Now to him who is able to strengthen you according to my gospel and the preaching of Jesus Christ, according to the revelation of mystery which was kept secret for long ages but is now disclosed and through the *prophetic writings* is made known to all nations, according to the command of the eternal God, to bring about the obedience of faith...to the only wise God be glory for evermore through Jesus Christ, Amen (Rom. 16.25-27 my emphasis).

In this passage, γραφῶν προφητικῶν is usually taken by commentators to mean the Old Testament.[29] In the light of this present study, however, the possibility of Christian writings in this earlier period is not at all inconsistent with what we have been finding in the Apostolic Fathers as in the New Testament.

The first fact one has to face with regard to this passage is that various manuscripts include the doxology in different places, after chs. 14, 15, or 16, suggesting its importance as a literary antipode to Rom. 1.1-6. This

---

28. Baird, *Comparative Analysis*, pp. 53-56.
29. See James Denny, in W. Robertson (ed.), *Expositor's Greek Testament* (5 vols.; New York: Dodd, Mead, 1897–1910), vol. 3; C.H. Dodd, *The Epistle of Paul to the Romans* (MNTC; London: Hodder & Stoughton, 1932); C.F.D. Moule, *The Gospel according to Mark* (The Cambridge Bible Commentary on the New English Bible; Cambridge: Cambridge University Press, 1965); W. Sanday and A.C. Headlam, *A Critical and Exegetical Commentary on the Epistle to the Romans* (ICC; Edinburgh: T. & T. Clark, 1895; 5th edn, 1902).

argues for its authenticity as Pauline and its original setting in Romans; whether at the end of chs. 14, 15, or 16 is somewhat academic for this discussion.[30]

The parallel between the two passages is a major key to the question of whether or not this is a reference to early Christian writing. There are seven units identifiable in each passage.

I. Romans 1.1-6	*II. Romans 16.25-26*
(1) 'Paul'	(1) 'my'
(2) 'gospel of God'	(2) 'gospel'
(3) 'promised beforehand'	(3) 'kept secret for long ages'
(4) 'through his prophets in the holy Scriptures	(4) 'through the prophetic writings is made known'
(5) 'designated son'	(5) 'the mystery...now disclosed'
(6) 'by his resurrection'	(6) 'the revelation of the mystery'
(7) 'to bring about obedience to the faith...among all nations'	(7) 'made known to all nations according to the command of the eternal God to bring about obedience to the faith'

The parallel between the two passages is clear. It is phrase (4) that is under question. Superficially, it would seem that since (4) in column I obviously refers to the Old Testament, then so also should (4) in column II. We should not only note the obvious similarities, however, but the more subtle differences; for that is where the crux of the matter lies. In passage I, the antecedent of phrase (7) is (6). In passage II, however, the antecedent of (7) is not (6), but (4). It is the prophetic writings which are the medium for making the mystery of the incarnation known in passage II, even as it is the resurrection that is the medium in passage I. So phrase (4) in II is really parallel to phrase (6) in I. Despite the similarity in wording, there is an incongruity between phrase (4) in the two passages, suggesting we are dealing not with a similarity but a contrast. This would argue that 'prophetic writings' refers not to the content of the Old Testament, but to the resurrection and incarnation as found in Christian literature. Actually, in Rom. 1.5 Paul is talking about his apostleship to all the nations, to bring about obedience to the faith through Christ. The real parallel with 16.25-26 is that through the (Christian) prophetic writings, as through Paul's apostleship, the nations are to be brought

---

30. A.M. Hunter (*The Epistle to the Romans* [Torch Bible Commentaries; London: SCM Press, 1968], ad loc.), on the other hand, suggests that Rom. 1.3-5 sounds like 'a potted creed'.

8. The Repository of the Word 179

into obedience to Christ. The point of the parallel is Paul's *apostleship*, not Old Testament prophetic Scriptures, which is in contrast to the γραφή referred to in 16.26. The source of Paul's faith is Christ, not the Old Testament.

As Godet has shown,[31] the passage that most properly parallels Rom. 16.25-27 is not Rom. 1.1-6, but Eph. 3.3-5, where the 'mystery' is not made known in the Old Testament, but rather is 'now revealed to his holy apostles and prophets'. Paul is recorded using the term 'prophet' nine times, five of which are clearly 'Christian prophets, and only twice does it obviously refer to the Old Testament (cf. Chapter 4). Prophetic writing could therefore easily be a reference to Christian prophets or to those writing in the 'prophetic' or spiritual mode, or to Christian scribes recording the 'traditions' of the Church, based as they were on the teachings of Jesus (*Hist. Eccl.* 1.2.27; cf. 2 Tim. 1.13, 14; 2.2; 1 Cor. 11.2; 5.8; 16.2; 2 Thess. 2.15; Rom. 6.17-18; 5.14-18; etc.).

Perhaps the strongest argument for this interpretation is found in the internal homiletic structure of the Greek of Rom. 16.25-26.

τῷ δὲ δυναμένῳ ὑμᾶς στηρίξαι
  (1) κατὰ τὸ εὐαγγέλιόν μου
    καὶ τὸ κήρυγμα Ἰησοῦ Χριστοῦ
  (2) κατὰ ἀποκάλυψιν μυστηρίου
    (a) χρόνοις αἰωνίοις σεσιγημένου
    (b) φανερωθέντος δὲ νῦν διά τε γραφῶν προφητικῶν
  (3) κατ' ἐπιταγὴν τοῦ αἰωνίου θεοῦ
    εἰς ὑπακοὴν πίστεως
    εἰς πάντα τὰ ἔθνη γνωρισθέντος

In the above, the parallel use of κατά puts phrases (1), (2) and (3) in balance. They all refer to the subject, Paul's gospel. Phrases (2)(a) and (2)(b) are, however, set in contrast to one another, χρόνοις αἰωνίοις and νῦν, and here is the crux of the matter. Here is the contrast between promise and fulfillment which is the theme of Rom. 1.1-6. Now γραφῶν προφητικῶν is part of the fulfillment theme in phrase (2)(b). It comes immediately after νῦν, its antecedents are ἀποκάλυψιν μυστηρίου and φανερωθέντος, and it follows διά strengthened by the enclitic copulative particle τε, which augments the connection between διά and γραφῶν. It would seem clear that γραφῶν προφητικῶν cannot refer to Old Testament promise, but in contrast refers to writings presenting the

---

31. F. Godet, *Commentaire sur l'épître aux romains* (2 vols.; Paris: Libraire Sandoz & Fischbacher, 1879–80).

theme of fulfillment in Jesus Christ. There is sufficient evidence from the early Fathers that Paul had gospel sources to add considerable credence to this thesis (cf. Tertullian, *Against Marcion* 4.3); and the probability of an abundance of writings containing 'prophetic' material, that is, παράδοσις, διδασκαλία, πιστὸς ὁ λόγος, is clear. It may be that we will have to take Eusebius more seriously in this regard: 'and it is said that Paul was want to mention his (i.e. Luke's) Gospel, whenever, in writing about some gospel of his own (as it were) he used to say: "according to my gospel"' (*Hist. Eccl.* 3.4.7; cf. Rom. 2.16; 16.25; 2 Tim. 2.8).

1 Timothy 5.18

This use of 'Scripture' for Christian writing is strengthened by two other passages. The first is 1 Tim. 5.18 where the exact Greek of Lk. 10.7 is quoted and called γραφή in the same context with the LXX of Deut. 25.4: 'For the Scripture says, "You shall not muzzle an ox when it is treading out the grain", and, "The laborer deserves his wages"'. This use of γραφή, along with that in 2 Tim. 3.16, strongly argues that it is also Christian Scripture that the author is talking about in 1 Tim. 4.13: 'Till I come, attend to the public reading of Scripture (ἀναγνώσει), to preaching, to teaching'. This term usually refers to the Old Testament (Acts 13.15; 2 Cor. 3.14), but in this case we seem to be in a later period where it now refers to Christian writings as well as the Old Testament.

Early Christian worship involved the rehearsal of the διδαχή, which could be either oral or written. In 1 Cor. 14.26, Paul lists five elements of worship: a hymn, a lesson (διδαχή), a tongue, a revelation and an interpretation. Luke in Acts 2.42 lists four elements: the apostles' teaching (διδαχή), fellowship, prayer, and the breaking of bread. The common element seems to be διδαχή, which is regularly a reference to the gospel of the Church about Jesus, but always based on his λόγια (Chapter 8). In Rom. 16.26 at least, this seems to have been in written form. Justin gives this kind of picture when he describes the church on Sunday, meeting in one place, where 'the memoirs of the apostles or the writings of the prophets are *read*' (*1 Apol.* 66; my emphasis). If the Christians possessed γραφή or γράμματα by now, which seems clearly the case, then their public reading would have been inevitable. Many New Testament books like Hebrews and Ephesians seem to have been composed for just his purpose. Surely they would have been read more

8. *The Repository of the Word*

than once. I think Fred Gealy is probably close to the mark when he writes that 'the minister would be constantly engaged in reading both old and new scriptures, the Old Testament, apocalypses, writings of the apostles and teachers, letters of officials, hymns and devotional lyrics composed by prophets, accounts of early beginnings of the church such as came to form in the Gospels and Acts'.[32] There seems little question but that the late first, early second century was a highly literary period within Christian circles. That this would not have been put to the service of worship seems highly improbable. In this context, Paul's request to Timothy to bring 'one book and above all the parchments' (2 Tim. 4.13) is most suggestive.

2 Timothy 3.14-15

The author of 2 Timothy, probably a disciple of Paul writing sometime after Paul's death, has given us further evidence of early Christian 'Holy Writings' (2 Tim. 3.14-15): 'But as for you, continue in what you have learned and have firmly believed, knowing from whom you learned it and how from childhood you have been acquainted with the *sacred writings* which are able to instruct you for salvation through faith in Jesus Christ' (my emphasis). This is of course a controversial passage. I accept it as a reference to Christian writings for the following reasons: (1) The above survey of late first-, early second-century apostolic literature indicated clearly that there would have been considerable precedent for referring to Christian writings as ἱερὰ γράμματα.

(2) As Gealy has pointed out, if the Pastorals were written by an ardent Paulinist, who knew Paul's letters well, and who intended to establish authority in the Church, it would be incredible if in his mind Paul's letters were not thought of as sacred writings.

(3) Paul's use of the term γράμμα is principally as a reference to the Old Testament, which might argue for such an interpretation in 2 Tim. 3.15, except for two striking facts. First, we note that never except in this passage is γράμμα preceded by the adjective ἱερός. That is, there is something different about this usage from other clearly Pauline uses (Rom. 2.27, 29; 7.6; 2 Cor. 3.6, 7). If this were a Pauline student, however, we could expect differences in word usage. The second fact is

---

32. F. Gealy, 'The First and Second Epistles to Timothy and the Epistle to Titus', in G.A. Buttrick *et al.* (eds.), *The Interpreter's Bible* (12 vols.; New York and Nashville: Abingdon Press, 1955), XI, ad loc.

even more striking. Everywhere that Paul refers to the 'written code', γράμμα (see references above), he does so in order to *deny* that it is a source of salvation. Rather it is for him a source of death. For us to accept even a later Pauline student as now saying that the Old Testament writings are a source of 'salvation through faith in Jesus Christ' is to posit a complete reversal of one of Paul's most basic teachings.

(4) Further evidence for this view comes from the distinction between ἱερὰ γράμματα (v. 15) and πᾶσα γραφή in v. 16. Their juxtaposition here suggests that the author intended a comparison between Christian writings and Old Testament 'Scripture'. Just such a distinction seems to have been made by Clement of Alexandria (*Strom.* 2.11), where he gives a comprehensive description of Christian 'learning' as 'being supplied out of the divine Scriptures (θείων γραφῶν), the sacred writings (ἱερῶν γραμμάτων), and out of the "God-taught wisdom" (θεοδιδακτουσοφίας) according to the apostle'. Here would seem to be a clear distinction between the three sources of Christian instruction: the Old Testament (γραφή), the Christian writings (ἱερῶν γραμμάτων) which for Clement would be the teachings of Jesus, and the Pauline tradition.[33] We are also reminded that γράμμα is often used in the general sense of education (Jn 7.15), and Paul is even accused of being turned mad by his 'great learning' (γράμματα). The use of πᾶσα in v. 16 would seem to refer back to γράμματα, and reflect the author's view that Christian 'sacred writings' are to be included also among 'Scripture', a statement that would need to be made at this time when Christian writings were just beginning to be so designated.

(5) The best evidence, however, comes from the thrust of the entire letter. Timothy is being reminded of three generations of Christian faith, from his grandmother Lois and his mother Eunice; and the whole letter is a rehearsal of the substance of Timothy's education which he is exhorted to remember:

> the Gospel...now manifested through the appearing of Jesus Christ... the pattern of sound words which you have heard from me... the truth which has been entrusted to you... what you heard from me... Jesus Christ...as

---

33. See *Exhortation to Heaven* 9: 'Thou, O Timothy, from a child thou hast known the holy letters which are able to make thee wise unto salvation through faith that is in Christ Jesus (2 Tim 3.15). For truly holy are those letters...and the writing of volumes that consist of these holy letters...' (my emphasis). This is equated with the 'words of the Lord himself' (Mt. 4.17), so 'holy letters' here refers to the teachings of Jesus.

preached in my Gospel... the word of God... the sure saying (πιστὸς ὁ λόγος)... the word of truth... the faith... God's firm foundation... the knowledge of the truth... my teaching... what you have learned...from childhood...

And then the author sums it all up in terms of the 'sacred writings which are able to instruct you for salvation through Jesus Christ'. This is hardly a reference to Old Testament teaching. And then he climaxes his summary by saying, 'all Scripture is...profitable for teaching...that the man of God may be complete' (2 Tim. 3.16). Seen in this light the word 'all' would seem to encompass the entire letter and to include Christian writings along with the Old Testament which contains the Grace God 'gave us in Christ ages ago' (2 Tim. 1.9). In other words, the source of your salvation is primarily Christ; but all of this, Paul, gospel material, the Old Testament, is 'inspired' and 'profitable', and can be called 'Scripture'. The term ἱερὰ γράμματα here would seem to refer to the basic substance of Timothy's Christian education, which, when linked with the Old Testament, becomes πᾶσα γραφή. From the succession of terms, gospel, the word of God, the sure saying, the word of truth, the faith, the knowledge of the truth, teaching (διδασκαλία), we would seem to have a reference here to all three major sources of Christian instruction: the gospel, the traditions (παράδοσις) and the Holy Word of Jesus.

2 Peter 3.15-16

The latest of these references to Christian writing is 2 Pet. 3.15-16, which one can date to approximately AD 90:[34] 'So also our beloved brother Paul wrote to you according to the wisdom given him, speaking of this as he does in all his letters. There are some things in them hard to understand, which the ignorant and the unstable twist to their own destruction, as they do the *other scriptures*' (λοιπὰς γραφάς; my emphasis). The key to this passage is found in the total argument of the

---

34. This date is debated, with A.B. Barnett, 'The Second Epistle of Peter', in Buttrick *et al.* (eds.), *The Interpreter's Bible*, XII, p. 164, putting it as late as 150. See B. Reicke, *The Epistles of James, Peter, and Jude* (AB, 37; New York: Doubleday, 1964), pp. 144-45, for what I consider a decisive argument for the earlier date. See *Hist. Eccl.* 3.4.7, where Eusebius sees Rom. 2.16 as a reference to a written Gospel of Luke. This is very tenuous. The evidence from the εὐαγγέλιον study in Chapter 1 above clearly points to this as a later usage.

book. This is basically a warning against heresy and 'cleverly devised myths' (1.16). It is presented in terms of a comparison between the false prophets in the Old Testament (2.1) and 'false teachers' (2.1) who are the 'ignorant and unstable' misinterpreters of Paul's writings (3.16), 'even denying the Master who bought them' (2.1). The substance of that which is being denied or twisted is then both Jewish and Christian, Old Testament prophecy, and the revelation of Jesus: 'the predictions of the holy prophets and the commandment of the Lord and Savior through your apostles' (3.2). It is 'these things', both Jewish and Christian, of which the author says in the introduction 'I intend always to remind you' (1.12); and it would seem that it is these things, all of them, that are referred to in the comparison in 3.16.

The phrase τὰς λοιπὰς γραφάς then implies two bodies of writings in the same category. The one would clearly be the Old Testament Scriptures which are being made a matter of 'one's own interpretation' (1.20). The other would seem by implication to be Christian γραφή. These would be Paul's letters which are being 'twisted' (3.16). But the argument of the book insists on a broader context, summarized in 3.2: 'the predictions of the holy prophets, and the commandment of the Lord and Savior through your apostles'. Paul's letters and his usage of the teachings of Jesus (cf. Chapter 4) are by implication both called γραφή in this comparison and given equal status with the Old Testament.

Conclusion

What is emerging here is the probability that by the time of the Pastoral Epistles, 2 Peter and the doxology in Rom. 16.25-26, Christian writings are being referred to as ἱερὰ γράμματα, γραφῶν προφητικῶν, and γραφή. 'Scripture' in the formal sense that it has with Tertullian comes later, and in this early period it is perhaps more accurate to talk of Christian 'writings'; but the formal sense is emerging, even with what must be primitive portions of Gospels or the Pauline corpus, and these writings are presented on a par with the Old Testament as sources of Christian faith. It is here that the holy Word, holy narrative, holy gospel and holy tradition found their formal and continuing home. It was this fact of an early and persistent written form that helped stabilize the oral

Christian consensus and provide the mechanism for the production of a written New Testament.[35]

---

35. For an excellent recent survey of the story of the development of the written canon, see B.M. Metzger, *The Canon of the New Testament: Its Origin, Development, and Significance* (Oxford: Clarendon Press, 1987).

Chapter 9

HOLY FATHERS:
THE TRANSMITTERS OF THE WORD

The process of literary preservation of the Holy Word, narrative, gospel and tradition continued with growing intensity and formality as the Church moved out into the first and second centuries. We are especially interested in the growing strength and widespread distribution of the written teachings of Jesus as evidenced from Clement of Rome to the writings of Eusebius. These Fathers reflect a universally high regard for Christian 'Scripture', the heart of which were the teachings of Jesus, the focal point of Church belief and practice.

Generally speaking, scholars today are inclined to agree with Birger Gerhardsson in his insistence that the Apostolic Fathers are mostly ambiguous about whether or not the Jesus material in these works was written or oral.[1] While it is clear that the oral nature of the Holy Word was its most basic and primitive form, still the evidence would seem to suggest much more early writing than is generally admitted. We shall 'sound' this material in two ways: through direct reference to written sources, and through indirect testimony coming from the quotations of gospel material by the Fathers. There are various ways this vast body of literature can be organized. We shall do so here in the simplest way, in relative chronological sequence.

The First Epistle of Clement to the Corinthians

Tradition has attributed the *First Epistle of Clement to the Corinthians* to the third or fourth bishop of Rome sometime in the last decade of the

---

1. B. Gerhardsson, *Memory and Manuscript: Oral Tradition and Written Transmission in Rabbinic Judaism and Early Christianity* (Lund: W.K.C. Gleerup; Copenhagen: Munksgaard, 1961), p. 198. Gerhardsson points to 'the skepticism of the authors of the early church toward the written word' (p. 199).

first century. He refers in his writings to 'the Holy Word' and the 'oracles' (λόγια) of God, but in all cases these probably mean the Old Testament (13.2, 3; 53.1; 62.3). Besides the Old Testament, his basis for doctrinal authority was 'the words of the Lord Jesus' (λόγον τοῦ κυρίου Ἰησοῦ; 13.1). Our question is whether or not these were in any sense written words. The word γραφή occurs five times, four of which are clearly Old Testament (34.6; 42.5; 45.2; 53.1). In doubt is the statement in 23.3-5: 'Let this Scripture be far from us in which he says "Wretched are the double-minded, who doubt in their soul and say we have heard these things even in the days of our Fathers, and behold we have grown old, and none of these things has happened to us"... as the Scripture also bears witness...the Lord shall suddenly come to his Temple...' The latter portion of this passage is clearly a free rendering of Mal. 3.1; but the first part is unknown. Quoted also in *2 Clem.* 11.2, it is very possibly a section from some lost apocalypse, perhaps, as the translator Lake says, that of Eldad and Modad. There is one clear reference to written material in 13.1: 'Let us do that which is written (τὸ γεγραμμένον), for the Holy Spirit says, "Let not the wise man boast in his wisdom..."' This, however, is clearly a reference to Jer. 9.23-24, despite the quotation of this same passage in 1 Cor. 1.31 and 2 Cor. 10.17. There is, therefore, no direct reference to written Christian material in *1 Clement*.

But there does seem to be indirect reference in three sets of quotations from the teachings of Jesus. The first is this same passage, *1 Clem.* 13.1-2, where he urges his readers to remember 'the words of the Lord Jesus', and then gathers together seven sayings under a thematic heading, all dealing with 'gentleness and longsuffering': 'Be merciful that ye may obtain mercy. Forgive that ye may be forgiven. As ye do, so shall it be done unto you. As ye give, so shall it be given unto you. As ye judge, so shall ye be judged. As ye are kind, so shall kindness be shown you. With what measure ye mete, it shall be measured to you.' There is a parallel in the Synoptics for every one of these sayings except the one about kindness (Mt. 5.7; 6.14-15; 7.12; Lk. 6.38a; Mt. 7.2a; 7.2b). The *1 Clement* versions are all shorter, except the last saying which has the same number of words as the Synoptics. The Greek of these six parallels agrees with 67.9% of the Greek in their Gospel counterparts. It would seem that the main reason for the change in Greek is a stylistic one. Clement has set up his sentences in a beautifully coordinate fashion by slightly modifying the Greek. The difference lies in lifting out seven sayings according to content similarity and bringing them together into a block, and then in slightly modifying the wording in order to get a stylistic, even homiletic, parallelism: ἵνα... ἵνα... ὡς... ὡς... ὡς... ὡς... ὡς. This has the effect of creating a slightly more legalistic (*quid pro quo*) sense than the Synoptic counterpart, but does not essentially alter the meaning of the sayings.

Now the point is this: in order to do such editing, I suggest the author must have had a written collection of Jesus' λόγια from which to pull together these similar units, and then edit them so cleverly, while still preserving 67.9% of the Synoptic Greek.[2] He may have made his own written collection of oral units, but we still have to account for the Greek similarity. Koester has suggested that he had an early Christian catechism, and this makes some sense. This collection is very much like the Beatitudes, and reflects the characteristic 'school' activity of the Christian community, gathering λόγια together under various rubrics, sometimes amending them for some practical purpose, but the key words, and the basic ideas, remain intact. In the above collection, it is the key words that do not change. Here what we have been discovering is the heart of the 'fixed' tradition. There must have been some kind of written connection between the Synoptics and *1 Clement*. What it was we can only conjecture. What is certain is that behind these quotations lay a solid body of oral and/or written teachings of Jesus, having immense authority, and wide coinage.

There is a second passage in *1 Clem.* 46.8: 'Remember the words of the Lord Jesus; for he said, "Woe unto that man: it were good for him if he had not been born, than that he should offend one of my elect; it were better for him that a millstone be hung on him, and he be cast into the sea, than that he should turn aside one of my elect"'. Here we seem to have a conflation of Mt. 18.6-7 and Mk 14.21. Somewhere along the line these two λόγια were connected because of the similarity in idea, and the catchword οὐαί. The verbal agreement with the Synoptics is especially striking. There is a closer agreement in the Greek between *1 Clement* and the three Synoptics as they report these two sayings (67.9%) than between the Synoptics themselves (56.6% between Mt.

---

2. B.M. Metzger (*The Canon of the New Testament: Its Origin, Development, and Significance* [Oxford: Clarendon Press, 1987], p. 43) points to an analogous collection in Clement of Alexandria (*Strom.* 2.18.91) and in Polycarp (*Phil.* 11.3). He is uncertain whether this is memory or written sources: 'Two or three times he speaks of the words of Christ, and seems...to have a written record in mind'.

18.6-7 and Mk 9.42; Lk. 17.1, 2; Mk 14.21). Koester suggests that *1 Clement* has not used the Synoptics, but a variant.³ The use of the catchword οὐαί as an occasion for conflation strongly suggests written sources. The verbal similarity is impressive, as is our impression of the stability of the tradition, whether written or not.

There is a third passage where Jesus' parable of the sower (Mk 4.3-9) is used as an illustration of the resurrection. The parable is highly abbreviated, and is not presented as a direct quotation, but rather as a summary and exposition. Still the catchwords and phrases persist: ἐξῆλθεν ὁ σπείρων... γῆν... καρπόν. Only 12% of the Greek of Clement can be equated with Mark. Here the author has taken one of the several points of the Markan parable and sharpened it into the only point, with some minimal doctoring, but the essential teaching remains intact. This must be said to be a free rendering of the tradition as Mark found it; but the fact that it is presented as a paraphrase rather than a direct quotation might soften this judgment. The important thing for us is the persistence of the catchwords.

The Epistles of Ignatius

In his *Chronicon*, Eusebius fixes the date of Ignatius's martyrdom in the tenth year of Trajan, AD 108. In the epistles of Ignatius, then, we are most probably penetrating into the first century. There is not a lot of evidence, but there is sufficient to indicate that Ignatius was familiar with the Gospel material, and could have had some written sources.⁴ The phrase 'it is written' (γέγραπται) occurs twice (*Eph.* 5.3; *Mag.* 12.1), and each time it introduces a quotation from the proverbs, although in *Eph.* 5.3, the proverb 'God resisteth the proud' also occurs in Jas 4.6 and 1 Pet. 5.5, and the Greek of Ignatius is closer to the New Testament than to the LXX. There are several indirect references to the teachings of Jesus where the sharp point of the reference is some Synoptic catchword like οἰκοδεσπότης (*Eph.* 6.1; cf. Mk 12.1-12; Mt. 21.33; etc.), δένδρον, καρπόν (*Eph.* 14.2; cf. Mt. 12.33), φυτεία πατρός (*Trall.* 11.1; *Phld.*

---

3. H. Koester, *Synoptische Überlieferung bei den Apostolischen Vätern* (TU, 65; Berlin: Akademie-Verlag, 1957), p. 19.

4. Metzger (*Canon of the New Testament*, p. 49) states: 'Most scholars agree that Ignatius was familiar with Matthew or a document closely akin to it... The primary authority for Ignatius was the apostolic preaching about the life, death and resurrection of Jesus. It made little difference to him if oral or written.'

3.1; cf. Mt. 15.13), suggesting oral data, or parallel Gospel written sources. There is a more direct quotation in *Smyrn.* 3.2-3: 'When he came to those with Peter he said to them: "Take, handle me and see that I am not a phantom without a body"'. Half of the words of this saying, ψηλαφήσατέ με καὶ ἴδετε ὅτι, derive from Lk. 24.39, suggesting that Ignatius may have had a written copy of the passion narrative, or portions of it, as found in Luke.

By all odds the most perplexing reference to these matters in Ignatius is *Phld.* 8.2:

> Do nothing in factiousness, but after the teaching of Christ (χριστομαθίαν), for I heard some men saying, 'If I find it not in the charters in the Gospel I do not believe', and when I said to them that it is in the Scripture, they answered me, 'That is exactly the question', but to me the charters are Jesus Christ, the inviolable charter is his cross, and death, and resurrection, and the faith which is through him; in these I desire to be justified by your prayers.

Now the critical question here is the meaning of 'charters', which are called 'Scripture'. If one punctuates this passage one way, charters could mean the gospel; but punctuated another way it most probably means the Old Testament. I would tend to agree with Lake that this refers to the Old Testament, and Ignatius is saying that he finds Christ in the Old Testament, but that the Old Testament should be replaced by the teaching, gospel, cross and resurrection of Christ. One should probably not therefore find here a reference to the teaching of Jesus as γραφή. What it does say is that the χριστομαθία is the new and 'inviolable charter', which for Ignatius is not only on a par with the Old Testament, but supersedes it. Whether or not this designates written material is impossible to say from this one passage. In the light of all the references in Ignatius, however, it could very well be. One thing is certain: for Ignatius, the teaching of Jesus and the passion narrative stand as solid traditions to which he can refer in a unitary way as the authoritative source, the 'inviolable charter' of his faith. There would also seem to be some written gospel data which he shared in common with the Synoptic editors (see above).

The Didache

The *Didache*, produced sometime in the late first or early second century, gives us a glimpse of the Church at a very early period when the 'apostles and prophets' were traveling about preaching in much the way described in the Gospels (Mt. 10.1-2). Such a one is 'to be received as the Lord', and is enjoined to 'receive nothing but bread till he reach his night's lodging'. And then he is to stay no 'more than one day, or if need be a second... but if he stay three days he is a false prophet' (11.4-6). The recipients are urged to appoint 'bishops and deacons worthy of the Lord', so the author is describing a very primitive time indeed, a transition period between the unstructured Church of Jesus' day, and the more ecclesiastically ordered Church of the Pastoral Epistles. Chapter one is a description of 'the way of life' as contrasted with 'the way of death'. There is only one direct reference to written Gospel material, 'reprove one another not in wrath but in peace as you find in the Gospel...in the Gospel of our Lord' (*Did.* 15.3), but there is much indirect testimony to such. This chapter is a compilation of twelve individual sayings. Four are from certain extra-canonical sources, but eight are sayings found in Matthew 5–7 and Luke 6. If one compares the Greek of the *Didache* with that of Matthew and Luke, it appears that exact duplicates of 60.7% of all the words in the *Didache* are found in the Synoptic counterparts. Some of these, while not paralleled exactly, are paraphrases of Synoptic material (3b; cf. to Lk. 6.32-33; 4d; cf. to Mt. 5.42), and there are also echoes of 1 Pet. 2.11 and Tit. 2.12. In *Did.* 9.5, 'This also did the Lord say, "Give not that which is holy to the dogs"', exactly parallels Mt. 7.6, with the exception that κυσίν becomes κυσί. *Didache* 15.3 is an indirect reference to Mt. 5.22-26 and 18.15-35, and *Didache* 16 is a series of allusions and partial quotations of apocalyptic sayings found in Matthew, Luke and 1 and 2 Thessalonians. Here the author is making what Koester would call 'free use' of the sayings material, blending it with Paul and others.[5] Koester points out

---

5. See Koester, *Synoptische Überlieferung*, p. 12. I am much indebted to Professor Koester for this, which formed the *Grundschrift* of my own study. *Did.* 16.1 is parallel to Mt. 24.42-44; Lk. 12.35-40, with 43% exact Greek, ὁ κύριος is substituted for ὁ υἱὸς τοῦ ἀνθρώπου (cf. Mk 13.35; Mt. 25.3). The Holy Word is changed. The *Didache* seems to be a composite of all Synoptic locations. *Did.* 16.3, parallel to Mt. 24.11, 12, 24; 7.15, exact Greek 21.7%. *Did.* 16.4a parallel to Mt. 24.12, 10, 50% exact Greek, a free use of a Synoptic theme. *Did.* 16.4b parallel to Mk 13.22; Mt. 24.24; Mk 13.19; Mt. 24.21, 17% exact Greek, free use with some similarities in idea differently expressed. *Did.* 16.5 parallel to Mk 13.13 44.4% exact Greek, same or similar ideas differently expressed, a free use. *Did.* 16.6-8 parallel to Mt. 24.30-31; Mk 13.26-27, 47.8% exact Greek with several similar ideas differently expressed.

that these allusions to the Synoptics do not need a written Gospel source, although he admits that the compiler of the *Didache* 'used the written Gospels during the first half of the second century as one of the many other sources for collections of the Lord's words without particular authority'.[6]

This suggests that there were many sources for the teachings of Jesus vying with each other for use and authority during this time. The canonizing process was that of deciding which were the 'best', and destroying the rest. The most important thing here is that despite some additions from dubious, and often highly Jewish, material, and some superficial changes in word form, wording or word order, the central message as found in the Synoptic sayings remains essentially intact. The over-all percentage of verbal agreement with the Synoptic sayings is 48%. The author seems to have not only had access to written material, but to have used it, freely at times, but at other times, in some of the compilations and more exact parallels, rather carefully. The bunching of these references into three main groupings, the sermon on the mount, the instructions to the twelve (Mt. 10 parallel to *Did.* 12) and the little apocalypse (Mk 13), suggest that perhaps what the author had here were some of the proto-sources lying behind the Synoptics. The compilation seems to be a blend of both oral and written sources, and exhibits a strong literary, scholarly and historical as well as apologetic concern.[7]

The Epistle of Barnabas

According to Metzger, most scholars suggest a date for this composition in the first half of the second century. There is some direct evidence that the author had written Gospel sources. Mostly he refers to the Old Testament as 'Scripture' (γραφή) (*Barn.* 5.4; 6.12; 13.2), but on one occasion he quotes *1 Enoch* (89.55, 66, 67) and calls it γραφή. Then at one point, where he has been referring to what the 'Scripture says' (*Barn.* 4.7, 11 = Old Testament), he includes in the same authoritative context this statement: 'Let us take heed lest as it was written (ὡς γέγραπται) we be found "many called but few chosen"' (4.14), an

---

6. Koester, *Synoptische Überlieferung*, p. 241.
7. For Koester (*Synoptische Überlieferung*, p. 240), the compiler of the *Didache* had *als seine Aufgabe* collections of instructions and rules under the authority of the twelve apostles, material which came out of the same tradition as the Synoptic material.

exact quotation of Mt. 22.14. The subtle distinction between γραφή and γέγραπται is perhaps important at this early period; but γέγραπται in this authoritative context suggests that written teachings of Jesus had authority similar to the Old Testament. In another indirect quotation, the author also gives us the exact Greek of Mk 2.17 with the slight substitution of ἦλθεν for ἦλθον, possibly a scribal error: 'He came not to call the righteous but sinners'. At still another point in this chapter (*Barn.* 5.12), he quotes a passage common to both Zech. 13.6, 7 and Mt. 26.31 (Mk 14.27), wherein the Greek is closer to that of the Gospel (54.5%) than it is to the LXX. There seem to be written Greek sources here strikingly close to the Synoptics.

Justin Martyr

Eusebius dates Justin's active period during the reign of Hadrian (AD 117–138). The teachings of Jesus are the source and authority for his theology, and they are clearly in written form. In his *1 Apology* he is recalling 'a few of the teachings which have come from Christ himself... (whose) sayings were short and concise, for he was no Sophist' (ch. 14). In the *2 Apology,* in his letter to the Roman Senate protesting the innocence of Christians to certain false charges, he complains that the philosopher Crescens 'assails us, without having read the teachings of Christ' (ch. 3). That these are written sources of Jesus' words is further certified by two other passages in the *Dialogue with Trypho*. In one passage he says, 'Our Lord in his teaching...proclaimed that...Elijah would also come', and then goes on to quote Mt. 3.11, 12, after which he says, 'And it is written "Then the disciples understood that he spoke to them of John the Baptist"' (Mt. 17.13). The second passage shows that sufficient copies of Jesus' sayings are available in written form for Trypho to have access to one, for he has Trypho say, 'I am aware that your precepts in the so-called Gospel are so wonderful...no one can keep them. For I have carefully read them' (ch. 10). Finally, in a memorable passage, Justin describes the use of such documents in the second-century Church: 'On the day called Sunday, all who live in cities or in the country gather together to one place, and the memoirs of the apostles or the writings of the prophets are read as long as time permits; then when the reader has ceased, the president verbally instructs, and exhorts to the imitation of these good things' (*1 Apol.* 67). Clearly, in the time of Justin, there were written Gospel records, which were prime sources for the life and theology of the Church. The term 'Scripture' (γραφή) for Justin, however, probably is reserved for the Old Testament (*Trypho* 8). The reference to 'writings of the prophets' may well indicate written tradition (παράδοσις), giving to the Christian prophets a literary role.

The Shepherd of Hermas

This work is variously dated to approximately the middle of the second century. Metzger sees it as 'probable' that the author according to the Liberian Catalogue was the brother of Pius, bishop of Rome (d. 154), although others say he was a younger contemporary of Clement of Rome.[8] It contains no direct quotations from the canonical Gospels, but there are many allusions and much similar material. What is especially interesting is that in four of the seven passages where such similarities can be seen, the Greek words that Hermas and the Synoptics have in common are the important catchwords. In *Vis.* 4.2.6, parallel to Mt. 26.24 and Mk 14.21, the two common words are οὐαί and the aorist passive of γεννάω. In *Sim.* 5.2.6, parallel to Mk 12.6-7, they are ἀγαπητόν and κληρονόμον. In Hermas's *Sim.* 9.20.2-3, where the parable of the sower (Mk 4.3-9) is elided with the theme of entering the Kingdom (Mt. 19.23; Mk 10.23, 24; Lk. 18.24), there are several key Synoptic terms dealing with basic metaphors and the Kingdom theme (ἀκάνθας, πλούσιοι, δούλοις, βασιλείαν τοῦ θεοῦ, μετάνοια). In *Sim.* 9.22.3, the one phrase ὑψοῦντες ἑαυτούς stands out linking this with a number of possible Synoptic references (cf. Mt. 23.12; Lk. 14.11; etc.).[9]

All of this suggests that the author of Hermas could have had written versions or portions of the Synoptics. Whether or not he considered them as authoritative 'Scripture' is, as Koester notes, difficult to say. Metzger does not think so. This work would seem to be from a period when the teachings of Jesus were authoritative, but the particular written versions that later became canonical, although perhaps known, were not as closely adhered to as they were later. The 'catchword' phenomenon is especially interesting in view of my contention elsewhere that it is

---

8. Metzger, *Canon of the New Testament*, p. 63.

9. See also *Mand.* 4.1.6 parallel to Mk 10.11; Mt. 5.32; 19.9; *Mand.* 12.6.3, indirect reference to Mt. 10.28; Lk. 12.5; *Sim.* 9.31.2, an indirect reference to Mt. 5.8, Mk 10.13.

these key words that reveal the most verbal patterns in a massive computerized analysis of the Synoptics.[10]

Polycarp, Epistle to the Philippians

Polycarp was martyred in AD 155, so in his letter to the Philippians we are probing the first half of the second century. According to Metzger, Polycarp had a collection of at least eight Pauline epistles, including two Pastorals, and the knowledge of 1 Peter and 1 John. In one place (12.1) Polycarp's *Philippians* includes what is probably a quotation from the letter of the Philippians to Polycarp:[11] 'For I am confident that you are well versed in the Scriptures *(sacris literis)*...as it is said in these Scriptures, "Be ye angry and sin not" [cf. Ps. 4.4] and "Let not the sun go down on your wrath?"' (cf. Eph. 4.26). The Old Testament and Paul seem here to be equally 'Scripture'. There is also a direct reference in 7.1 to 'the oracles (λόγια) of the Lord' as the basis of the Christian confession. As I have already shown, the term is probably to be distinguished as a written collection from λόγοι, which would be the oral words of Jesus.

This suggestion that Polycarp possessed written copies of portions of the New Testament, including the teachings of Jesus, is strengthened by two quotations and one paraphrase of Jesus' words in this letter. In 2.3, Polycarp writes, 'remembering what the Lord taught when he said, "Judge not that ye be not judged, forgive and it shall be forgiven unto you, be merciful that ye may obtain mercy, with what measure ye mete, it shall be measured to you again", and "Blessed are the poor, and they who are persecuted for righteousness' sake, for theirs is the Kingdom of God"'. This collection of sayings is from Matthew and Luke (Mt. 7.1, 2, 12; 5.7, 3, 10; Lk. 6.20, 37, 38, 21; cf. Mk 11.25), and represents a sufficiently close Greek parallel (84.4%) to suggest the presence of Synoptic documents or their immediate sources. Each of these λόγια is shorter than its Synoptic counterpart, but without impairing the essence of its meaning.

---

10. J.A. Baird, *Audience Criticism and the Historical Jesus* (Philadelphia: Westminster Press, 1969).

11. See K. Lake (trans.), *The Apostolic Fathers* (LCL, 24-25; London: Heinemann; Cambridge, MA: Harvard University Press, 1912–13), I, p. 299; Metzger, *Canon of the New Testament*, p. 60.

In another such collection, Polycarp has brought together three different sayings, only two of which are paralleled in the Synoptics: 'Let us turn back to the word which was delivered to us in the beginning, "watching unto prayer", and persevering in fasting, beseeching the all-seeing God in our supplications "to lead us not into temptation", even as the Lord said, "The spirit is willing, but the flesh is weak"'. Matthew and Luke still seem to be the controls (Mt. 6.13a; 26.41; Lk. 11.15b; cf. Mk 14.38), and the reproduction of their Greek this time is 100%. The third example is not presented as a quotation, and we are impressed with Polycarp's concern always to so indicate if he is quoting Jesus directly. This seems to be a conflated paraphrase of Mt. 5.44, 48 and Lk. 6.27 with echoes of several of Paul's letters, James and John. 'Pray...for those who persecute you and hate you, and for the enemies of the cross, that your fruit may be manifest among all men, that you may be perfected in him'. Even here the theology of the Synoptic Jesus is intact, suggesting someone who was indeed 'well versed in the Scriptures', and careful in their handling.

Papias

Almost nothing is known of this one whom Irenaeus called 'a man of long ago who heard the apostle John preach and was a friend of Polycarp' (*Adv. Haer.* 33). His date is variously given between AD 70 and 140. He is best known for his treatise in five books, 'Expositions of the Sayings of the Lord', of which only small fragments have survived. From the preface to this work (*Hist. Eccl.* 3.39.4), it is clear that 'the sayings of Jesus were drawn not only from written documents but from oral tradition'.[12] We note his focus upon the Holy Word of Jesus (λογίων κυριακῶν ἐξηγήσεως), what seems to be his knowledge of Mark's Gospel and his preference for the oral form of that word.

---

12. See Metzger, *Canon of the New Testament*, p. 52; see also J.A. Kleist, 'Re-Reading the Papias Fragments on St. Mark', *St Louis University Studies: Series A: Humanities* (1945), pp. 1-17; J. Kurzinger, 'Das Papias und die Erstgestalt des Matthaus Evangeliums', *BZ* 4 (1960), pp. 19-30; R.H. Gundry, *Matthew: A Commentary on his Literary and Theological Art* (Grand Rapids: Eerdmans, 1982), pp. 609-22.

Irenaeus

Irenaeus, Bishop of Lyons, born about AD 130, quotes voluminously from every book in the New Testament except Philemon and 3 John. The four Gospels are the chief authorities for Christian doctrine, and he quotes these under the names of their authors, as distinct from earlier authors who referred not to what 'Mark said', but to what 'Jesus said'. For him the very heart of the Gospels, and so of Christian doctrine, were the parables of Jesus (*Adv. Haer.* 4.27). As Metzger points out, the apologists (Justin to Athenagoras) are content with quoting the Old Testament prophets and the Lord's own words in the Gospels as proof of divine revelation.[13] By this time (AD 175) the New Testament is clearly 'Scripture' (γραφή) (cf. *Adv. Haer.* 1.3.6; 1.6, 8; 2.27; 3.2.1), and the Gospels are considered to have a central place of authority (*Adv. Haer.* 3 preface). These are 'the Gospels of the apostles' and are authoritative because the apostles have been made 'truly perfect' by the Holy Spirit (*Adv. Haer.* 3.19.9, 11). Despite the objections of such heretics as Marcion, in Irenaeus's day New Testament Scripture seems to have been clearly understood and generally accepted in the form in which it was later canonized.

Montanus

From this period come echoes of the followers of Montanus, 'Who caused the church to take its first step toward the adoption of a closed canon of scripture'.[14] One theologian (no name given) who attacked this charismatic, apocalyptic movement around AD 192–193 is quoted by Eusebius (*Hist. Eccl.* 5.16.2–17.4). He has hesitated to draw up an anti-Montanist treatise, 'not through lack of ability, but from fear that I might perchance be adding a new article or precept to the *word of the new covenant* of the Gospel (τὸ τῆς τοῦ εὐαγγελίου καινῆς διαθήκης λόγον), to which no one in accordance with the Gospel itself can add and from which one cannot take away' (my emphasis). He does not specifically identify this 'word', but it would seem likely that he is referring to the λόγος as we have defined it above.

---

13. See Metzger, *Canon of the New Testament*, p. 154.
14. Metzger, *Canon of the New Testament*, p. 106.

Kerygma Petrou, Acts of Peter

From this same period (AD 80–180) come other fragmentary and possibly apocryphal suggestions that the earliest writings recognized as authoritative by the Church are written Gospels. In the *Kerygma Petrou*, Peter urges James and the Jerusalem church 'not to pass on to any of the Gentiles the books of my preachings'. The *Acts of Peter*, coming from approximately AD 180, pictures Peter going into the dining room where he sees the 'Gospel' being read: 'So he rolled up the book and said, "you men...must know how the holy Scriptures of our Lord should be declared"'.

The Second Epistle of Clement to the Corinthians

More a sermon than a letter, and probably not written by Clement of Rome, this work is indistinctly dated between AD 120–170. It gives much more certain evidence for written sources. The clearest indication of this is *2 Clem.* 2.4: 'and another Scripture (γραφή) also says, "I came not to call righteous but sinners"'. This is an exact duplication of the Greek of Mk 2.17b (Mt. 9.13b; Lk. 5.32). Here we have an exact replica of a written Gospel saying. Having just quoted Isaiah, the author by ἕτερα...γραφή would seem to place his written version of Mark on a par with the Old Testament. This same phenomenon occurs in *2 Clem.* 19.1: 'Pay attention to that which is written (τοῖς γεγραμμένοις) that you may both save yourselves and him who is the reader (ἀναγινώσκοντα) among you'. In 17.2 he has said 'pay attention to the commands of the Lord' (Old Testament); but in 17.7 the author talks of 'the commandments of Jesus Christ', and in 19.3 he quotes Eph. 4.18. The reference here is probably to the written Old Testament, Paul and the teachings of Jesus; but one cannot be absolutely certain whether all of these would be τοῖς γεγραμμένοις. In *2 Clem.* 14.1, he labels as 'Scripture' a quotation from Jer. 7.11, which also occurs in Mt. 21.13; and in *2 Clem.* 14.2, 'Scripture' clearly refers to the Old Testament, in distinction from 'the books and the apostles', seemingly a reference to 1 Pet. 1.20. There seems to be little doubt that the author of *2 Clement* had written Christian sources and sees at least some of them as holy Scripture. He cites the words of Jesus eleven times, of which five are not

9. *The Transmitters of the Word* 199

in the canonical Gospels. As Metzger puts it, 'The words of Jesus are taken as supreme authority'.[15]

An even more exact indication of this comes from a comparison of other λόγια quotations in *2 Clement*. In 3.2, Jesus 'also says, "whosoever confessed me before men, I will confess him before my father"'. This is very close to Mt. 10.32 (Lk. 12.8); 83% of the Greek words are the same or similar, and although some words are different, the meaning is the same. There is an interesting case in *2 Clem.* 4.2 (par. Mt. 7.21): 'Not everyone that saith to me Lord, Lord, shall be saved [Mt.: "shall enter the Kingdom"], but he that doeth righteousness' [Mt.: "that doeth the will of my father in heaven"]'. We note here an exact Greek duplicate except for the two phrases where one word in *2 Clement* replaces several in Matthew (84.6% agreement). The same abbreviating technique where the idea remains intact can be found in the *Gospel of Thomas* (9, 75), coming from that approximate period. The λόγιον in *2 Clem.* 4.5 has echoes of the parable of Abraham's bosom (Lk. 16.19-31), the parables of the ten virgins (Mt. 25.1-13), the wedding garment (Mt. 22.11-14) and the closed door (Lk. 12.36): 'If ye be gathered together with me in my bosom, and do not my commandments, I will cast you out, and will say to you, depart from me, I know not whence ye are'. The wording is somewhat garbled (43.3% Greek parallel), and there is considerable shortening of Synoptic detail, but the ideas do not change. This seems to be a separate tradition here with some genuine Synoptic pattern elements. In *2 Clem.* 6.1-2, we have an illustration of where the author seems to have both Matthew and Luke in hand: *2 Clem.* 6.1 repeats 58.8% of the Greek of Lk. 16.13, while *2 Clem.* 6.2 echoes 78.6% of the Greek of Mt. 16.26: 'And the Lord says "No Servant can serve two masters". If we desire to serve both God and Mammon it is unprofitable for us, "for what is the advantage if a man gain the whole world but lose his soul?"' There is a shortening of the Synoptic version, with some ambiguity as to where the quotation stops. The second sentence, 'If we desire...', is a commentary on the quotation.

---

15. 'In *2 Clement* the development can be seen even more clearly, the Gospel changes into holy Scripture'. See E. Hennecke and W. Schneemelcher (eds.), *New Testament Apocrypha* (2 vols.; Philadelphia: Westminster Press, 1963), II, p. 30. See Metzger, *Canon of the New Testament*, pp. 7, 73. The author of *2 Clement* 'certainly knew and used Matthew and Luke, 1 Corinthians and Ephesians'.

There is a nice illustration of careful conflation technique in *2 Clem.* 9.11: 'For the Lord said, "My brethren are those who do the will of my father"'. All of the Greek words in *2 Clement* can be duplicated either in Mt. 12.50 or Lk. 8.21 (cf. also Mk 3.35). We note here again the abbreviation of the Synoptic saying. An even more dramatic illustration of conflation occurs in *2 Clem.* 13.4: 'For when they hear from us that God says, "It is no credit to you if ye love them that love you, but it is a credit to you if ye love your enemies, and those that hate you"'. Here we have a conflation of Lk. 6.27, 32 and Mt. 5.44, 46, with an exact agreement of 72.2% with the Greek of both sources. The essential Word of Jesus remains intact and key words persist while the whole is shortened. One reason for rearranging the phrases in *2 Clement* is to provide an enhanced literary structure with the repetition of εἰ ἀγαπᾶτε τοὺς ἀγαπῶντας... εἰ ἀγαπᾶτε τοὺς ἐχθρούς...

There is an apophthegm reported in *2 Clem.* 5.2, which appears to be a conglomeration of ideas from Jesus' mission instructions at a preliterary level, held together by the catchword 'lamb' and the idea of the death of the body:

> For the Lord said, 'Ye shall be as lambs in the midst of wolves', and Peter answered and said to him, 'If then the wolves tear the lambs?' Jesus said to Peter, 'Let the lambs have no fear of the wolves after their death; and do ye have no fear of those that slay you, and can do nothing more to you, but fear him who after your death hath power over body and soul, to cast them into the flames of hell (cf. Lk. 12.4-5; Mt. 10.16, 25; Mk 8.15-16).

There are fifteen Greek words exactly parallel in Matthew and/or Luke, and eleven that are very close, with the same root but different grammatical form or close synonym (57.8%). As an apophthegm, the ideas, basic imagery and 'mode' conform closely to the Synoptic pattern (88.9%).[16] Another quotation in *2 Clem.* 8.5 gives us an illustration of material found in Lk. 16.11-12 where the nineteen words in the Synoptics become twenty-three words in *2 Clement*: 'For the Lord says in the Gospel, "If ye did not guard that which is small, who shall give you what is great. For I tell you that he who is faithful in that which is least is also faithful in that which is much."' Koester posits an apocryphal gospel behind this λόγιον, and certainly this would be true of *2 Clem.* 12.2, which is quite close to the *Gospel of Thomas*.

---

16. J.A. Baird, *A Comparative Analysis of the Gospel Genre: The Synoptic Mode and Its Uniqueness* (Lewiston: Edwin Mellen Press, 1991), Chapter 2.

In all the above, the evidence points to the author of *2 Clement* possessing written copies of at least portions of Matthew and Luke, Ephesians and 1 Peter (?), as well as certain other apocryphal gospels. He quoted his Synoptic materials with an average 71.8% exactitude; and even though there is some redactional activity, the essential message and the key words of his sources remain intact. His redactional efforts followed three main patterns: (1) grouping independent units under some rubric such as theme or catchword; (2) abbreviating, summarizing, and infrequently elaborating; and (3) stylistic changes. He regularly conflated various sources, and most often shortened as he did, but on at least one occasion there is a lengthening of his source. The obvious center of his theological authority is the teachings of Jesus which he treated with great care.[17]

Dionysius of Corinth

From the same period comes further evidence in an interesting passage in the *Epistle to the Romans* by Dionysius of Corinth (AD 161–180). Here the Gospels as Scripture (γραφή) are contrasted with spurious writings: 'It is not marvelous, therefore, if some have set themselves to tamper with the dominical Scriptures as well, since they have also laid their designs against writings that do not class as such' (*Hist. Eccl.* 4.23.12). Tatian's *Diatessaron* comes from the same period, and underscores the scholarly interest in the four Gospels, all equally authoritative.

Theophilus of Antioch

It was at this time (c. 180) that Theophilus of Antioch referred to the Gospel of Matthew as Holy Word (ἅγιος λόγος), and saw Matthew and John, along with the Old Testament, as inspired. It is interesting to note how many of these early Fathers quote Matthew as their primary authority.

---

17. Koester (*Synoptische Überlieferung*, p. 240) sees *2 Clement* using not the Gospels of Matthew and Luke directly, but rather a written collection of *Herrenworter*, based on Matthew and Luke, and similar to that of the Oxyrhynchus papyri.

Athenagoras

A Christian philosopher of Athens, whom some call one of the ablest of Christian apologists of the second century, Athenagoras cites words and phrases from both Matthew and Luke, and says that he has been brought up on such teachings (λόγοι) as 'love your enemies' (*Leg.* 11.2). He introduces the teachings of Jesus on divorce in Matthew by the simple formula 'he says', and refers to the Gospel of John as 'the Word' (as I infer from *Leg.* 10.17). The guiding control of the written 'words... word... WORD' of Jesus is clear.

Clement of Alexandria

By the end of the second century, Clement of Alexandria was able to refer to both Old and New Testaments as 'the venerable canon', 'the divine Scriptures (*Strom.* 2.9). He quotes fairly accurately from all the New Testament except Philemon and 2, 3 John, and calls it 'Scripture' (cf. *Instructor* 2, 3, 5, 9). In one classic statement, he seems to divide his authoritative written sources, 'that alone which is true', into three categories: (1) that which is supplied out of divine Scripture (θειῶν γραφῶν), probably Old Testament; (2) the sacred writings (τῶν ἱερῶν γραμματῶν), very probably the Gospels and especially the teachings of Jesus; and (3) the God-taught wisdom according to the apostle (θεοδιδάκτου σοφίας), which is probably a reference to Paul (*Strom.* 2.11).[18]

Origen

At this time (c. AD 185), Origen declared the four Gospels as 'the only indisputable' source (*Hist. Eccl.* 6.25.3-4), and insisted that 'We take... for the proof of our statements, testimonies from what are believed by us to be divine writings (γραφή), the standard of the heavenly church of Jesus Christ according to the succession of the apostles' (*De Principiis* 4.1, 9). For Origen, authoritative Scripture was at least Old Testament, Gospels and the epistles of Paul (*Hist. Eccl.* 6.38.1).

---

18. The rest of section 11 is filled with quotations from the teachings of Jesus. If 'God taught wisdom' refers to Paul, then 'sacred writings' must refer primarily to these dominical teachings in written form.

Tertullian

Converted in AD 195 and writing at the end of the second and early third centuries, Tertullian shows the centrality of the Gospels for the faith of the Church, what he calls 'the rule of faith' (*Against Marcion* 4.17-19). He understands that Paul had a written gospel from the apostles, and made this available to Luke, 'a genuine text of the apostles' writings' (*Against Marcion* 4.3; cf. *Hist. Eccl.* 3.4.7). The apostolic churches are those in which 'Their own authentic writings are read' (*Against Heresies* 36). By this time the entire New Testament is called 'Scripture' (*On Idolatry* 5), is widely known (except Jude and 2, 3 John; cf. *Against Heresies* 36), and is appealed to (especially the Gospels) as final authority (*Against Praxeas*).

Serapion of Antioch

At the turn of the second century, Serapion, successor to Theophilus as Bishop of Antioch, reflects not only the controversy over the *Gospel of Peter*, but also the continued stabilizing activity of the Holy Word: 'Most of it (Peter) is indeed in accordance with the *true teachings of the Savior* (italics mine), but some things are additions to that teaching' (*Hist. Eccl.* 6.2).

Hippolytus

Bishop of Rome, pupil of Irenaeus, Hippolytus (d. 235) quotes all the New Testament, except Philemon and 2, 3 John, and reduces all heresy to one common ground, antagonism to the Scripture, which for him means both Old and New Testaments (*Treatise on Christ and Anti-Christ* 67). He introduces the New Testament texts with the phrases, 'as the Lord says', and 'as the apostle says', and assumes his readers know the teachings of Jesus and respect scriptural authority. It may well be that some such written New Testament material is what is meant by the brief inscription of Obercius (AD 216) found in Hierapolis: 'He taught me (Christ)...the faithful writings.'[19]

---

19. J. Quasten, *Patrology*. I. *Beginnings of Patristic Literature* (Utrecht: Spectrum, 1950; repr. Westminster, U.K.: Newman, 1983).

Novatian, Cyprian of Carthage

By the time of Novatian (AD 210–280, *On the Trinity* 16) and Cyprian of Carthage (d. 258), both Old and New Testaments are 'Divine Scripture'. Cyprian is fond of quoting both Testaments, especially Matthew, and Novatian the teachings of Jesus as the final authority.

Eusebius

By the fourth century, as reflected in the writings of Eusebius, there seems to be a universally high regard for Christian 'Scripture' (γραφή) as a basis for the Church's life and doctrine. These books are 'sacred' (ἡ ἱερὰ τοῦ εὐαγγελίου διδάσκει γραφή; *Hist. Eccl.* 1.8.3) and 'divine' (ἡ θεία γραφή; 1.10.2). They are 'the rule of the primitive faith' (πίστεώς τε ἀρχαίας κανόνα; *Hist. Eccl.* 5.28.13), 'spoken by the Holy Spirit' (*Hist. Eccl.* 5.28.18), and so the final authority in matters of faith and doctrine. For Eusebius there are three classes of Christian literature: canonical, disputed and rejected. The first is called γραφή, 'scripture', to distinguish it from the rest. Sometimes this refers to one 'scripture of the Gospel' (*Hist. Eccl.* 1.10.6; cf. 1.8.3; 1.10.11; 3.37.2; etc.), or to 'the scripture of the divine Gospels' (τὴν τῶν θείων εὐαγγελίων γραφήν; *Hist. Eccl.* 7.15.4; cf. also 2.6.5), suggesting a single collection of several Gospels. At other times he cites 'Gospels' in the plural and attributes them to one or another of the Evangelists:

> Matthew had first preached to Hebrews, and when he was on the point of going to others he transmitted in writing in his native language the Gospel according to himself... Mark and Luke had already published the Gospel according to them, but John it is said, used all the time a message which was not written down, and at last took to writing for the following cause. The three Gospels which had been written down before were distributed to all including himself; it is said that he welcomed them and testified to their truth, but said there was only lacking to the narrative the account of what was done by Christ at first and at the beginning of the preaching (*Hist. Eccl.* 3.24.6-7; cf. 2.15.1; 3.39.15; 4.23.12; 5.8.1, 3; 5.20.4-8).

At times Eusebius can refer to other portions of the New Testament as γραφή, for example the book of Acts (*Hist. Eccl.* 2.1.8; 2.9.4), or 1 Peter, which is 'unquestioned', and one of 'the divine writings which are undisputed'; but this is to be distinguished from 2 Peter, which, although useful, is not 'canonical' (*Hist. Eccl.* 3.3.1, 2, 7; cf. 3.25.1, 6; 3.31.6; etc.). At other times Eusebius can speak of both Old and New

Testaments interchangeably as γραφή, thus giving them equal authority (*Hist. Eccl.* 4.23.6; 4.29.5; 5.28.8, 13-14; etc.). He tends to begin his thinking about the composition of the Gospels with the Evangelists producing the full Gospels (2.15.1-2; 3.39.15). There are no clear references to Gospel proto-sources in Eusebius. Rather, he goes out of his way to describe 'the apostles...paying little heed to the desire for writing books' (*Hist. Eccl.* 3.24.3).[20] Eusebius reflects the common view of that day that the only apostles who wrote were Matthew and John, who got their material directly from their own experience with Jesus. In the case of Mark and Luke, these were derived from the verbal recollection of the apostles via these disciples of Peter and Paul.

Summary and Conclusions

(1) There is a fairly close verbal agreement between the Greek text of λόγια quotations in the Fathers, and that of their Synoptic parallels. A more exact study of the Apostolic Father collection reveals a development from modest agreement to one that is quite high, as one moves further and further away from the first century. This would seem to be an indication of the increasing control the written Synoptics exercised over the reproduction of the Holy Word. The following chart makes this clear.

Apostolic Fathers' Agreement with Synoptics	
First Epistle of Clement to the Corinthians (AD 81–96)	67.9%
Epistles of Ignatius (AD 98–108)	50%
Didache (AD 100)	48%
Epistle of Barnabas (AD 90–110)	54.5%
Second Epistle of Clement to the Corinthians (AD 150)	71.8%
Polycarp, *Epistle to the Philippians* (AD 150–155)	92.2%

The over-all average in the above is 64.1%, and compares with the 86% agreement between Matthew and Luke in the double tradition.[21] On occasion, the verbal agreement between the Apostolic Fathers and

---

20. This is the translation in H.J. Lawler and J.E.L. Oulton (eds.), *Eusebius, Bishop of Caesarea: The Ecclesiastical History and the Martyrs of Palestine* (London: SPCK, 1927). K. Lake (*Eusebius: The Ecclesiastical History* [LCL, 153; London: Heinemann; Cambridge, MA: Harvard University Press, 1926], p. 251) translates this 'the apostles...cared little for attention to their style' (σπουδῆς τῆς περὶ τὸ λογογραφεῖν μικρὰν ποιούμενοι φροντίδα).

21. Baird, *Audience Criticism*, p. 61.

the Synoptics in λόγια quotations is higher than that between one Synoptic Gospel and another (e.g. *1 Clem.* 46.8). The percentage progression tends to follow a rough historical pattern. The later works agree more closely with the Synoptics in their λόγια quotations than do the earlier, although one must also account for the fact that certain individuals, like Clement of Rome, though early, have a high agreement with the Synoptics.

(2) Throughout this survey of the Christian Fathers, there is a universally high regard for Christian Scripture (γραφή) as the basis for the Church's life and doctrine, at least as far back as Irenaeus, and perhaps extending to the time of the *Epistle of Barnabas* (c. AD 100).

(3) It is clear that the teachings of Jesus as both oral and written material were the heart of Christian Scripture from the time of Clement of Rome and continuing through Eusebius, adding support to the evidence of Chapter 7 that such was also the case with the New Testament. What 'the Savior said' was the court of last appeal, the proof of divine revelation, 'the Word of the New Covenant', what Theophilus of Antioch called ἅγιος λόγος. As Metzger succinctly put it, 'Jesus' words were their own warrant'.

(4) The evidence suggests that various written collections of gospel material were available to the Fathers as far back as Clement of Rome, including the whole or portions of those that later became canonical. Many of these were probably what we have called proto-sources, with sayings or events gathered together under various rubrics such as theme, catchword, situation, etc. These various written sources seem to have vied for authority, along with some material contained in the apocryphal New Testament. The Fathers sometimes quote them indiscriminately, although at least by Irenaeus's day our four Gospels were generally accepted as canonical. They are the most often quoted, especially Matthew and then John. It would seem that the unofficial canonization of the Gospels took place within the Church before that of the rest of the New Testament.

(5) There is evidence that merely being able to say 'it is written' is a source of authority, and consequently being 'unwritten' can on occasion be synonymous with being spurious. This seems true of Papias, who, as Eusebius says, 'quoted other things also, as coming to him from unwritten tradition...strange parables of the savior and teaching of his, and some other things of a mythical character...through misrepresentation of the apostolic accounts' (*Hist. Eccl.* 3.39.11).

(6) Despite this veneration of that which was written, during this period it was not a particular set of writings but rather the teachings of Jesus as such that were most authoritative. The canonization process was that of deciding which written sources were best, among what must have been many collections, both large and small, public and private, spread around the Mediterranean world. Koester's judgment is a good one, that the Apostolic Fathers stand 'next to', rather than following the Synoptics in time.[22]

(7) I find no concern on the part of these Fathers to trace the history of the Gospel literary tradition behind the apostles. Rather, there is such an uncritical acceptance of the oral recollections of the apostles as their ultimate origin that one might almost talk of an 'apostolic barrier' to such further critical investigation. This is the kind of thing the heretics were more inclined to do; and one is reminded that Tatian, who 'spent his time with the heretics', is often called the father of modern criticism!

(8) In this material, certain redactional activity appears in handling the teaching of Jesus. λόγια are gathered together under various rubrics as suggested. There are sometimes changes in word form and order, for literary or homiletic effect. There is evidence of paraphrasing, shortening, expanding (seldom conflating) and summarizing Jesus' sayings. There is also the combining of material found in the Synoptics with that which is not, and a few actual changes in wording. That is, there is evidence of a free use of the teachings of Jesus, depending as much on the individual as on the period. All of this gives evidence of the fluidity of the λόγια tradition before it was stabilized by the widespread dissemination of written and 'canonical' Gospels. One can see here the need for some such authoritative collection, that is, one judged by all to be the most accurate. One thing, however, is clear. In this early period, the source of authority was not so much what was written as what was said by Jesus. That it was 'written' became more and more important; but the Fathers, especially in the earlier period, did not seem to make much of this distinction. They felt they could say with certainty that it was the 'Word of the Lord', whether it was written or not.

(9) Along with this free circulation of many collections of gospel data, one must also recognize on the part of these Fathers a carefulness with the Jesus material. They usually make a clear distinction between a λόγιον quotation, an allusion and a third-person description of an event or saying. They seem to want to keep the teachings of Jesus 'clean'.

---

22. Koester, *Synoptische Überlieferung*, p. 258.

Such a concern is reflected in the reference by Eusebius to Papias, 'who quoted other things also, as coming to him from unwritten tradition'. Despite the mixing of Synoptic material with non-canonical, despite the changes in wording, word form and order, despite the paraphrasing, shortening, expanding and indirect references to λόγια, the Holy Word in these Fathers comes through essentially as reported in the Synoptic Gospels. I see little evidence of theological tampering with the sayings material. There are indeed some ideas added to Synoptic theology that could be said to represent an intrusion of certain first-, second-, third-century emphases; but in every case under scrutiny here this is clearly distinguishable from the Synoptic-like material. It resides in separate sayings of Jesus or in clearly theological treatise material, but not in the changing of Synoptic teachings to suit the particular theological interest. Some dubious material is said to be part of the 'teaching of these words... the way of life' (*Did.* 1.3, 2); but this is not said to be the teaching of Jesus.

(10) One of the largest insights in this study is that it is the key words and ideas which persist. It is they that are the core of the stability of the Jesus tradition, as they are of any individual saying. Without these, the material falls apart or loses its characteristic Jesus quality and identity. This again suggests, as it has been doing throughout this book, that the pattern words and ideas of Jesus are the heart of what came to be called the Holy Word. It is these that formed the hard core of the early Christian consensus, in either oral or written form, and gave stability to the life and thought of the primitive Church.

Chapter 10

THEOLOGICAL TRAJECTORY:
IMPLICATIONS OF THE PARADIGM FOR THEOLOGY

It is now time to summarize the theological and historical implications of the data that have been presented above in order to crystallize our research into the formation process of the New Testament. The New Testament was a compound of theology and history which interacted and interwove so intimately as to be the warp and woof of the same fabric. But the evidence clearly suggests that the historical trajectory as narrative and generating process was secondary in both precedence and priority to the theological trajectory of the Word. The situation from which the New Testament emerged was the logical and very natural working out of the paradigm of the Holy Word. This is why we know so much more with certainty about the theology of and about Jesus than about his history and the details of Gospel formation. It was the dictates of that theology, the Word which Jesus proclaimed, and what the Church believed about that Holy Word and the Holy One who proclaimed it, that set the character of the Church and led it to report Jesus the way it did. The Word, as spoken, existential and incarnate, was God's vehicle of revelation; and the trajectory of that Word constitutes the very foundation principle for the development of the New Testament and the history of the Christian Church. So in approaching the historical process of New Testament formation we must reverse the usual program and begin with the most 'known' which is the Holy Word, and then proceed to the less known, the process itself; for in the analysis and understanding of Christian history, theological substance precedes historical process.

Theological Trajectory: A Living and Abiding Word

We began by quoting C.H. Dodd to the effect that the problem in historical Jesus research is 'to discover the starting point of the development which the New Testament writings exhibit'. The major insight of these pages is that the starting point of this development was not only a series of overt events of the birth, life, death and resurrection of Jesus Christ, but even more importantly the event of the Holy Word as it was proclaimed by Jesus and then by the Church, and as it was believed, preserved, interpreted, applied and experienced as Kingdom power by those who saw themselves as ministers of that Word. It was this trajectory of the Word within the Christian community that provides us with the dynamic key to the process that called the Church into being, constituted its life and thought, produced its New Testament and preserved its identity throughout those crucial first centuries.

So for us who are attempting to reconstruct the history of the early Church and the formation of the New Testament, we must first write the theology of that Church as it can be induced from the mass of New Testament and apostolic data. There is of course some episodic historical information, especially in Acts, and much can be gained from external sources; but we must begin by deducing the history of the early Church and especially the formation of the New Testament from the results of our theological induction. This kind of interactive induction and deduction is the essence of the scientific method, and so entirely appropriate to scientific historiography. Our investigation then points first of all to the following characteristics and implications of this theological trajectory.

a. *The Centrality of the Word*

The survey of the New Testament and the Christian literature of the first four centuries presents us with one clear pattern. It is the 'words of Jesus', the 'word of Jesus', or simply 'the living and abiding Word' that formed the nucleus of the life and thought of the early Church from the beginning. Patterns of key words and ideas in the teachings of Jesus gave the material the stability necessary to survive. Without them the written Gospels would have lost their focus, and the Christian kerygma its Jesus quality and identity. The person of Jesus was supremely important, but primarily as the proclaimer and incarnation of the Holy Word. Narratives of his birth, life, death and resurrection give a vitality, a humanity, a depth and eternal perspective to the Jesus story, but ultimately they are the framework for the holy words of Jesus. The cross was important, but primarily as the unfolding of the meaning and compelling power of the Word. The resurrection was important, but primarily as the validation of the Word. The Holy Spirit was important, but primarily as the empowering, chastening, directing, instructing presence of the Word. Gospel was the interpretation of the Word. Written Gospels were the formal repositories of the Word. Traditions were the application and extension of the Word into the life of the Church. Paul, the apostolic company, the Christian prophets and teachers through the years all saw themselves as custodians, proclaimers, interpreters, guardians and administrators of the Holy Word. Christian schools provided the environment in which the Word was preserved, examined, recorded and transmitted. The Fathers saw themselves primarily as transmitters, interpreters and facilitators of the Holy Word of Jesus. Neither a particular set of writings, nor a special group of individuals, but these 'commandments of Jesus' in both oral and written form would seem to have been the ultimate authority for the life and thought of the Church, and the nucleus of the New Testament.

b. *The Sanctity of the Word*
The most important thing about this Word for the early Church was its sanctity as 'Holy Word'. Seen throughout the present study, this sanctity is the function of several elements. (1) First of all, it is seen in the carefulness of the Church in distinguishing the Word of Jesus from the narrative, gospel and παράδοσις which cradled, interpreted and applied it. An important aspect of the sanctity attributed to the apostles from a very early period was their function as the 'apostolic pipeline' to the holy words of Jesus. The apostle Paul's concern to distinguish his own opinions from the 'commandments' of the Lord is his testimony to their sanctity. The activity of the Christian prophets as mediators of the παράδοσις, based on the Word, but carefully distinguished from it, is a further expression of this phenomenon.

(2) This holiness is illustrated by the rapid formalization of the λόγος in the New Testament from the 'words of Jesus' to 'the word of Jesus' to the Word which 'will not pass away', and then in later writings to the 'Holy Word'.

(3) The sanctity of this Word in the interpretation of the Church was formalized in the 'word of the Gospel' which is 'the word of truth' (Eph. 1.13), the 'word of life' (1 Jn 1.1), the 'word of God' (Acts 4.29;

Rom. 9.6), the 'word of his grace' (Acts 20.32), the 'word of reconciliation' (2 Cor. 5.19). Underlying all of the fourteen New Testament terms used to identify the gospel lie the teachings of Jesus about the Kingdom of God, which constitute the heart of the gospel's holiness.

(4) This sanctity is seen in the dependence of the entire New Testament upon the Holy Word, in the secondary character of the narrative, and in the constant return of the Church Fathers to the words of Jesus as the final test of their theological authority, and the basis of their hermeneutic. There is a close relation in the New Testament between the terms ἅγιος and ἐξουσία. Authority was a function of holiness. These were not words to be debated, but only accepted and obeyed. Any authority the apostles had within the early Church was derived from their special function as the custodians and administrators of the Holy Word.

(5) What I have called elsewhere the 'oracular quality' of Jesus' teachings illustrates this sanctity which is intrinsic to the Word itself:[1] 'heaven and earth will pass away, but my words will not pass away' (Mk 13.31), 'whoever is ashamed...of my words' (Mk 8.38), 'verily I say to you'.[2] This is reflected in his unique use of the formula ἀμὴν λέγω ὑμῖν, and in the recorded responses of his audiences: 'No one ever spoke like this'. I have identified this as a product of the nature and significance of the content of Jesus' words, the self image or consciousness of the speaker, and the conception of the speaker in the eyes of his hearers and reporters.[3]

(6) The sanctity of this Word was a function of its content, the center of which in the teachings of Jesus was the sovereignty of God. Irenaeus put it succinctly describing the Gospel as that 'in which is recorded the doctrine regarding God' (*Adv. Haer.* 2.4.1). Paul referred interchangeably to 'the gospel of Christ' and 'the gospel of God'. John focused his narrative theology upon the Word who 'was God'. Mark introduced Jesus 'preaching the gospel of God, and saying, "The time is

---

1. J.A. Baird, *A Comparative Analysis of the Gospel Genre: The Synoptic Mode and Its Uniqueness* (Lewiston: Edwin Mellen Press, 1991), pp. 33-37.

2. See J.A. Baird, *The Justice of God in the Teaching of Jesus* (London: SCM Press; Philadelphia: Westminster, 1963), pp. 237-53; *idem, Rediscovering the Power of the Gospels: Jesus' Theology of the Kingdom* (Wooster, OH: Iona Press, 1982), pp. 127-30.

3. Baird, *Comparative Analysis*, p. 33.

fulfilled, and the Kingdom of God is at hand; repent and believe in the gospel'" (1.14-15). Jesus summarized his word by instructing his disciples to 'seek first the Kingdom of God and his righteousness' (Mt. 6.33). In whatever ways we have examined the Holy Word, in the teaching of Jesus, underlying all the terms used throughout the New Testament to describe the gospel, in the thought of his disciples, Paul, the early Christian schools and those Fathers who represented the early Christian consensus, the focus was ultimately upon the Word of and about the sovereign and Holy God. And whether we are talking about the Holy Word of Jesus, the narratives of his birth, death and resurrection, the gospel, the apostles, the traditions, the work of the Scripture schools or the sermons and treatises of the Fathers, it is all as an expression of the Word of God made flesh. Ultimately, the source of all holiness is God himself, who is the very essence of holiness, whose holiness is a description of the fullness of his being and nature, and especially of that which makes men and women fear and tremble and stand in awe before him.[4]

(7) This sanctity was furthermore a product of the spiritual character of the Word itself. Jesus described the Kingdom as not only a word to be understood, but a presence to be accepted, a seed to be received within the soil of the soul.[5] In these fourteen words used to describe the gospel there is a complementary tension between the rational and the spiritual, between the Word as heard and understood, and the Word as an experience of the power of God. This reflects the growing awareness of the Church that the Word of Jesus about God and his Kingdom, the power of God as indwelling Spirit, and the presence of the risen Christ were somehow inseparable in him who 'came to cast fire upon the earth' (Lk. 12.49).[6]

(8) The sanctity of the word is also derived from its source in Jesus, whom John and Peter, reflecting the view of the Church, called 'the Holy One' (Jn 6.69; Acts 3.14). Jesus himself was the source of authority within this Word. It was his conscious identity with God and the Kingdom which caused some to complain that 'you teach yourself', and

---

4. Baird, *The Justice of God in the Teaching of Jesus*, p. 177; see also *idem*, *Rediscovering the Power of the Gospels*, Chapter 3.

5. Baird, *The Justice of God in the Teaching of Jesus*, p. 177; *idem*, *Rediscovering the Power of the Gospels*, p. 98.

6. Baird, *Rediscovering the Power of the Gospels*, p. 124.

drove others to their knees in awe and reverence.[7] So it is perfectly consistent that John should bring his treatment of the λόγος to incarnate focus in Jesus Christ. λόγος Christology is powerfully inherent within this entire Christian concept of the Holy Word as the inevitable extension of this normative center of Christian faith and life.

And so the quest for the historical Jesus ultimately becomes a theological one. For behind the Holy Word was the record of Jesus' consciousness of a special relationship with God, and a special mission to perform.[8] Out of this sense of his own holiness, he taught as no one had ever done before.[9] And he was remembered by a growing number of adoring disciples in ways that made his teachings and then his life immediately authoritative and normative for the followers of 'the way'. The revealer of the Holy Word is the Holy One, and the sanctity of that Word is inescapably a function of Christology.

c. *The Consensus of the Word*
The constant pointing back to the words of Jesus within the New Testament as throughout the Church until the time of Eusebius clearly reveals a basic theological consensus within that community.[10] In

7. Baird, *Rediscovering the Power of the Gospels*, pp. 127-30.
8. Baird, *Rediscovering the Power of the Gospels*, pp. 117-40.
9. See Baird, *Comparative Analysis*, pp. 127-43.
10. As Schubert Ogden comments ('Sources of Religious Authority in Liberal Protestantism: For Van A. Harvey on his 50th Birthday', *JAAR* 44 [1976], pp. 403-16): 'It is not Scripture as such but the earliest stratum of Christian witness, the so-called *kerygma,* that is the real canon of Christian community'. See also *idem*, 'The Authority of Scripture for Theology', *Int* 30 (1976), pp. 242-61, esp. pp. 258-60. Ogden's instincts are, I think, on target; but in my opinion he does not go far enough in centering this Jesus *kerygma* on the words of the historical Jesus himself. Jeremias is closer to the evidence when he insists that there is a connection between all major New Testament themes and the proclamation of Jesus. The recent literature on this subject reveals a sharp division as to whether or not a distinction can be made between the core of the tradition and its later elaboration. Nils Dahl would agree that such a distinction should be made. See N.A. Dahl, 'Kerygma and History', in H.K. McArthur (ed.), *In Search of the Historical Jesus* (New York: Charles Scribner's Sons, 1969), pp. 131-38, esp. p. 132. See also H. Anderson, *Jesus and Christian Origins* (New York: Oxford University Press, 1964), p. 90, writing about William Manson. Also H. Riesenfeld, *The Gospel Tradition* (Philadelphia: Fortress Press, 1970); A.B. Barnett, 'Jesus as Theologian', in A. Wikgren (ed.), *Early Christian Origins* (Chicago: Quadrangle Books, 1961), pp. 16-23. Those in the form-critical tradition tend to reject this thesis. See Anderson's (*Jesus and Christian Origins*,

10. Implications of the Paradigm for Theology

Chapter 3 we identified a layer of Christian consensus in the interweaving, interconnected and often interchangeable usage within the New Testament of fourteen terms having a common theological coherence. These identified the gospel as a stable body of material, widely understood and consistently accepted. Their consensus was based upon that deposit of Jesus' teaching and focused upon the patterns of key words, phrases and ideas within them as found in their most widely accepted form in the canonical Synoptic Gospels.

I have dealt at length with the compatibility of various verbal and theological patterns within the Synoptics in my book on audience criticism.[11] Elsewhere I have noted the theological congeniality of the Synoptic teachings of Jesus with the theology of John and Paul.[12] Certainly some such consensus existed in Paul's mind in the parallels in Galatians between fulfilling 'the law of Christ', being taught 'the word',

---

p. 99) three objections. Geza Vermes (*Jesus the Jew* [New York: Macmillan, 1974]) points to the miracles as the center of Jesus' ministry rather than his teachings. His attempt to identify Jesus as a charismatic Jewish rabbi like Hanina Ben Dosa is instructive, but misses the point. There were certainly healing incidents, but the textual evidence shows Jesus trying to avoid this function. The evidence of great crowds who wanted him to do this, and even his disciples, supports Vermes's description of Galilee as a place where charismatic rabbis were wont to practice the healing arts. But a more careful reading of the Synoptics shows Jesus focusing on the Holy Word, and avoiding this popular Jewish image. The crowds misunderstood him then just as Vermes is doing now. If one denies Jesus any deeper significance, then what is left is a charismatic Jew who strangely avoided that healing function. The fact that many in the Church looked constantly for 'signs' is a further indication of the Jewish expectation, and Jesus also rejected this. It is part of the understanding of religion as *mizvoth* which Jesus soundly rejected; but Vermes ignores most of this evidence. W. Kelber (*The Oral and the Written Gospel* [Philadelphia: Fortress Press, 1983], p. 30), quoting E. Schillebeeckx, insists that we can no longer start from 'the single *kerygma*' of a Jerusalem mother church as we used to. 'One must declare unworkable the model of a tightly knit community of early Christians committed to the preservation and transmission of a single Gospel.' This is only partly true. The evidence presented here for the Holy Word consensus refines this 'flat' statement and shows that it is more complicated than this. Within this admitted complexity, there is a stable core. David Aune (*Prophecy in Early Christianity and the Ancient Mediterranean World* [Grand Rapids: Eerdmans, 1983], p. 200) is proceeding in the right direction. I go further to describe those 'accepted customs and norms' he talks about which lay behind the prophecy and the teaching of the early Church.

11. J.A. Baird, *Audience Criticism and the Historical Jesus* (Philadelphia: Westminster Press, 1967).

12. Baird, *Rediscovering the Power of the Gospels*.

keeping 'the law' and walking 'by this rule' (τῷ κανόνι; Gal. 6.2-16). This is what Metzger calls 'the basic Christian tradition recognized as normative by the church',[13] and is what seems to have prevailed. Metzger sees the ecclesiastical canon evident in the Church as early as the *Martyrdom of Polycarp*. My evidence suggests that the concept of 'Canon' represented the working out of the logic of the Holy Word of the gospel, and can be traced back to the person of Jesus himself.

How exactly compatible the various expressions of this Holy Word were within the Synoptics, between the Synoptics and the rest of the New Testament, or within the writings of the Apostolic and Ante Nicene Fathers is an important critical question. The evidence from early Christian 'heresies', the witness of the apocryphal New Testament, and the theological battles involving the various councils of the Church, all point to differences in understanding and emphasis in the handling of the Word. But the evidence also points to a basic continuity of understanding, and to the words of Jesus as the self-conscious core of that consensus which held the New Testament together, and was the stabilizing center of the life and thought of the Church from the first to the fourth century. Consensus within diversity seems to have been the picture.

d. *The Paradigm of the Word*

We are now at the point where we can draw together the four concentric circles of the λόγος trajectory as this 'living and abiding word' moved out from the words of Jesus in ever widening circles to include the narrative context, the gospel interpretation and the παράδοσις application of that Holy Word. All of this was going on concurrently, with movement from the Holy Word to narrative, to gospel to tradition, as the growing needs of the Church demanded more and more exposition, interpretation and application. The determination to canonize the New Testament put a formal limit on this expansion, but through the years the needs and concerns of the Church as it faced the exigencies of its tortuous history prompted a continued expansion: of narrative in the apocryphal New Testament, of gospel in the ever-expanding theology of the Church, and παράδοσις in the escalating traditions, which eventually rivaled all the rest in abundance and importance. The one stabilizing element seems to have been the Holy Word, which at least until the fourth century, the terminus of this study,

---

13. Baird, *Rediscovering the Power of the Gospels*, p. 125.

10. Implications of the Paradigm for Theology

was the center and focus of the life and thought of the Church. One might picture it in the following way:

    Tradition (παράδοσις)
      Gospel (εὐαγγέλιον)
        Narrative (διήγησις)
          Word (λόγος)
            New Testament (διαθήκη καινή)

It is this theological-historical paradigm which is the chief product of our lengthy research project. Every portion of the New Testament represents one or the other type of material. It is not a matter of different books, but of different strains of material, concentrated in certain books, but running throughout the New Testament. We have seen the very 'natural' way in which these theological circles have radiated out from their center in Jesus, 'the Holy One'. The teachings of Jesus are the focal point, the 'starting point of the development'. The narrative context of birth, life, death and resurrection, the importance of the audience to whom he addressed his words, the many ties to actual events, all point to the character of the Gospels as elaborate 'biographical apophthegms'. The narrative was important in its own right and as a framework for the Word; but the Word was central, and in the life and person of Jesus in presenting that Word the early Church saw the profoundest mystery of the incarnation. As John put (1.1), 'In the beginning was the word'.[14]

But this Word about God and his Kingdom within that historical context immediately demanded interpretation; and throughout the New Testament we find many efforts to understand and explain the 'mystery' of this gospel, chief among them the epistles of Paul, the Gospel of John, the letter to the Hebrews and the Apocalypse.

Such natural theological progression then led to the activities of the Christian prophets and others in creatively applying this Word and gospel to the practical problems of the Church, ethics, liturgy and Church discipline. Such παράδοσις rapidly multiplied, from Jesus' own efforts as codified in the sermon on the mount, to Paul's various statements about such matters, to the concentration on such in the Pastoral and Catholic Epistles, and to a later compendium in the *Didache*. All of this was part of the perfectly natural and inevitable

---

14. I am not intending to present here a new interpretation of the source of the λόγος doctrine in John, but the possibilities here are intriguing.

progress of the theological extension of the Word. This sequence is more observable looking back upon the total picture than it was a matter of conscious awareness while it was going on. But even as one can detect years later certain movement and direction in history, so in the theological history of the Word one can observe subtle patterns forming a 'trajectory' from early to late, from simple to complex, from oral to written, from Word to narrative, to gospel, to παράδοσις within this evangelical stream.

These four basic theological-historical strata differ from each other in ways that set them apart. They differ functionally in their relation to the Word, as exposition, context, interpretation and application. They differ in their emphasis, whether on Jesus' word about the Kingdom of God, or the narratives of life, death and resurrection, or the word about the risen Christ and the redemption found in him, or the function of the Word in providing an ethical framework for the life of the Church. They differ in their sanctity, with the Holy Word elevated beyond debate, and then the gospel, over which there is some conflict in authority, especially with Paul, but also within other portions of the New Testament. Then came the παράδοσις, over which considerable disagreement is revealed in the New Testament.

These four circles of the extension of the Word also differ in their authority, with the Word as primary, then the gospel, then the traditions of the Church, probably what Clement of Alexandria meant by 'the secondary constitutions of the apostles' (*Strom.* 1.1; cf. Chapter 5). Paul summarized it accurately, describing the Church 'built upon the foundation of the apostles and the prophets, Christ Jesus himself being the chief cornerstone' (Eph. 2.20). The Church was the 'body of Christ', within which God has appointed 'first apostles, second prophets...' (1 Cor. 12.28). The apostles were the chief custodians of the Word, the prophets were primarily concerned with the traditions, but all deferred in their interpretation and application to Jesus as the source and very incarnation of the Word itself.

They differ finally in the process of their origin and preservation, with a movement from oral to written, from primitive Jesus sayings to the activity of apostles, prophets, Christian scribes, ministers of the word and schools of the apostles and later Scripture specialists in preserving, recording, editing, expounding and applying that Word. We shall say more about this historical process below.

10. Implications of the Paradigm for Theology

But despite these various differences, there is a core of unity within all four blocks of New Testament material that derives from their absolute fixation upon the 'words... word... WORD' of Jesus about the Kingdom of God, and this continued throughout the Church at least until the time of Eusebius. They are one in their most fundamental theological orientation, and this is the basis of that consensus to which we have referred. As Papias correctly observed, this was 'a living and abiding voice'.

It is this paradigm of the Word that not only gives us the starting point and primary control of the development which produced the Synoptics, the New Testament and the early Church, but also is the guiding principle in the interaction of the early Church's historical recollection and its theological conviction. The history of the early Church was the history of the dynamic shifting of emphasis, struggle for survival, degeneration, continuation, formalization, extension and at times prostitution of this basic paradigm. Its theological 'ripple-effect' continued unabated throughout the history of the Church, and continues to this day in the ever-expanding attempts to exploit the narrative, elaborate the gospel and multiply the applications of its παράδοσις. The constant danger throughout Christian history has been that the Holy Word of Jesus would be smothered in the process. But all of the evidence we have seen points to the determination of the central leadership of the Church from Jesus to Eusebius to maintain in its theology and life the centrality and controlling significance of that Word.

e. *The Canon within the Canon*

Such an approach raises again the old question as to whether or not one can find a 'canon within the canon'. There has been a recent revival of this concept on the continent where the second canon is the standard or center within the New Testament. It 'Means to find in Scripture a principle of hermeneutic that enables one to draw a line of demarcation between what is authoritative within the canon and what is not'.[15] Werner Kümmel attempts this, which he finds in three areas: in the message and figure of Jesus, in the oldest kerygma which explains the

---

15. B.M. Metzger, *The Canon of the New Testament: Its Origin, Development, and Significance* (Oxford: Clarendon Press, 1987), p. 276. See I. Lonning, *Kanon im Kanon: Zum dogmatischen Grundlagen Problem des neutestamentlichen Kanons* (Forschungen zur Geschichte und Lehre des Protestantismus, 43; Oslo: Universitetsforlaget; Munich: Chr. Kaiser Verlag, 1972).

significance of the death and resurrection, and in the theology of Paul.[16] For Herbert Braun, the canon is located in the preaching of Jesus, in Paul and in the Fourth Gospel.[17] Willi Marxsen believes we come closer to it in the proto-sources behind the Synoptics, but for him the real test of canonicity is a more existential one.[18] Bruce Metzger recognizes some differences, but argues for the diversity of all twenty-seven books as necessary to the canon. The divergences are often the result of a specific message to a specific situation, and these are healthy. Krister Stendahl rejects entirely the idea of a canon within the canon, calling it a 'hermeneutical mirage'. He sees the canon as a key ring and each of the New Testament books as one key on the ring.[19]

The evidence of this study points to a more complex answer to this question, which incorporates both sides of the debate. We need a more adequate model than 'canon within the canon'. The very word canon tends to be misleading and creates an artificial dialectic, depending more on later ecclesiastical conceptions of canonicity than on the witness of the primitive texts. The paradigm of the Word as developed above both supports and opens up the concept of canonicity in ways that provide for both a center and a perimeter, both continuity and diversity. It cuts across all of the twenty-seven books from quite different angles, and shows a new kind of dialectic emerging out of the natural logic of the Word and the historical environment in which it arose. It is not so much a matter of certain books, but of certain types of material which arranged themselves quite naturally in a hierarchy as we have described, and which then were contained in certain books whose authority was based upon this deeper paradigm. If one must use these terms, then the data of this entire study point to the Holy Word of Jesus, in all the ways we have described it above, as the canon within the canon. The

16. W.G. Kümmel, 'Notwendigkeit und Grenze der neutestamentlichen Kanons', *ZTK* 47 (1950), pp. 227-313. See also *idem*, *The Theology of the New Testament according to its Major Witnesses: Jesus, Paul, and John* (Nashville: Abingdon Press, 1973).

17. H. Braun, 'Hebt die heutige neutestamentliche Forschung den Kanon auf?', in *Gesammelte Studien zum Neuen Testament und seiner Umwelt* (Tübingen: Mohr Siebeck, 1962), pp. 310-24.

18. W. Marxsen, *Introduction to the New Testament: An Approach to its Problems* (trans. G. Buswell; Philadelphia: Fortress Press, 1968), p. 282. See Metzger's rebuttal (*Canon of the New Testament*, pp. 275-80).

19. K. Stendahl, *The Bible as Document and Guide* (Philadelphia: Fortress Press, 1984), pp. 55-68.

immediate, natural and consistent way in which this Word was enhanced with narrative, gospel and παράδοσις, however, places these all within the larger canon which became the New Testament. It was the sanctity and authority of that Word which provided the 'canonical' element, which was a product not of the decision of any ecclesiastical body, but of the intrinsic character of this as the Holy Word of the Holy One.

It has long been recognized that conformity to the 'rule of faith' was one of the three basic prerequisites for canonization. Metzger defines this as 'the congruity of a given document with the basis of Christian tradition recognized as normative by the church'.[20] My further refinement of this would be to suggest that this 'rule of faith' was a compound of gospel and tradition, with the Holy Word at its center.

The centrality of the Holy Word is the basis for all the books in the larger canon, and did not shift for at least the first three hundred years. This then recognizes a center, but places it within the expanding witness of the New Testament, whose canonizing was a function of the quality of the material, its proximity in time to the person of Jesus, the witness of the apostles, the testimony of the Holy Spirit, the practical necessities of the Church to 'fix' this witness as a hedge against encroaching heresy, but most of all the fidelity of these twenty-seven books to the Holy Word of Jesus.

We must therefore analyze the problem in a different way, for these very twenty-seven books present us with artificial divisions, which confuse the issue. The canonicity concept I suggest was first of all one of Word, narrative, gospel and παράδοσις, that is, of the various ways in which the theological basis of the Church was preserved and implemented; for in this particular Christian history, theological substance precedes process. This was the product of the inevitable logic of the Word. That it was contained in certain books was secondary, and more an accident of history than of canonical necessity. We do indeed need all twenty-seven books in the New Testament, but only because they are the best expressions of various aspects of the paradigm of the Word to come out of that early period. The canonicity of the Word then suggests that, within the New Testament, there is not only consensus but diversity, and also a scale of relative authority the closer any particular book is to the canonizing center, the Holy Word.

---

20. Metzger, *Canon of the New Testament*, p. 251.

f. *The Torah Parallel*

This then leads us to suggest another model which is more congenial to the New Testament textual evidence, coming as it did originally out of a community dominated not by ecclesiastical 'canons', but by the Old Testament, the rabbinic schools and the Hebrew orientation of that earliest Church.[21] It was not until later that the consensus of the Word began to be called κανών. The earliest record comes from Paul (Gal. 6.16), who is urging his readers to 'walk by this rule' (κανόνι), describing what he calls 'the law of Christ', or the 'word' (6.2, 6, 13). This was consistent with the later use of λόγος and παράδοσις but was not a common usage.[22] Birger Gerhardsson points in the direction of this Torah parallel when he likens the teachings of Jesus to the sayings of the rabbis in the Mishnah.[23] My own evidence suggests that within that highly charged Hebrew situation, the Holy Word of Jesus was comparable not so much to the sayings of the rabbis in the oral tradition, as to the Word of God in the written Torah. As I have demonstrated elsewhere, the quality of the sayings of Jesus is on a significantly different level from that of the oral Torah of the rabbis. Jesus spoke of God, his Kingdom and himself in such theological proximity that we are not surprised to find the closest parallels to the 'oracular mood' of his words in the God sayings in the Old Testament.[24] The Synoptics are closer to the written than to the oral Torah, closer to the Old Testament than to the Mishnah. One might diagram the comparative relationships in this Torah Parallel as follows:

New Testament	Old Testament	Talmud
Holy Word	Torah	Torah
Gospel	Nabi'im	Midrashim
Tradition	Kethubim	Mishnah

The process of Old Testament canonization and that of New Testament formation was going on at exactly the same time in the first century as was that of the finalization of the Mishnah; and it would appear that the same 'feeling' for this dynamic relationship between the various strata of Old Testament and rabbinic material is evident within

21. See Baird, *Comparative Analysis*, Chapter 1.
22. See Baird, *Comparative Analysis*, Chapters 1, 4.
23. B. Gerhardsson, *Memory and Manuscript: Oral Tradition and Written Transmission in Rabbinic Judaism and Early Christianity* (Lund: W.K.C. Gleerup; Copenhagen: Munksgaard, 1961), pp. 209, 325.
24. Baird, *Comparative Analysis*, Chapter 4.

this Hebraic Christian community from the many hints at a Christian Torah.

Jesus seems to have had some such awareness in mind: 'You have heard it said... but I say unto you' (Mt. 5. 21-48); 'I am come not to destroy the law... but to fulfill it' (Mt. 5.17). It is commonly observed that the Gospel of Matthew in its editorial arrangement presents Jesus as a new Moses, structuring his teaching into five great discourses in a roughly pentateuchal fashion. We see this reflected in the incident of the transfiguration, where Jesus is pictured in the succession of Moses and the prophets (Mt. 17.3), and echoed in John: 'We have found him of whom Moses in the law and also the prophets wrote' (1.45). The language of the last supper reflects such thinking with the use of the term διαθήκη (καινὴ διαθήκη) to describe the blood of Jesus (Lk. 22.20). Paul then picked up this Torah language and described the gospel as the 'new covenant' (1 Cor. 3.16; 11.25) and the 'law of the Spirit of life in Christ Jesus' (Rom. 8.2; 10.4; 13.10), followed by the author of Hebrews where the new covenant is couched in more priestly language.

The distinction made within the early Jewish community between written and oral Torah is the same made by the early Church between the Word and the traditions, which, like the rabbinic *Halakah*, interpreted and applied the Word. The παράδοσις within Christian circles was oral law even as the Holy Word was the New Torah. Harald Riesenfeld's insight is close to the mark: 'The words and deeds of Jesus, although originally transmitted by word of mouth, were conceived from a very early date to be the New Torah, and hence as the word of God of the new eschatological covenant'.[25] It is therefore no surprise that very early we find the model for Christian worship to be the pattern of the Jewish synagogue, with exposition followed by the reading of Old Testament Scripture and the reciting or the reading of διδαχὴ ἀποστόλων, a parallel term for the gospel, based as it was upon the teachings of Jesus (Acts 2.42).[26]

25. Riesenfeld, *The Gospel Tradition*, p. 22; Baird, *Comparative Analysis*, Chapter 1; J.C. Meagher (*The Way of the Word: The Beginning and the Establishing of Christian Understanding* [New York: Seabury Press, 1975], pp. 18, 184, appendix B) sees 1 Jn 2.24 as 'the first commandment of the law of Christian thought'.

26. See Riesenfeld, *The Gospel Tradition*, Chapter 4. C.H. Dodd (*Gospel and Law: The Relation of Faith and Ethics in Early Christianity* [New York: Columbia University Press, 1951]) observed years ago that διδαχή and διδασκαλία are more appropriate renderings of *Torah* than is νόμος.

But once we have said this, we must beware of typological models that risk doing violence to the living, unstructured, somewhat amorphous data of history. Jesus is described seeing himself as greater than Moses (Mt. 5.21), greater than the Temple (Mt. 12.6), greater than Solomon (Lk. 11.31), Lord of the Sabbath (Mt. 12.8).[27] As Gerhardsson and others have reminded us, for the early disciples the teachings of Jesus were understood as inspired revelation (*bat qol*) from one who was more than a rabbi, more than a prophet. This is consistent with the evidence of Chapter 1, and further illustrates what I have documented elsewhere, that the 'oracular' words of Jesus are most closely parallel not to those of the rabbis in the Mishnah, but to the words of God in the Old Testament, and especially in Ezekiel.[28]

Furthermore, as we have seen, the Holy Word was understood by Jesus and the Church, not as an extension of Torah as law, but as the fulfillment of the revelation of the prophets, for whom there was a 'new law', written upon the fleshy tablets of the heart (Jer. 31.33).[29] This is what Paul called 'the new law of the Spirit of life in Christ' which set him free from the 'law of sin and death' (Rom. 8.2). Despite this use of Torah language, both Jesus and the early apostles warned against substituting the old legalism with another legalism based on what Jesus called 'the leaven of the Pharisees' (Mk 8.15) and Paul a 'yoke of slavery' (Gal. 5.1). Actually, the similarity of the paradigm of the Word to the three-fold division within the Old Testament is a later typological insight, probably not seen by those who put together the New Testament. There is a certain awkwardness in the parallel, with the Holy Word in the New Testament paralleling both law and prophets, and involving the various books from a theological rather than an historical, even literary, direction as in the Old Testament.

What then of the New Torah? Given the basic differences between Judaism and early Christianity, and between these two models, one could say there is a certain 'natural affinity' between them that pointed toward the canonizing of the New Testament in Christianity's own 'Jamnia', whose location and details have been lost to historical view. As we look back, what we see is probably a very 'natural', unconscious sense of a New Torah emerging in the minds of many who were trained in the

---

27. See Baird, *Rediscovering the Power of the Gospels*, p. 129.

28. Baird, *Comparative Analysis*, Chapter 4; Gerhardsson, *Memory and Manuscript*, p. 209.

29. See Baird, *The Justice of God in the Teaching of Jesus*.

Torah mentality of that day. That is the way they thought, but it took time for a self-conscious Christian Torah or 'canon' to emerge. The very nature of the Holy Word both prompted and resisted this Torah parallel: prompted it because of the sanctity of the Word and the Jewish mentality of early Christianity; resisted it because of the intrinsic opposition of that Word to the legalism of the synagogue tradition, and the determination of the early Church to go beyond its Jewish roots to the New Torah of life in Christ. With these reservations, the Holy Word really is similar to the Pentateuch, the gospel to the prophetic material of the Old Testament, and παράδοσις to the Writings. The point is that the Christian Torah like its Hebrew counterpart had a center and concentric extensions with varying degrees of authority. Most importantly, for Christians, the Holy Word was parallel to the Word of God in Torah, and constituted the starting point and primary control of the development which produced the guiding paradigm for the interaction of the early Church's theological conviction and historical recollection.

g. *The Trajectory as Basic 'Shift'*
From time to time in this study we have pointed to a trajectory in the theological process within the early Church in the movement from 'the words of Jesus' to the 'word of Jesus', to 'the Word', to the 'Holy Word' of and about Jesus. This represented a subtle shift from a less formal to a more formal treatment of the teachings of Jesus, from the oral to the written form, from the Hebrew to the Greek mode of reporting history,[30] from the reporting of the words of Jesus to their theological interpretation in the gospel and their practical and ethical application in the παράδοσις.

The difference between Word and gospel begins with the distinction between the 'memoir' (teaching of Jesus, narrative) and διήγησις (sermon, interpretation, application). The shift continues with the movement from the Word as spoken to the Word as Spirit and power. We have also seen a shift from the Synoptics, where the Word and the narrative are closely related, yet clearly separate, to the later New Testament where the Holy Word and holy narrative have become merged into the narrative theology of John, and to Paul where Jesus' emphasis on the Kingdom of God has become the theology of the crucified and risen Christ. More subtle movement can possibly be seen from the earlier attention to 'realistic' history in the Synoptics, to the

---

30. Baird, *Comparative Analysis*, p. 23.

later stylized and legendary narratives in the apocryphal New Testament, but this raises critical questions which would cloud the issue at this point.[31] Primarily the 'shift' was one of emphasis from the words of Jesus to the words about Jesus, to the words that apply the Holy Word to the needs of the first-century Church. We have seen this in the broadening conception of the λόγος, but without losing its hold on the holy words of Jesus. We have seen it in the growing emphasis on the death and resurrection of Jesus, and the doctrine of the atonement which developed within the gospel to understand it. I have tried to show elsewhere that the basic ingredients for that early atonement theology were indeed contained in the Synoptic teachings of Jesus;[32] but one would have to admit considerable extension and elaboration of those ideas in Paul and Hebrews, as well, perhaps, as in the Gospel of John. We have also seen this shift in the development of the παράδοσις to include a wider and wider list of practical and theological concerns.

The causes of this shift were no doubt many and varied, reflecting the changing conditions and needs of those early years. The author of Hebrews reflects this in his determination to lead his readers beyond 'the elementary doctrine of Christ and go on to maturity'. For him the point (8.1) was to deepen their understanding of the work of Christ as mediator and High Priest, to relate his new covenant to Torah (10.1), to understand the meaning of faith (11.1) and the place of Jesus as its 'pioneer and perfecter' (12.2). Some of this shift was inevitably due to the death and resurrection of Jesus, the novelty of the gospel and the practical needs of a Church developing within a hostile environment. Immature Christians needed to 'grow up' (Eph. 4.15) in their understanding and ability to function as followers of a dramatically new way of life. Some changes were no doubt due to the influence of dominant personalities like Paul, John, Peter or the author of Hebrews. Some could have been due to cultural influences, but such cause and effect is harder to document. From this theological perspective, it would seem that this trajectory of the Word was the perfectly logical, natural, and so inevitable working out of the doctrine of the Word of God within this community of the Word.

The question of how successful the earliest Church was in abiding by the norm of this Holy Word would involve a detailed comparison of the

---

31. See what I call 'the degeneration of the Synoptic Mode' in the first three centuries. Baird, *A Comparative Analysis*, pp. 101-26.

32. Baird, *Rediscovering the Power of the Gospels*, pp. 141-48.

Synoptics and the rest of the New Testament, and the theology of the first few centuries, and that is too large a subject for this book. What we have documented is the self-conscious *intention* of the Church to be true to the words of Jesus, their belief that they had done so, and the theological evidence for this conviction in the consensus of the Church around the Holy Word. The 'shift' as we have described it seems to have been more a matter of emphasis, style and vocabulary than of substance, and was in this way in tension with the sanctity of the Word, and as such was essentially part of the 'trajectory' of that Word. The further out we move in history from this ground zero, the more diversity we have observed, but always in tension with the consensus around the Word, and the determination to retain its purity. My own assessment of this shift contained in another publication is that most of what is made explicit in the gospel was already implicit and partially explicit in the words, assumptions and actions of the Synoptic Jesus. His own self-understanding was the bridge between the words 'of' Jesus and those 'about' Jesus in the gospel and παράδοσις of the Church.³³

Hermeneutical Application of the Paradigm

What is the guiding principle in the interaction of the early Church's historical recollection and its theological conviction? This hermeneutical question which we raised at the beginning of the study needs now to be answered in the light of all that has emerged in our research. As I see it, several hermeneutical principles have surfaced from these data. (1) First and foremost is that which guided the early Church through those difficult days when the Christian message was initially being formulated, interpreted, applied and proclaimed: the words of Jesus are the proper beginning point and standard for the life and theology of the Church. It is in the key words, phrases and ideas of the Holy Word of Jesus that the Church found its consensus and Christian theology its starting point. In the internal debates over doctrine and tradition, the principle that resonated with that 'living and abiding voice' was enunciated by Polycarp in his letter to the Philippians (*Phil.* 7.1-2): 'Whoever perverts the oracles of the Lord... let us turn back to the word which was delivered to us in the beginning'. When in doubt, go to the Holy Word.

---

33. Baird, *The Justice of God in the Teaching of Jesus*; idem, *Rediscovering the Power of the Gospels*.

(2) The substance within this first principle was that the sovereignty and justice (righteousness) of God are the heart of the Word, and that is the place to begin one's thinking about all aspects of Christian faith and life.[34] It is here that the Church began its understanding of the birth, life, death and resurrection of Jesus. It is the person and nature of God that is the beginning and focus of the 'gospel of God'. It is the Spirit of God that informs and empowers that λόγος, which is more than a spoken or intellectualized tool of communication. It is the sovereignty and justice of God that are the bases of the Christian παράδοσις. And so it is that theology is properly described as the understanding of the Word of God.

(3) This means then that Christology is an extension of the doctrine of God, whether we are talking about Jesus' statements about himself in relation to the Kingdom, or the Church's description of him as the Word made flesh. Any characterization of Jesus that does not begin with his Word about God risks the trivialization of the Gospel. However important may be the historical life of Jesus, any attempt to understand him by beginning with the historical process runs the risk of never really arriving at the heart of the Word made flesh.

(4) The hermeneutical implication of the above is that the working out in the gospel of the theological implications of the Holy Word and the Holy One for the life of the Church, bringing together the Word, life, death and resurrection with the faith experience of the community, however inspired by the Spirit, is a human exercise that stands in a secondary relation to the primary revelation of God in this Holy Word.

(5) The further extension of this logic suggests that the παράδοσις application of the gospel to the practical problems of the Church and the lives of its members must be an extension of the theology of the Word if it is to be true to the Church's primary witness. Any Christian ethic that begins not with the Word, but with some cultural, parochial or historical congeries, however important they may be to the resolution of the problem, risks the distortion of the ethic of the Word into something remade in the image of those very factors.

(6) The gospel and especially the παράδοσις represent the theological and ethical contextualization of the Word. They are both needed, but the priorities must be maintained to preserve the original revelation in Jesus. The danger is that we canonize this contextualization and parochialize the universality of Jesus' word of the Kingdom. The momentum toward

---

34. See Baird, *The Justice of God in the Teaching of Jesus*; idem, *Rediscovering the Power of the Gospels*.

10. Implications of the Paradigm for Theology

parochialization was begun early, formalized within the ecclesiastical canons and traditions of the Church, and continues to this day. The universal message of the Gospel became the kind of exclusivist theology that has been the curse of Church division through the centuries, as the Church periodically found itself clinging to an outmoded theology and ethic, imposing an inquisition, burning a Servetus, persecuting a Galileo, or distorting Christian theology in terms of some culturally or temporally determined popular movement. What is needed is to distinguish the Torah of the Word from the gospel and its παράδοσις, and relativize those aspects of the New Testament, Christian theology and ethics in general which are tied to the particularities of either the first century or the present century. The distinction is essential for an adequate hermeneutic; for whenever παράδοσις becomes gospel, or gospel becomes the Holy Word, then Christian ethics and theology are in danger of creating some form of distortion. The key is the closeness to the Holy Word of Jesus, and the early Church seems to have been concerned to preserve this all-important distinction. That is why the New Testament gospel and παράδοσις were canonized in those twenty-seven books, and why other candidates were excluded. The hermeneutical need here is to liberate the universality of the Holy Word, to de-parochialize it in the awareness that in the New Torah of the Christian faith we have a focal point of divine revelation that is unique to Christianity as a light to the world, transcending the parochial entrapments of time and human circumstance, and freeing the gospel for the universal and eternal present to which it is committed.[35]

---

35. See Baird, *Rediscovering the Power of the Gospels*, pp. 77-78.

Chapter 11

HISTORICAL TRAJECTORY:
IMPLICATIONS OF THE PARADIGM FOR HISTORY

The question now is what does all this say to the historical dimension of the Word? If the Word does indeed precede the process in the history of the Christian faith, then what can we learn from the Holy Word about the historical process of its survival and proclamation? What this line of approach says initially is that the theological trajectory as detailed above was the generating force and single most determining agent for the formation of the early Church and for the New Testament as its basic document and most definitive product. Sifting through the mass of evidence for this theological fundament, there are two types of data which emerge as having relevance for our understanding of the historical trajectory that actually produced the Church and its documents. The first is evidence for the historical process, and the second is that for or against the historical authenticity of that process as described or implied by our evidence. The one is a matter of historiography; the other of epistemology. These are two distinct ways of approaching the historical question, but they are also inevitably interrelated as the two sides of the larger investigation of history. I shall treat them separately, but with this interrelationship in mind. This is not intended to be a complete exposition of either the process or its validation, but rather what the evidence of this book contributes to that history.

The Formation Process

a. *Motivating Factors*
We must begin then with the person of Jesus, the 'Holy One', with his immediate circle of disciples, and with the motivating factors that contributed to this historical process. John Meagher concludes that the transition from the words of Jesus to the Word about Jesus was built into

11. Implications of the Paradigm for History

the plan of Luke and into the theology of Paul. I see it as inevitably built into the theology of the Holy Word itself,[1] most particularly in the practical movement within the Church in its use of the concept of λόγος. Meagher further believes that the earliest Church was not 'altogether

---

1. J.C. Meagher, *The Way of the Word: The Beginning and the Establishing of Christian Understanding* (New York: Seabury Press, 1975), pp. 198, 202. See A. Harnack, *History of Dogma* (New York: Dover, 1961), pp. 45-46. Meagher is concerned to show that the New Testament is one in assuming that authentic Christian understanding is conditioned by what was ἀπ' ἀρχῆς; trans-historical in its beginning but historical in Jesus: 'It is by the standards of ἀπ' ἀρχῆς, and only under such combined conditions that it can finally be determined which interpretation of Christianity may be called authentically Christian, and only thus can we discern in what way, and possibly even whether, Jesus is the one'. He believes that the basic truths about this salvation-historical interpretation of Christianity may be called authentically Christian, and only thus can we discern in what way this practical canon and new order were adequately understood by the first followers of Jesus and faithfully committed by them to those who followed them: 'There is a remarkable degree of agreement concerning the ways in which right understanding was thought to be constituted, and reliably achieved...this was an identifiable court of appeal'. But ultimately the Word is a community product, 'finally determined by the communal court of appeal' (p. 196). For him the historical Jesus is one important constituting factor of the 'Way of the Word', but by no means the only one, or even the norm within the norm: 'The ultimate practical canon is to be found within the living and cumulative consciousness of the Christian community not outside it'.

In this excellent book, the author is concerned to free himself from old critical orthodoxies, and in his observation of detailed evidence he does break out of some old stereotypes. But he never quite escapes the critical orthodoxy of the Bultmannian era. He identifies in a particularly creative way many of the key issues, and in his detailed evidence his observations are objective and often original; but his conclusions do not always follow his evidence. He slips back ultimately into the *Urkirche*, sociological thought frames of Bultmann where the 'Way of the Word' is ultimately a 'sociological product' (Bultmann). Agreeing with Meagher in many ways, granting that there are other norms for the early Christian witness, the main point at which we differ is the extent to which the teachings of Jesus were the primary norm for early Christianity and the formation of the New Testament. Throughout, Meagher overestimates the divergences within the New Testament, and underestimates the controlling character of the Holy Word and the consensus that surrounded it. The entire evidence of this present book gives a new picture of the Holy Word that demands the priority of the teachings of Jesus. What is needed here is not just a discussion about individual units of evidence or particular conclusions, but an entirely new framework for the discussion, which my study attempts to provide. This, I think, would eliminate some of the confusion between new evidence and conclusions in Meagher's discussion, which is perhaps the best current book on this subject.

successful' in abiding by the norm as they saw it, being impatient to resolve disagreements, careless about history, inventive in their use of the Old Testament and too confident about the direct guidance of the Spirit. This is a matter that needs to be carefully considered, and it is to this historical dimension that we finally turn.

The evidence of this book points to three basic sources of motivation: (1) the nature of Jesus in his person and message; (2) the peculiar character of the early Christian community of faith, involved as it was in both the Hebrew and the Hellenistic dimensions of that early period; and (3) the needs of that community as it faced a hostile environment with a gospel that, although similar in some ways, was significantly different from anything in the Hebrew or Hellenistic world. More exactly, these were the natural needs for theological understanding of this new gospel in the face of burgeoning heresy and the challenges of Greco-Roman and oriental philosophy and religion, for spiritual expression of this gospel in worship, and for personal growth among a people whose level of spiritual maturity left much to be desired. There was also the need for applying this gospel to the ethical, ecclesiastical and even political exigencies of a Church under persecution, filled with controversy and fumbling for the answers to old questions put in a very new light.

b. *The Historical Setting*
The setting out of which this process of New Testament formation arose and through which it moved was initially that of Jesus and the audiences to which he spoke. This was primarily that of the twelve, but also that larger group of disciples which included men and women of wealth and education, some of whom were probably skilled in writing, and concerned to preserve a record of what was transpiring among them.[2] Using the term in its broader sense, this original 'school' of Jesus set the pattern for what became after his death a school of the apostles in Jerusalem, and then various schools of certain apostles and their disciples in Rome and Ephesus, in Caesarea, Antioch and elsewhere, leading eventually to such larger and more formal schools as those in Alexandria and Caesarea. The setting involved preaching, worship and debate; but it was this teaching situation, this didactic ethos, with dominant apostles, prophets, teachers, Christian scribes, traveling missionaries and catechetical instruction, that was most central to the preservation,

---

2. J.A. Baird, *Audience Criticism and the Historical Jesus* (Philadelphia: Westminster Press, 1967), pp. 37-38.

11. Implications of the Paradigm for History

interpretation, reproduction and dissemination of the Holy Word. This all reflected a Church with a strong literary, scholarly, historical and theological concern that was both ordered and organized in the handling of that Word. The worship setting further helped to express and develop the dual nature of the Holy Word as something to be not only remembered and understood but also proclaimed and experienced as the power and presence of the Word of God. It was in these situations that the passion narrative was rehearsed, and the Word became sermon, hymn and creed. Although this story needs much more research, it would seem at this writing that the major centers for this developing experience were Jerusalem, Capernaum, Nazareth, Caesarea, Antioch, Ephesus, Corinth, Rome and Alexandria, with the intermingling of the Hebrew, Hellenistic and oriental cultures, all of which are evident in the process.

c. *Historical Dynamics*

The dynamics operating within this historical trajectory began with the peculiar nature of the Word itself, with its revelation of the sovereign God by him whom they believed to be God's son. This Word had about it an 'oracular quality' that commanded attention,[3] a shocking character illustrated by Jesus' description of it as 'fire' cast upon the earth (Lk. 12.49).[4] So the word of Jesus took priority over the narrative, and it was the key words and phrases of his teaching that formed the primary focus of their remembering, remained essentially intact throughout the formation of the New Testament, and continued as a 'living and abiding word' at least until the time of Eusebius.

There was a 'naturalness' to this process, a mundane logic to its progression from the more primitive attention to Jesus' words to the more sophisticated theology of the Church, that suggests a certain inevitability to this trajectory we are describing. The words of Jesus were intrinsically related to the audiences to which he was speaking,[5] inescapably tied to the narrative of his life, death and resurrection, immediately needing careful interpretation, and continuously demanding inspired application to the exigencies of life in the early Church. So it

---

3. J.A. Baird, *A Comparative Analysis of the Gospel Genre: The Synoptic Mode and Its Uniqueness* (Lewiston: Edwin Mellen Press, 1991), pp. 33-34.

4. J.A. Baird, *Rediscovering the Power of the Gospels: Jesus' Theology of the Kingdom* (Wooster, OH: Iona Press, 1982), pp. 124-25.

5. Baird, *Audience Criticism*.

was that the Word was augmented by narrative, gospel and tradition, protected from major distortion by the authority of the apostles and their successors, and eventually canonized within the ecclesiastical councils of the Church. All of this is a procedure that is compatible with what we know about the early Church, and its social-religious environment.

There was both variety and consensus within the early community, to be expected from different minds under different circumstances attempting to understand and relate this Word to the changing and varied needs of the Church. The 'shift' in this progression, from the words of Jesus to the Word about Jesus, seems then to have been primarily a shift in emphasis and vocabulary in response to the changing needs and ethos of the Church rather than one of theological substance. Nevertheless, we can see in this process the beginnings, even within the New Testament, of a kind of 'creeping παράδοσις' that led in later centuries to a more radical distinction between Scripture and tradition. In these earlier days, canonization was the natural outworking and necessary response to internal threats of heresy and external dangers of extinction. The whole heresy controversy was a testimony to the determination of the Church to preserve the consensus of the Holy Word.[6]

d. *Historical Means*

The means whereby this process was accomplished have been emerging subtly in this study. In the beginning, the teachings of Jesus were so constructed, and the audiences so constituted, that his words were contained in memory, especially those 'catchwords' and phrases, stories, metaphors and characteristic ideas that repeated themselves in patterns throughout the Synoptics. The apostles were particularly concerned to remember and later to remind their disciples of these words of Jesus, and to rehearse enough of his life to give them a necessary framework, especially the events surrounding his death and resurrection. Certain of the early apostles and especially the larger group of disciples could well have had both the motivation and the skill necessary to record these as notes (ὑπομνήματα) and later as more extended memoirs (μνημονεύ-

---

6. The dynamics of controversy also played a part in this theological-historical trajectory. The classic study of this is still that of Walter Bauer (*Orthodoxy and Heresy in Earliest Christianity* [Philadelphia: Fortress Press, 1971]), which is coming back into the center of attention, having been translated by a team from the Philadelphia Seminar on Christian Origins.

11. *Implications of the Paradigm for History*

µατα), and to form a coterie of Christian scribes (ὑπηρέται) whose mission it was to pull together all of these sources and proto-sources into what Luke called 'orderly accounts'.

The evidence for such early writing back to the time of Jesus is I think clear, and the description of such reporter-historians by Eusebius and Clement of Alexandria is apt. We shall discuss this point more below. The continuing evidence for proto-sources, the agreement on certain legends like the passion narrative, the existence of lacunae, and the significant agreement between the Synoptics and the λόγια quotations among the Fathers, all point to the process of early writing. By the time of the Pastorals, 2 Peter, and Rom. 16.22, the reference to Christian writings as ἱερὰ γράμματα is I think defensible, and it was this early and persistent written form that helped stabilize the oral Christian consensus. Most of the Apostolic Fathers seem to have had access to some of this growing body of written material, and its use in worship and catechetical instruction is clearly reflected in 2 Tim. 3.14-15 and elsewhere.

We have described the school situation extensively, and it would seem that here is the major track for the production of the New Testament, extending from the simple, loosely-structured school of Jesus and those of his apostles to the later highly sophisticated schools in Alexandria and elsewhere with resident teachers, buildings, and the kinds of libraries to which Eusebius had access in Caesarea. The testimony of Eusebius and others and the internal evidence of the texts point, I think clearly, to this school environment in the clustering of New Testament literature around the dominant disciples and their pupils. That of Paul produced Luke–Acts and editions of his letters; the school of Peter generated Mark and the Petrine letters. The school of John edited the Gospel, letters and possibly the Apocalypse, and that of Matthew put together the Gospel so dependent upon its founder. The abundance of books in the apocryphal New Testament attributed to these and other early leaders, and such collections as those of Nag Hammadi and the sayings of the Desert Fathers,[7] further testify to this school phenomenon. Again there is something rather simple, sensible and mundane about such a procedure.

The manner in which it came about involved certain types of individuals, each of whom had some particular interest, opportunity, or skill which called him or her to play a special role in the process of New Testament formation. We have identified of course the apostles and that larger group of disciples which included men and women of substance,

7. Baird, *Comparative Analysis*, pp. 119-20.

training and literary skill.⁸ Within this circle there were Christian scribes (ὑπηρέται), ministers of the word, and traveling evangelists who followed the pattern originally set by Jesus himself. Next in authority to the apostles were the prophets who applied the Word to the practical life of the Church, to ethics, liturgy and ecclesiastical concerns through what they believed to be divine 'revelation'. Their opinions were highly valued, gathered together like those of the rabbis in the Mishnah, and then circulated throughout the Church, some appearing in the New Testament itself, and others in collections like the *Didache*. These and others acted as ethical teachers, who instructed the Church on practical as well as theological matters. And behind all of these there functioned the living and abiding Word of Jesus in both oral and written form which gave continuity, focus and authority to the teachings of this complex and sometimes conflicting company of enablers of the Word.

And so it was that sometime in those early years, perhaps around the time of Constantine,⁹ the twenty-seven books were formally canonized much as had been the Hebrew Torah before them. But what had already happened was that the Holy Word, probably to be identified with the so-called 'rule of faith', had been operating from the beginning as the core of Christian faith and life. Bruce Metzger has put it well: 'It is not surprising therefore that in the early church the remembered words of Jesus were treasured and quoted taking their place beside the law and the prophets, and being regarded as of equal or superior authority to them'. According to my evidence, this process had been generating naturally and inevitably, according to the most simple and sensible internal logic, a trajectory of Word, narrative, gospel and tradition. This was contained rather haphazardly in these twenty-seven books which seemed to represent most adequately what the Church remembered as that which had been delivered to them from the beginning. The canonizing Fathers then simply formalized this and called it the New Testament.¹⁰

---

8. Baird, *Audience Criticism*, pp. 37-38.

9. See W. Farmer, *Jesus and the Gospel: Tradition, Scripture and Canon* (Philadelphia: Fortress Press, 1982), p. 178.

10. B.M. Metzger, *The Canon of the New Testament: Its Origin, Development, and Significance* (Oxford: Clarendon Press, 1987), pp. 2-3. This part of the story has been dealt with many times elsewhere, and it would be redundant to rehearse it here.

Historical Authenticity

The question, finally, is how seriously can we take these evidences as the history of what actually happened? In Bultmannian terms, how much *Historie* is there within this formation process as we have described it above?

a. *The Epistemology of Historiography*

To begin with, we must acknowledge the philosophical problem that has haunted historians as well as philosophers, scientists and theologians, from the days of Gorgias to the present. How can we be absolutely certain about anything?[11] Let us lay this ghost to rest immediately with the flat affirmation that given the nature of human thought, given the epistemological process, given the character of reality, whatever it may be, there is no possibility of *absolute* certainty about anything. All we can seriously talk about within the intellectual world is relative degrees of probability. Too long has the discussion of the historical Jesus for example been hung up on what is in my view a philosophically naive search for absolute certitude. Biblical scholars tend to be good linguists, but not very good philosophers. This is an important field of study, but for the business of historiography it is a side track with many blind alleys. All we shall pretend to discuss here is the relative probability of bed-rock, absolute historicity, with the assurance that not only is this all we or any other researcher into the empirical world can discover, but that for the normal purposes of practical life and religious faith, this is enough. What we are concerned about is not absolute, but rather 'sufficient' certainty that will enable us to talk reasonably about the historical Jesus and other important empirical matters of New Testament historiography.

In the course of our study, many hints have emerged that speak to this question. No one of them is definitive, but taken together they tell a consistent story. They involve one or another of the various criteria that have arisen in the quest for the historical Jesus, but cluster around three major points of focus: the Holy Word, the Christian consensus, and the several environmental probabilities.[12]

---

11. See D.R. Hall, *The Seven Pillories of Wisdom* (Macon, GA: Mercer University Press, 1990), for a common-sense analysis of this whole enterprise.

12. In the literature of recent years, there are at least fifteen historical criteria used by those engaged in this discussion of the historical Jesus: dissimilarity, uniqueness,

b. *The Epistemology of the Holy Word*
The first of these is the Holy Word. There is a historical logic that is intrinsic to the fundamental historiographic phenomenon which we have documented throughout this study. The unbroken straight line of attention to the words of Jesus throughout the New Testament, the Apostolic and Ante Nicene Fathers presents us with a hard core of historical data that stand as a historiographic 'benchmark'. Whatever is true to this stable point has the probability of historical authenticity. This is strengthened by the many evidences that this Word functioned as the core of the gospel and the traditions.

One of the historical criteria most widely used by New Testament historians following Bultmann is that of dissimilarity. If something in the Gospels can be shown to be dissimilar to the thought of the early Church or the Gospel editors, then it has the probability of authenticity. This can be a useful criterion, but it is only one among many that must be employed, and its excessive, extreme and exclusive use has been misleading. This single-criterion fixation simply dismisses the evidence that might contradict it on the basis of certain doctrinaire presuppositions, and represents the extension of a healthy skepticism into historical nonsense. Used in this way, it simply begs the question by rejecting the possibility that someone could have gotten it right. The criterion of dissimilarity as popularized by German form criticism is therefore a type of reductionism which exposes New Testament historiography to the charge of bad methodology. Anyone dealing scientifically with the empirical world knows that one set of empirical patterns must be cross-correlated with other different types of patterns, before one can talk seriously about an empirical 'fix'. I find at least fifteen different historical criteria being used by one and another New Testament historian. There is validity in all of them, but no one can be relied upon without being correlated with the others.

c. *Patterns of Probability*
The logic of probability works, I think, this way. Everything that is real in nature, including human beings, is a bundle of recurrent patterns, of

---

environmental probability, closeness to Jesus, continuity, a stable point, sanctity/ authority, Aramaic quality, early writing, compatibility, logic, naturalness, redactional probabilities, multiple attestation, agreement. See my unpublished manuscript, 'Historical Skepticism and Gospel Renewal', for a full discussion of these individual criteria.

11. Implications of the Paradigm for History

phenomena that occur more often than chance would allow. I have elsewhere suggested three characteristics of what can be called a 'pattern': uniqueness, regularity and permanence.[13] It is in the occurrence of a single pattern that some aspect of reality identifies itself. The combination of these single patterns into recognizable complexes then further delineates the nature and character of that phenomenon, and objects, persons and events can be recognized and identified. In the case of a human being, it is patterns of size and shape, but more importantly of speech, thought and action, that constitute these clues to identity. And so it is with a figure of history, like Jesus of Nazareth. If combinations of patterns recur that cannot be better explained by being attributed to some other individual, redactor, group or external factor, then probability points to a particular historical individual who thought, taught and acted in these ways. In this manner, the use of the dissimilarity criterion becomes an examination of the uniqueness of the individuality of Jesus, but within the evidence for the patterns of continuity that reflect his identity. This is a modified use of the dissimilarity criterion, along with others such as multiple attestation, continuity, compatibility, enabling this historical test to function more adequately and, incidentally, more positively. The many indications of the carefulness of the Church in preserving in the New Testament the distinctions between the words of Jesus, the gospel about Jesus and the traditions which applied his Word to the life of the Church, are positive indications of the uniqueness, regularity and permanence of the λόγος. This Word was unique and different from anything else upon which the Church based its faith and life. The sanctity of that as Holy Word in the eyes of the Church from the beginning until the time of formal New Testament canonization gave this Word an authority that has been evident in the deference to it by apostles, ministers of the Word, prophets and teachers, and in their apparent carefulness with it.

The Fathers of the late second and third centuries continued the pattern of deferring to the Holy Word of Jesus as supreme authority, what Serapion of Antioch called 'the true teaching of the savior', and this is evident in their treatment of the Word. We have shown several typical examples, like that of *2 Clement*, revealing a careful conflation technique where the essential Word of Jesus remains intact and key words persist, even though in this case the whole is shortened from the

---

13. Baird, *Audience Criticism*, pp. 25-26.

Synoptic version, and there is some re-arranging of phrases to provide a more literary structure.

The New Testament and the Fathers therefore agree in their adherence to the λόγος of Jesus as the basic substance of the Gospel and the traditions. We must never forget that for those who put together the New Testament, and who interpreted and applied its message throughout the early centuries, this was the 'living and abiding' Word of the son of God. It was therefore something to be remembered, treasured and handled with a carefulness certainly not seen in the aretalogies of the ancient Mediterranean world, and perhaps never before or since in history.

d. *The Epistemology of Consensus*

Behind the individual written Gospels, and undergirding the oral gospel, lay a stable, enduring understanding of Jesus, what he said about the Kingdom, what this meant to the faith of the Church, and how men and women should act within that context. What we have called this consensus within variety does not give absolute proof of the historical authenticity of the Word. As we have seen, there are many complexities to this picture. But the probability of authenticity would seem to be supported by the stability, unique integrity and sanctity of this Word. There are at least three types of phenomena pointing in this direction.

1. *Continuity*. The first is that of continuity. All of the New Testament presents the λόγος as a coherent body of teaching containing the substance of the Church's theology, distinct from παράδοσις, and immediately grounded in the primitive teachings of Jesus. The logic of the interrelation between audience and Word reveals a continuity cutting across all three Synoptics.[14] The shift in emphasis, orientation and vocabulary in the handling of the words and theology 'of' the reported Jesus as it moves to the Word and theology of the Church 'about' Jesus, further illustrates this continuity throughout the rest of the New Testament and the literature of the early Church. The orthodox Fathers are in general agreement that this λόγος is the basic substance of the apostolic preaching and the heart of the gospel.

More exactly, it is the persistent patterns of key words, phrases and ideas which formed the heart of this λόγος consensus. We have seen this

---

14. Baird, *Audience Criticism*.

in the internal continuity and compatibility of the Synoptic teachings of Jesus.[15] The phenomena of multiple attestation, of verbal agreement between the sources, of discontinuity between the λόγια and the editorial material all point to this consensus.[16] The 64.1% agreement between the Apostolic Fathers and the Synoptics in reporting the words of Jesus continues this theme. It is the verbal agreement, and the theological continuity-within-variety of language, style and emphasis, that constitute what we are describing.

The phenomena of consensus and continuity are further illustrated in the institution of apostleship that has its basis in the most primitive Jesus account, and continues without a break with disciples of disciples throughout the New Testament and the testimony of Christian literature up to and including Eusebius. The sanctity, authority and function of the apostles continues unchanged throughout the entire literature of this study in a Church that claimed to know what the apostles taught, and treated this knowledge with utmost respect. And the key to it all was their knowledge of and self-conscious fidelity to the Holy Word of Jesus.

2. *Compatibility*. The criterion of compatibility further contributes to this theme by dealing with the logical and theological relationships between large blocks of data that are different in some detail but similar in ways that reveal continuity between the units. In a previous study, I demonstrated at length the ways in which the λόγια of Jesus were consistent and so compatible in the ways in which the words and ideas within them correlated positively with the audiences to whom they were directed in the text. This continued in the regularity and compatibility of verbal, theological and praxis patterns cutting across all three Gospels and all of their major sources.[17] I have pointed in this study not only to the differences between the Holy Word, the gospel and the traditions, but also to their compatibility in their constant and self-conscious focus upon the λόγια of Jesus. We have seen this occurring in the Pauline material where the transition from the 'gospel of God' to 'the gospel of Christ' is a matter of a growing emphasis on Christ due, it would seem, to a shift in the ethos of the Church, rather than a basic change in theology.

---

15. Baird, *Audience Criticism*.
16. See Baird, *Audience Criticism*, pp. 74-135.
17. Baird, *Audience Criticism*.

A subtle illustration of this continuity within diversity comes from the difference between Paul's use of εὐαγγελίζομαι, which centers on the content of the Word, stressing the cross, death and resurrection, and that of Luke whose use of the verb stresses the gospel as activity. Despite this difference, for both the basis of their usage is the Word of Jesus about the Kingdom of God. They are different, but compatible, both showing the Church's awareness of a solid core of belief commonly understood and widely proclaimed.

The strong correlation between the New Testament use of κηρύσσω and εὐαγγέλιον/εὐαγγελίζομαι both reflects the escalation of atonement theology about Jesus and the Kingdom, and continues the Kingdom theme of the Synoptics unabated. So the emphasis is not so much changed as broadened to include atonement theology as well as a continuous dedication to the Holy Word.

Perhaps the clearest illustration of this phenomenon comes from the correlation between various words describing the gospel. Paul for example interweaves terms like λόγος, ἀλήθεια, κήρυγμα and many others, which have their own peculiar emphasis, but which come together in their interchangeability in describing the gospel based upon the Holy Word of Jesus (Chapter 3). The widespread theological consensus involved in the cluster of fourteen such terms and their interweaving throughout the New Testament is the primary historical witness to this phenomenon of compatibility. It comes out in bursts of clarity within Paul's thought in passages like 1 Cor. 2.1-16, where the secret wisdom of God, spiritual truths, the gifts of the Spirit, the mysteries of God, the Kingdom of God, the power of God (4.20) all combine into a brilliant synthesis of the Word of Jesus about God and the Word of God as a living presence. This interplay between the intellectual and the spiritual achieves special brilliance in New Testament books like Ephesians, a summary of Pauline theology, bringing together concepts like mystery, word, truth, gospel, Spirit, wisdom, in a blend of the intellectual and the spiritual, of theology and experience, of the teachings of Jesus and the faith of the Church, of the mind of God and the minds of men and women.

3. *Discontinuity*. The phenomenon of discontinuity further refines this concept. Compatibility as we are using it means continuity within diversity, and any assessment of historical authenticity must take this seriously. I first came across this phenomenon in my study of the

11. *Implications of the Paradigm for History*

audiences to which Jesus is recorded speaking.[18] It became apparent that there was a clear and persistent difference between the vocabulary and theology of the sayings of Jesus and the obviously editorial material. The striking thing is that, despite these patterns of discontinuity, the editors reported the λόγια with sufficient fidelity to permit the survival of patterns of verbal, theological and praxis continuity within the λόγια. These patterns cut 'horizontally' across all three Gospels and their sources, and at times contrasted with the perspective of the editor. We have seen this repeated in the present research in the 'shift' from the theology of Jesus about God to the theology of Paul and the early Church about Jesus and his relation to God. It appears in what we have called the 'creeping παράδοσις' as the traditions applying the understanding of the Church about Jesus and the Kingdom multiplied, and at times may even have strayed from the Holy Word. It appears in the many heresies competing for dominance in the early centuries. But throughout, this diversity in vocabulary, emphasis and point of view is stabilized and ultimately reconciled by the continued dependence on the Holy Word of Jesus as the basis for the thought and life of the Church, however adequately they may have understood and explained it. Compatibility is continuity in tension with discontinuity.

e. The Epistemology of Environmental Probability
A third major historical criterion around which cluster various other criteria of historical validity or non-validity is that of environmental probability. Given our knowledge of the social, religious and personal characteristics of the early Christian community and the age in which it existed, what are the 'probabilities' for the historical authenticity of this material? There are many possible types of data that could be used in this approach, and it has been a popular avenue of investigation in the current quest for the historical Jesus. It is also a slippery set of criteria, for they tend toward circular logic, and involve data that are more hypothetical than what one finds in a printed text. We still do not know a great deal about the details of life in that first-century Church. But we do know some things with a fair degree of probability, and we are learning more. These have a special value because they represent a different type of external data that can be correlated with the more internal data of the text to give us another check on the accuracy of our

---

18. Baird, *Audience Criticism*, pp. 74-75.

conclusions. Without trying to cover this large field of possibilities, there are at least five such criteria emerging in this particular study which have relevance to the more general criterion of environmental probability.

1. *Closeness to Jesus*. The first is that of the closeness to Jesus. There are many historical hints, both internal and external, that suggest a closeness or a distance from the original Jesus situation as it is described in the Gospels, or as it has emerged from the logic of the data. The first that surfaced in this study is the use of the plural λόγοι in all four major sources of the Synoptics (Mark, Q, M and L). The logic of seeing the 'words' of Jesus as a more primitive reference to his teaching than the more collective and formal 'word' of Jesus is I think clear. This primitive usage occurs most often in Mark (6 of 13). If one sees Mark as the most primitive of the Gospels, then this would correlate with that logic, but certainly not prove the priority of Mark.

The fact that the Synoptics always record this plural usage in teaching to the disciples, and mostly (10 times) to the twelve, again points to the closeness of these data to bed-rock history. In my audience study, the λόγοι to the apostles are those wherein Jesus spoke his mind most clearly and completely on subjects like the Kingdom, the eschaton, the Jews, the judgment of God.[19] The internal logic of that primitive situation suggests that it is they who would be most likely to remember particular 'words'. Indeed the Church assumed that and made them authorities on the holy words from the beginning. The institution of the apostleship, their sanctity and leadership, their function as what we have called the 'pipeline' for the Holy Word, has its justification in the widespread occurrence of these phenomena, with testimony to this effect traceable back through the Church Fathers to the earliest sources. It was their proximity to Jesus and to his holy words that gave them this authority.

2. *Oral Tradition*. A second criterion dealing with environmental probability is that of the oral tradition. If, as is commonly accepted, the earliest form of the Jesus material was that of orally transmitted data, then we must pay attention to the tendencies of oral folklore and its transition to literature. Our modern print-oriented bias does not always

---

19. Baird, *Audience Criticism*, p. 125.

take into consideration the differences between spoken and written words. We have been warned that early writing does not necessarily show fidelity to the substance of the original word, and some, like Kelber, have pointed to certain 'tendencies' toward distortion within that primitive process. There is a circularity to this logic, however, which suggests that we cannot take it too seriously as a general indictment of Christian historiography. Given the nature of language, and the almost inevitable subtle changes that take place when something visual or oral is translated into written communication, any historian, or for that matter any scientist, philosopher or reporter, is subject to this same built-in problem. It is all part of the universal and perennial problem of epistemology, and we are not going to try to solve that here. Nor do we need to, for what we are concerned about is the 'probabilities' within the limits of practical reason rather than some kind of absolutistic knowledge of historical perfection. This is what I would call 'sufficient knowledge' as distinct from 'perfect knowledge'.

The major evidences to which we have pointed within the oral dimension of the Jesus data have been those patterns of key words and phrases, characteristic ideas and typical habits of action which are too consistent to be interpreted as the product of individuals other than Jesus.[20] We have also tried to show that the highly developed art of memory existing within Jewish circles carried over into the Christian community. Remembering accurately and with understanding was an important activity within the Church, and seems to have been a basic key to the stability of the Holy Word, and those portions of the narrative most widely proclaimed. We have suggested that this memory-pattern picture of the disciples, Christian scribes and evangelists points to them first of all as reporter-historians, and only secondarily if at all as theologians or ethicists. Those latter functions were reserved for the apostles and the prophets.

One of the most consistent applications of this criterion of environmental probability is that proposed by Birger Gerhardsson in his book *Memory and Manuscript*. According to him, Jesus used a method similar to that of Jewish and Hellenistic teachers: that of text and interpretation. He made his disciples learn certain of his sayings by

---

20. See Baird, *Audience Criticism*, pp. 136-52.

heart.[21] The impression given by the teachings of Jesus is that of condensed memory texts, delivered with a fixed wording. The words of Jesus then became stamped upon the memories of the disciples, and in view of the attitude of Jewish disciples to their masters it is unrealistic to suppose that forgetting or pious imagination had much to do with the changing of this tradition. This earliest period was no doubt primarily an oral period, but for the Jew this meant a highly disciplined process of retaining and transmitting the words of the master, whether Hillel, Aquiba or Jesus. Along with the oral material also probably went written notes (ὑπομνήματα) for the purpose of aiding memory, and also written tractates or collections of sayings organized again for ease of memory. It was these that formed the beginning of the larger and larger collections that were eventually edited into Gospels. The earliest transmission of these collections Gerhardsson describes as a direct methodological delivery of the kind regularly used by the rabbis and their pupils: repetition, a concern for the exact words, condensation, abridgment, use of mnemonic techniques, written notes and various other methods to forestall forgetting. Variations between parallel versions would then be the result either of Jesus' own variation on particular themes, or of the fact that 'most of the Gospel material is haggadic material' and is often transmitted with a wider margin of variation than is halakic material. Sometimes variations occur due to translation or to faulty memorization, or finally sometimes due to 'the principles of redaction used by different evangelists'.

Gerhardsson has, I think, demonstrated the probability of a distinct parallel between the rabbinic schools and the school of Jesus. This careful treatment of the words of one's master was part of the environment out of which the earliest Jesus material emerged. His insight that the tradition from and about Jesus represented a distinct and stable body of material, partly memorized and partly written, forming the basis of a Christian Torah, is an anticipation from an entirely different line of research of one of the major conclusions of my own study. The parallels between the process of presentation, fixation and transmission of the sayings of the rabbis and those of Jesus are natural and convincing at many points, and one must suppose that pharisaic Judaism, whether early or late in the

---

21. B. Gerhardsson, *Memory and Manuscript: Oral Tradition and Written Transmission in Rabbinic Judaism and Early Christianity* (Lund: W.K.C. Gleerup; Copenhagen: Munksgaard, 1961), pp. 328-29.

first century, had significant influence on Jesus and the early Church in these matters of methodology. In the language of the Synoptic mode, the independence (SM-1), brevity (SM-2), direct discourse (SM-3), ease of memorization (SM-4) and evidence of seams separating individual units (SM-9) are clearly Jewish modal characteristics which Gerhardsson shows are paralleled in the rabbinic tradition.[22]

Emerging from Gerhardsson's study of the parallel rabbinic tradition is the concept of a 'Holy Word' which represented a 'fixed, distinct tradition from and about Jesus, a tradition which was partly memorized and partly written down in notebooks and private scrolls, but invariably isolated from the teachings of other doctrinal authorities'.[23] It was this that represented the early Christian oral Torah, and was the basis of the theology of Paul. It was a kind of 'Christian Mishnah', to which the rest of the apostle's preaching was the Talmud. As the central locus of this Holy Word, the Synoptic Gospels therefore represent a carefully preserved tradition that can be presumed to be essentially accurate. This is an anticipation of my own conclusions, but from quite a different line of evidence.

Nevertheless, I think Gerhardsson may have gone too far with the rabbinic analogy. My evidence points to the Gospel genre as being *sui generis*, and although couched primarily in 'the Hebrew mode' it also contains much that I have elsewhere called the 'Greek mode',[24] and diverges significantly from rabbinic literature. The rabbinic methods of interpretation probably strongly influenced the Gospel writers and the praxis of Jesus, but the Synoptic Gospels are closer to Torah than they are to Mishnah; and in the eyes of his disciples, as Gerhardsson would no doubt agree, Jesus was more than just a New Moses. The rigor of the school of Jesus was, I would guess, much more relaxed and informal than that of the rabbinic schools, and the memorization more a function of Jesus' constant repetition of his basic message as he and his disciples carried out their mission together. That they would have used some of the interpretive techniques of the rabbis and their students seems to me,

---

22. Gerhardsson, *Memory and Manuscript*, pp. 148-49. See also Baird, *Comparative Analysis*.
23. Gerhardsson, *Memory and Manuscript*, p. 335.
24. Baird, *Comparative Analysis*.

however, to be most natural and in keeping with the evidence as I have found it.[25]

25. The most vigorous rejection of Gerhardsson's thesis has come from Morton Smith and Moses Hadas in their book *Heroes and Gods: Spiritual Biographies in Antiquity* (Religious Perspectives, 13; New York: Harper & Row, 1965). Smith's critique makes some valid points, but it is marred by a dogmatism that is based on too many deeply entrenched presuppositions. See the critique of this book in my *Comparative Analysis*, pp. 92-93. An earlier book by C.K. Barrett (*Jesus and the Gospel Tradition* [Philadelphia: Fortress Press, 1968]) rejects Gerhardsson's thesis on what I think are only partially valid grounds. Barrett's work, though brilliant, is thoroughly conditioned by his presuppositions, and to refute his conclusions necessitates a critique of the entire generation of post-Bultmannian scholarship (see Baird, *The Justice of God in the Teaching of Jesus*; idem, *Audience Criticism*; idem, *Rediscovering the Power of the Gospels*; idem, *Comparative Analysis*). For a more recent and flexible critique of Gerhardsson, see W. Kelber, *The Oral and the Written Gospel* (Philadelphia: Fortress Press, 1983). Kelber is concerned about the print-oriented bias of western hermeneutics. He is searching for the original form of oral materials. He is critical of Gerhardsson's thesis, arguing that Jesus did not teach according to the rules of mechanical memorization. Rejecting Gerhardsson's concept of the centrality of Jerusalem, he dismisses as 'no longer tenable' the unity of the message around the λόγος τοῦ κυρίου. He quotes C.K. Barrett to support his rejection of the apostolic college thesis, not seeming to realize that Barrett's arguments are based on his assumption that the Synoptics are written in the 'Greek Epic', while Kelber has argued for a more Hebraic orientation. Basically Kelber sees the Synoptics as just another illustration of oral folklore turned into writing, and distorted in the process. For him, orality seems to be a genre whose rules are fixed and according to which we must interpret the Gospels. He dismisses the school orientation of the Gospels, and ignores the literary element in his justifiable enthusiasm for the oral dimension. A vigorous critic of Bultmann, he argues that the beginnings of what came to be Christian tradition undoubtedly go back not to the *Urkirche* but to Jesus' own speaking, whose words were destined to be remembered not by authorities, but by ordinary people and close followers. One of his major concerns is the blurring of the beginning of the process of both oral and written material as it became text.

In this work we seem to have a clear movement away from Bultmann and form criticism, away from the Greek classical orientation of *theios aner* scholarship to a more Hebraic emphasis, away from a literary fixation to a more oral orientation, and away from a rigid redaction criticism, showing that many of the phenomena we had explained in rather tortuous literary ways are more easily explained as oral. He seems thus to be part of what I have called a 'New Paradigm' of scholarship which has broken free from some old critical molds. All of this is in my opinion productive and helpful.

There are, however, several major problems with this creative book which give me pause in accepting its thesis completely. To begin with, Kelber never really extricates

3. *Early Writing*. A third historical criterion within this general category of environmental probability is that of early writing. As memory became written memoir, then proto-source, Gospel and New Testament, so were these primitive data fixed in a form that stabilized them in their use within the Church. There is abundant evidence for the continuing ministry of the written word from the earliest times in the phenomenon of lacunae, in verbal and theological agreement between the Synoptic sources, in the activity of Paul, Luke and other ὑπηρέται, and in the long tradition of concern for the literary heritage of the Church (Chapter 7). We have pointed to evidence that by the time of the Pastoral Epistles, 2 Peter, and the doxology in Romans, Christian writings were being referred to as ἱερὰ γράμματα, γραφαὶ προφητικαί, and γραφή on a par with the Old Testament. This is what Timothy had available to him 'from childhood' to instruct him in his faith in Christ (2 Tim. 3.14-15). It was this fact of early and persistent written form that helped stabilize the oral Christian consensus and provide the mechanism for the production of a written New Testament. This does not prove the accuracy of the material, but it does create the probability that it was stabilized at a very early period.

himself from what I have called 'the Bultmannian captivity' (see *Audience Criticism*). Despite his rejection of Bultmann and form criticism, like so many dazzled by that brilliant school, he still clings to many of the Bultmannian presuppositions that logically undercut his own thesis. His insistence on the oral character of the early period for example echoes Bultmann's 'strictly oral' argument. He shares Bultmann's prevailing 'historiophobia' which warps the use of his evidence, and shuts off the possibility of new evidence to the contrary. What is needed here is a method that is more inductive, more objective, more comprehensive, and more aware of new types of evidence. His analysis needs a wider scope, including not only a careful study of the narrative, but also of the sayings material, not only of the Synoptic Gospels, but also the rest of the New Testament, and the testimony of the Fathers. Most importantly, this thesis needs an awareness of the special data presented in this book. The sanctity of the hard core of Jesus λόγια as detailed above, the evidence of the school activity out of which the New Testament emerged, the early consensus around the Holy Word, and the primitive literary activity that reflected, promoted and stabilized it. Perhaps most of all, this book needs an appreciation of the uniqueness of the Synoptics, and the existence of motives and forces at work within the early Christian community that were different from 'ordinary' folklore tradition (see Baird, *A Comparative Analysis*). Despite these weaknesses, this is an excellent study, and actually points in the direction of my own work above.

4. *Redactional Probability*. A fourth criterion that follows hard upon the above is that of redactional probability. Given what we think we know about the redactors, what is the most logically probable in terms of their function as accurate historians? This is a criterion that has been explored and exploited widely in recent years by redaction critics. It is highly speculative and therefore quite controversial. Generally speaking there are two levels at which this historical criterion is mined for evidence: (1) the overt evidence for literary style, historical carefulness and patterns of bias that might skew the results; and (2) the attempt to discover subtle patterns of motivation that give to these ὑπηρέται a hidden agenda which can be discovered, and needs to be corrected in order to arrive at the historical truth. The so-called 'paranetic motive' is the one most often identified. In this present study, the evidence seems to operate mostly on the first level.

The major observation of this study with regard to this matter is that the editorial process as described by Luke (1.1-4), Clement of Alexandria and Eusebius is probably accurate (Chapter 7). The redactional activity of ὑπηρέται, Christian scribes, ministers of the Word, whether at the level of ὑπομνήματα, proto-sources or larger Gospel collections as seen in the Synoptics did not reflect the artful design of a theologian or a literary stylist, but the act of a reporter-historian, striving for accuracy of detail. The probability then arises that we are talking at this point about what Bultmann called *Historie*. The rabbinic parallel as described by Gerhardsson is consistent with this, although it would seem that the process within Christian circles was not as formal and rigidly controlled as with their rabbinic counterparts.

The many sources and proto-sources lying behind the larger collections, like the so-called Q material, the sermon on the mount, the gathering together of parables under a theme as in Luke 15, collections of παράδοσις like the *Didache*, all point to an early redactional activity that supports Luke's statement that 'many have undertaken to draw up an orderly account...' (see Chapter 7).

One large facet of the redactor question is the whole matter of the genre of the Gospels. Were the editors guided by the force of some literary convention within the Greco-Roman world? This has important connotations for the ways in which we interpret Synoptic historicity, involving at least two historiographic criteria—those of dissimilarity and environmental probability. This is a problem too large to add to the burden of this book, so perhaps it will be permitted to summarize a

11. *Implications of the Paradigm for History*

recent work in which I have examined this question at length. Reversing the usual methodology, I began by examining the Synoptics in order to work out an adequate picture of their inner, literary, modal structure. I found nine literary characteristics typical of all three Synoptics and all of their sub-sources. They are made up of independent units that tend to be short and easily remembered. The sayings are couched in direct discourse and separated by literary or historical 'seams' which highlight their individuality. The mood of Jesus' words is distinct as 'oracular', and these sayings are significantly related in content and application to the clearly identified audience to which they are directed. These sayings finally are surrounded by a realistic historical narrative context, suggesting that the editors at least believed they were describing authentic history. I called these nine literary characteristics 'the Synoptic mode', and with that as a basic standard I compared the Synoptic Gospels to all ancient literature, Hebrew, Greek, Roman, Christian, which were in any way similar to these Gospels. The results tended to support the findings of this present study.

There are indeed many works in the ancient Middle East comparable to the Synoptic Gospels in their literary modality: the *Gospel of Thomas*, Lucian's *Demonax* and the Old Testament book of Ezekiel, to name only three of the closest.[26] Nevertheless, I find no duplicate in the descriptions of the lives and teachings of religious figures of the ancient Near East close enough to be considered the source of the literary genre called Gospel. There are many detailed similarities, but generally the Synoptics stand out as significantly different in both degree and kind. Collectively or individually they do not seem to follow any one genre so much as to have arisen out of the peculiarities of the Jesus situation, producing a unique and temporary genre that in some ways is similar to many different genres, but contains its own special genius in the total combination of its modal factors. It is not a pure so much as a 'composite' genre, created out of a particular short-lived situation, a genre which survived for a time, but which gradually and then completely disappeared.[27]

In an earlier study, the many patterns of vocabulary and theology running throughout the Synoptic λόγια set the words of Jesus apart as distinct from the editorial narratives.[28] A comparative genre analysis sets

---

26. Baird, *Comparative Analysis*.
27. Baird, *Comparative Analysis*, pp. 127-43.
28. Baird, *Audience Criticism*.

them apart from any other literature of antiquity. There is simply nothing like the oracular quality of Jesus' Word in all the comparable literature of antiquity.[29] The evidence of this present study points particularly to the carefulness of the Church in distinguishing that Word from the narrative, gospel and παράδοσις which cradled, interpreted and applied it, and from the literary quality of the ancient genres available to the Gospel editors and redactors. It is this distinctiveness which points to the very special character of this Word.

The data presented here have also pointed to the redactional activity of the Synoptic editors, which complicates but does not negate these conclusions. This consisted in the choice of words, arrangement of material, editorial insertions and the interaction between the narrative and the words of Jesus. All of this gives these Gospels their character as what I have called complex biographical apophthegms. With the words of Jesus, these redactional activities are minimal, can usually be detected, are theologically innocuous, and are disciplined by the evidence for the various patterns of continuity and compatibility to which we have already referred. On the other hand, the clearly editorial stratum containing legendary material, especially the highly theological birth and infancy narratives, are much harder to document. At those points, we are probably talking about a blend of objective *Historie* and interpretive *Geschichte*. The impression gained here is that throughout the New Testament the Holy Word of Jesus was that which is most documentable in terms of its historical authenticity.

As we move to those New Testament books stressing the gospel and the traditions, the editorial purpose has changed. In John the Word swamps the narrative with the increase in narrative theology, especially the atonement theology that became so prominent in later Christian centuries. Here again, we must speak of historical authenticity in the broader sense of interpreted history, bearing in mind the difference in intention between these books and the Synoptics. But always this redactional concern for what Jesus actually said and did remains high, and focused upon the Holy Word, whose key words and ideas remain essentially intact. There is also much to be said for the common insight that in some ways 'interpreted history' is the most adequate history.

The Fathers continue this same redactional environment. The author of *2 Clement* is not untypical. He quoted his Synoptic materials with a 71.8% exactitude, and his redactional efforts followed three typical

---

29. Baird, *Comparative Analysis*.

patterns: (1) grouping independent units under some rubric such as theme or catchword; (2) abbreviating, summarizing and infrequently elaborating; and (3) certain stylistic changes for the purpose of clarity or literary finesse. It was a process of fluidity and carefulness. But always the center of his theology was the Holy Word of Jesus crystallized in key words, phrases and ideas which he treated with great care (Chapter 8).

5. *Holy Schools*. An important historical element surfacing in this study is that of the holy schools of Word, gospel and tradition. It is in the character of these that we see concentrated the didactic environment within which the Holy Word of Jesus was nurtured, and out of which the New Testament emerged. Luke it would seem gives us an accurate and typical summary of the process (1.1-4). Any assessment of New Testament formation and its historical authenticity that does not take this process into careful account is not dealing with the history of the Christian Church. It was the teaching situation, the unbroken line of the Christian school, from the loosely organized group of apostles around Jesus, and those around Paul like Luke, to the most highly developed schools of Alexandria and Caesarea, that formed the nexus of the New Testament process. The historical implication of this is clear. The environment out of which the Gospels and the entire New Testament emerged was an organized and disciplined one, concerned for accuracy and adequacy (cf. Lk. 1.1-4: παρηκολουθηκότι, ἄνωθεν, πᾶσιν, ἀκριβῶς, καθεξῆς), and dedicated to the stabilizing of the reception, retention, interpretation, recording and transmission of the Holy Word (Chapter 6). The probability then emerges that this same disciplined, pedagogical, even scholarly ethos would carry over into the treatment of the narratives, the various Gospel summaries and collections of traditions. This does not prove historical authenticity, and the Holy Word is the easiest to document; but this 'stable point' creates the presumption that, given the differing needs, intent and circumstance, at least an approximation of the same concern would have applied to all data which stemmed immediately from it. As we have shown throughout, the Holy Word of the Holy One bequeathed its sanctity upon the holy narrative, the holy gospel and the holy traditions, and that was the environment within which this process of New Testament formation took place.

6. *Heresies*. One final element of the formation environment needs to be acknowledged. That is the abundance of heresies to which Jesus, Paul,

the Catholic Epistles and the apocryphal New Testament refer, and against which the Church set itself with a passion that blazed within the schools of Scripture, and disturbed the entire Roman Empire. As the gospel moved into the sophisticated Greco-Roman world, the temptation was great to accommodate it to one or another of the many philosophies and religions struggling for dominance. I would not doubt that on occasion this did indeed happen. But this is a study too vast to encompass in this book. My evidence suggests that this kind of thing was probably at a minimum.[30] It was the challenge of Judaism that caused Jesus to insist upon his gospel as a whole garment that must not be patched onto older ones. It was this threat that led to some of the sternest denunciations within Paul's letters. It was the danger of the perversion of the Holy Word of Jesus that led the Church to sanctify the apostles as the authorities. It was the variety of ethical points of view that led to the institution of the prophets, and their supervision by the apostles. And it was in the schools of the Church that these matters were debated, and out of which came the New Testament, whose very existence and eventual canonization is a testimony to the concern of the Church to correct, validate and stabilize its witness. The entire testimony of this study points to an intense attachment to the Holy Word of Jesus. This was first and foremost the product of the nature of that Word and the person of him who gave it; but a secondary function of that fixation was to steer the Church through the tumultuous and dangerous waters of those early centuries as its chief defense against heresy.

So the historical authenticity of this New Testament material is a mixed picture, a blend of *Historie* and *Geschichte*. The story of the early Church is a compound of unity and disunity. The trajectory of the New Testament is one of movement from Word to narrative to gospel to

---

30. Bauer's *Orthodoxy and Heresy* is a study which will probably continue to emerge as required reading for any one working in this field. There is not space to deal with this adequately here. The detailed theological comparison of the Synoptic Holy Word with the substance of the teaching within the Church of the first four centuries is another study which needs to be done. On the basis of the evidence within this more historical study, all we can say at this point is that the early Church as reflected in the New Testament and the later theologians *claimed* to be faithfully representing the Holy Word of Jesus. Beyond that we must talk in terms of probabilities, based upon a series of historical and theological criteria, no one of which by itself is definitive. See Baird, *The Justice of God in the Teaching of Jesus*; idem, *Audience Criticism*; idem, *Rediscovering the Power of the Gospels*; idem, *Comparative Analysis*.

tradition. But running through it all, like a golden thread, was the living and abiding Word of Jesus which gave unity, stability, direction and authority to it all.

Index of Ancient Sources

Old Testament

Deuteronomy					
25.4	180	52.7	87	*Malachi*	
		57.7	82	3.1	187
		61.1	82		
Psalm				*Zechariah*	
4.4	195	*Jeremiah*		13.6	193
		7.11	198	13.7	193
Isaiah		9.23-24	187		
40.6-9	87	31.33	224		

New Testament

Matthew		7.6	191	12.42	168
3.2	32	7.12	187, 195	12.44	36
3.11	193	7.15-23	156	12.45	168
3.12	193	7.15	191	12.50	200
4.17	182	7.20	137	13.19	48
4.23	32, 83, 89	7.21	199	13.52	170
5–7	191	7.28	47, 168	13.53	47, 168
5.3	195	8.19-20	170	15.3	108
5.7	187, 195	9.13b	198	15.6	108
5.8	194	9.29	101	15.13	190
5.10	195	9.35	83, 89	16.12	36, 93
5.17	223	10	192	16.17-19	125
5.21-48	223	10.1-2	191	16.26	199
5.21	224	10.2	122	17.13	193, 223
5.22-16	191	10.5	115	18.6-7	188, 189
5.25	171	10.16	200	18.15-35	191
5.32	194	10.25	200	18.18-19	125
5.42	191	10.28	194	18.34	122
5.44	196, 200	10.32	199	19.1	47, 168
5.46	200	11.1	47, 168	19.4-6	168
5.48	196	11.2-6	82	19.9	194
6.13a	196	11.5	82	19.23	194
6.14-15	187	12.6	224	19.27-28	125
6.33	213	12.8	224	20.24-28	125
7.1	195	12.28	36	21.13	198
7.2	195	12.33	189	21.33	189
7.2a	187	12.39	71	22.11-14	199
7.2b	187	12.41-45	168	22.14	193

Index of Ancient Sources

22.33	93	4.19	49	13.31	46, 212
23.8-12	125	4.20	49	13.35	191
23.8-10	153	5.16	175	14.9	83
23.12	194	6.8	115	14.12-16	168
23.23	71	6.12	90	14.21	188, 189, 194
24.10	191	6.30	122		
24.11	191	7.1-23	71	14.22-24	173
24.12	191	7.1	73	14.27	193
24.14	83, 89	7.3-4	108	14.3-9	168
24.21	191	7.17-23	168	14.9	83
24.24	191	7.27	73	14.38	196
24.30-31	191	8.15-16	200	14.54	171
24.31	48	8.15	224	15.43	32, 170
24.35	46	8.18-21	161	16.11	74
24.42-44	191	8.22-33	140	16.15	83, 89
25.1-13	199	8.27-33	126	16.20	50, 128
25.1-2	26	8.27-30	138	16.21	38
25.3	191	8.27-28	161		
26.1	47	8.33	32	*Luke*	
26.24	194	8.35	83	1.1-4	5, 57, 72, 102, 175-77, 250, 253
26.31	193	8.38	46, 212		
26.41	196	9.9	175		
26.58	171	9.14	170		
27.9	12	9.37	168	1.1	27
28.17	74	9.42	189	1.2	50, 128, 170
		10.6-9	168		
Mark		10.11	194	1.4	47
1.1	83	10.13	194	1.19	88
1.14-15	32	10.18-26	168	1.33	32
1.14	83, 84, 89, 90	10.23	194	2.10	88
		10.24	194	3.18	88
1.15	84	10.29	83	4.2	72
1.22	93	10.42-43	125	4.18	82, 84, 88, 89
1.38	71	11.10	32		
1.45	89	11.18	93	4.20	171
2.5	101	11.25	195	4.22	47
2.14-15	213	11.27-35	168	4.32	47, 48, 89
2.17	193	12.1-12	189	4.43	88, 89
2.17b	198	12.6-7	194	5.32	54, 114, 198
3.14	122	12.12	36		
3.35	200	12.14	94	6	191
4.1-9	99	12.32-34	170	6.1-4	57
4.1-2	97	12.32	94	6.20	195
4.2	93	12.38	93	6.21	195
4.3-9	189	12.44	168	6.27	196, 200
4.10-12	29, 39, 99, 100, 126, 140, 142-43	13	192	6.32-33	191
		13.10	83	6.32	200
		13.13	191	6.37	195
		13.19	191	6.38	195
4.14	48, 49	13.22	191	6.38a	187
4.16	49	13.24-27	168	7.1-10	145
4.18	49	13.26-27	191	7.3	170

258   Holy Word

7.7	48, 50	22.20	223	12.16	162
7.18-23	82	22.28-30	125	12.36	102
7.22	82, 84, 88	22.31-34	124	12.42	101
7.29	32	22.61	48, 77, 162	12.47	54, 102, 114
7.36-50	170	23.42	32	12.48	49
8.1	32, 88, 89	24.10	122	13.16	122
8.11	48	24.13-53	124	13.34	94
8.18	36	24.16	74	14.1	102
8.21	200	24.19	48, 49	14.7-11	102
8.39	175	24.37	74, 190	14.17	96
8.41	170	24.44	46	14.23-24	49
9.6	88	24.46-47	91	14.23	56
9.11	32			14.24	56
9.26	46	*John*		14.26	161
9.28	47, 168	1.1-2	56	15.3	49
10.7	180	1.1	217	15.17	94
10.24	47	1.12	102	15.20	49, 78, 161
10.29-37	32	1.14	55, 96		
10.39	48	1.17	95	15.25	49, 57
11.15b	196	1.45	223	15.26	96
11.24-26	168	1.77	98	16.4	161
11.25	168	2.11	101	16.13	96
11.26	168	2.22	49, 96, 162	17.6	56, 57
11.31	168, 224			17.8	102
11.32	168	2.23	102	17.14	56, 58
11.49	122, 128	3.2	101, 102	17.17	57, 96
12.4-5	200	3.7	102	18.36	171
12.5	194	3.12	102	18.37	94
12.8	199	3.16	102	18.38	94
12.35-40	191	3.21	96	20.27	74
12.36	199	3.36	102	20.31	75, 102
12.47-48	124	4.23	95	21.4	86
12.49	213, 233	4.39	102	21.5	86
13.31	170	4.41	49		
14.11	194	5.24	49, 56	*Acts*	
15.2	50	5.33	95	1.16	76
16.10-12	85	5.38	56	1.21	76
16.11-12	200	6.29	102	1.22	76
16.13	199	6.69	55, 213	1.24	76
16.16	88, 145	7.15	182	1.26	154
16.19-31	199	8.31	49	2.20	118
17.1	189	8.32	94	2.42	93, 103, 126, 128, 180, 223
17.2	189	8.37	49		
17.5	122	8.40	94		
18.1-8	124	8.43	49	3.1	76
18.24	194	8.47	49	3.14	55, 213
19.1-10	73	10.25	102	4.4	101
19.11	33, 36	10.35	57	4.13	76
20.1	88	10.37-38	102	4.27	76
20.39	170	11.25	102	4.29-30	76
21.33	46	11.52	98	4.29	51, 211
22.14	122				

4.30	76	13.48	50	2.27	181		
4.33	76, 126	14.1	101	2.29	181		
4.37	124	14.7	87	3.7	96		
5.12	126, 128	14.14	122	5.14-18	179		
5.28	93, 103	14.21	87	6.17-18	110, 179		
5.42	87	15	112	6.17	93		
6.1-6	145	15.7	84, 85, 92	6.25	99		
6.2	51, 57, 172	15.32	118, 119	7.6	181		
		15.36	50, 87	7.9	108		
6.4	51, 92, 172	16.10	87	8.2	223, 224		
		17.3	76	8.6	98		
6.6	124	17.11	51	8.27	98		
6.7	170	17.18	76	9.1	95		
7.52	147	17.19	94	9.6	52, 58, 212		
8.1	146	17.31	94				
8.4	51, 87, 92	18.25	102	9.9	58		
8.11	103	19.10	92	10.1-17	101		
8.12	84, 87, 89, 90, 92, 101, 145, 147	19.36-37	51	10.4	223		
		20.21	51	10.8-13	90, 91		
		20.24	51, 84, 85	10.8-9	90		
		20.25	51, 91	10.8	89		
8.14	146, 147	20.31	97	10.14	90		
8.20	103	20.32	51, 89, 212	10.15	82		
8.25	50, 87, 147			10.16	84		
		20.35	47	11.13	117		
8.33	175	21.9	117, 119, 146	11.25	99, 100		
8.35	87			11.28	84		
10.34-43	75	21.10	119	11.33-34	100		
10.36-43	90	21.21	102	11.33	98, 100		
10.36-37	51	22.3	134	11.34	97-99		
10.36	50, 51, 87	24.23	171	12.4	117		
10.37-38	90	24.24	101	12.16	98		
10.37	89	25.19	76	13.7-8	61		
10.42	115	26.16	171	13.7	59		
10.43	90	28.23	75	13.9	58		
10.44	51	28.31	51, 75, 90	13.10	223		
11.1	51, 56, 124			14	177, 178		
		Romans		15	177, 178		
11.14	56	1.1-6	177-79	15.6	98		
11.16	162	1.1	84, 124	15.8	96		
11.19	51	1.3-5	178	15.14	98		
11.20	87	1.5	178	15.16	84		
11.27	118	1.9	84	15.19	84		
12.24	51	1.15	87	15.20	87		
13.1-3	118	1.16	84, 101	16	177, 178		
13.1	119	1.18	96	16.7	122		
13.5	170	1.25	96	16.22	170, 235		
13.10	50	2.2	96	16.25-27	177, 179		
13.12	51, 93	2.16	84, 180, 183	16.25-26	178, 179, 184		
13.15	180						
13.32	82, 87	2.18	102	16.25	84, 92, 180		
13.36	171	2.21	91				

16.26	99, 179, 180	13.2	98	1.6	84		
		14.3	118	1.7	84		
		14.6	94, 98	1.9	103		
1 Corinthians		14.19	102	1.11	84, 87		
1.1	124	14.26	94, 180	1.12	87, 103		
1.4–2.16	56	14.29	156	1.14	108		
1.5–2.16	52	14.30	117	1.18-19	125		
1.5	52, 53	14.37	52, 117	1.18	87		
1.17–2.16	97	15	84	1.19-20	124		
1.17	87	15.1-11	163	2.1-2	126		
1.18	52, 92	15.1-8	136	2.2	84, 89, 91, 126		
1.21	97	15.1	52, 87, 102				
1.24	97			2.5	84, 95		
1.30	97	15.2	87, 93	2.7	84		
1.31	187	15.3-8	76	2.14	84, 95		
2.1-16	97, 242	15.3	102	5.1	224		
2.4	92	15.14	92	5.11	91		
2.5	102	15.51	48	5.14	58		
2.13	98	16.2	109, 179	6.2-16	216		
2.14-16	100	16.21	170	6.2	222		
2.16	53, 98, 112, 126			6.6	51, 102, 222		
		2 Corinthians		6.11	170		
3.4	134	2.12	84	6.13	222		
3.16	223	2.14	98	6.16	113, 222		
4.3	99	2.17	172				
4.15-16	126	3.6	181	*Ephesians*			
4.15	85	3.7	181	1.9	97, 99, 100		
4.20	97, 242	3.14	180				
5.8	95, 109, 179	4.2	95	1.13	52, 84, 93, 95, 97, 211		
		4.3	84				
7.10-12	112	4.4	52, 84				
7.25-26	112	4.5	89	1.17	97		
8.1-2	99	4.6	53, 98, 99	1.18	101		
8.1	98	5.19	52, 92, 12	2.11-13	162		
9.1-2	124			2.19-20	120		
9.1	126	6.7	50, 95	2.20	103, 218		
9.2	126	7.14	95	3.3-5	179		
9.12	84	8.7	98, 99	3.3-4	100		
9.16	87	9.13	84	3.3	99		
9.18	84, 87	10.5	98	3.4	99		
9.27	91	10.11	59	3.5	103, 123, 126		
11.2	109, 179	10.13	113				
11.17	115	10.14	84	3.6	85		
11.23	102	10.15	113	3.7	97		
11.25	223	10.17	187	3.9	97, 99, 100		
12.4	57	11	95				
12.8	52, 57	11.4	91	4.15	96, 226		
12.10	156	11.6	99	4.17	51		
12.28	103, 117, 118, 124, 218	13.8	96	4.18	198		
				4.26	195		
		Galatians					
13.2-4	99	1.1	124	5.9	96		

5.32	100	2.15	95, 109, 111, 179	2.2	109, 170, 179
6.14	95			2.8	84, 162, 180
6.19	52, 99, 100	3.4	115		
		3.6	103, 109, 115	2.11	115
Philippians		3.10	115	2.14	162
1.16	84	3.14	59	2.15	50, 54, 57, 95, 172
1.27	84	3.17	170		
2.16	52, 98			3.7	95
2.22	84	*1 Timothy*		3.8	95
3.8	99	1.1	124	3.14-15	181, 235, 249
3.16	113	1.6	113		
4.7	98	1.10	57, 113	3.15	181, 182
4.9	103	1.11	84, 113	3.16	180, 182, 183
		1.15	54, 114, 118		
Colossians				4.2	89, 93
1.5	52	1.17-18	113	4.3	57, 113
1.7	103	1.19	118	4.13	181
1.9	97	2.2	59, 61		
1.15	95	2.4	95	*Titus*	
1.23	84, 89	3.1	115	1.1	92, 95
1.25	52, 172	3.15	95	1.3	54, 92
1.26-27	99, 100	4.1	113	1.9	57, 113-15
1.28	100	4.5	54	1.14	95
2.1-5	100	4.6	54, 114	2.1	57, 113, 114
2.2	84, 98, 99	4.9	114, 115		
2.3	97, 98	4.11-16	115	2.7	113
2.4	84	4.11	115	2.10	113
2.6	102	4.13	113, 180	2.12	191
2.7	98, 101	4.15	113	3.1-11	115
2.8	108	4.16	113	3.1	162
2.22	113	5.1	113		
3.16	51, 52, 97	5.7	115	*Hebrews*	
4.3	52, 99, 100	5.17	54, 57, 113, 172	2.9	76
				2.10	58
4.18	162, 170	5.18	180	4.12	56
		6.2	113	4.14	76
1 Thessalonians		6.3	47, 54, 57, 95, 113	5.12	172
1.5	85			5.13	58
1.8	48, 51	6.5	50	6.1	58, 93
2.2	84	6.17	115	6.2	116
2.6	122	6.20	99	7.28	172
2.8	84			8.1	226
2.9	84, 89, 91	*2 Timothy*		9.11	58
3.2	84, 85	1.8-14	54	10.1	226
4.2	110	1.9	183	10.11	58
4.15	48	1.11	56, 124	10.16	76
5.14-18	110	1.13	47, 54, 56, 109, 179	12.2	76, 226
				12.23	58
2 Thessalonians		1.14	56, 109, 179	13.1-3	110
1.8	84			13.7	58, 162
2.5	162			13.9	116

13.12	76	1.19	58, 116, 117	4.6	96
				5.7	96
James		1.20	184		
1.18	95, 96	2.1	184	*2 John*	
1.21	95, 96	2.20	128	1	95, 96
1.22	54, 56, 95, 96	3.1-4	128	5	94
		3.1	162	6	94
3.14	95	3.2	11, 128, 184	9	95, 116
5.10	117			10	116, 162
		3.5	58		
1 Peter		3.7	58	*Jude*	
1.19	117	3.15-16	183	5	162
1.20	198	3.16	184	17	162
1.22-23	95				
1.23	5, 11, 54	*1 John*		*Revelation*	
1.25	5, 11, 87	1.1	50, 54, 55, 93, 211	1.9	54
2.11	191			2.20-22	119
3.8-9	110	1.6	96	3.10	49, 54
3.8	97	1.8	96	11.18	119
5.1	149	1.10	49, 50, 54	14.6	82
5.5	189	2.3-5	48	16.6	119
		2.7	58	18.20	119
2 Peter		2.14	58	18.24	119
1.1	149	2.20	55	19.13	55
1.12	162, 184	2.24	223	20.4	54, 172
1.16	184	3.19	96	22.6	119
		4.1-3	156	22.9	119

CHRISTIAN AUTHORS

1 Clem.		6.1	199	Athenagoras	
2.1	59, 85	6.2	199	*Legatio*	
13.1-4	59	8.5	85, 200	10.17	202
13.1-2	187	9.11	200	11.2	202
13.1	187	11.2	187		
13.2	187	12.2	200	Augustine	
13.3	5, 11, 187	13.4	200	*Tract.*	
23.3-5	187	14.1	198	7.17	174
34.6	187	14.2	198		
42.5	187	17.2	198	*Barn.*	
45.2	187	17.3	60	1.9	94
46.8	188, 206	17.6	173	4.7	192
53.1	187	17.7	198	4.11	192
62.3	187	19.1	173, 198	4.14	192
		19.3	198	5.4	192
2 Clem.				5.9	85
2.4	198	*Acts of Pilate*		5.12	193
3.2	199	1.1-2	174	6.12	192
4.2	199			8.3	85
4.5	199	*Acts of Thomas*		9.9	94
5.2	200	79	157	13.2	192
6.1-2	199				

Index of Ancient Sources

Clement of Alexandria		15.4d	191	3.25.1-7	157
Exhortation to Heaven		16	191	3.25.1	87, 89, 204
9	182	16.1	191		
		16.3	191	3.25.6	112, 204
Frag.		16.4a	191	3.29.4	155
1	86, 149	16.4b	191	3.31.6	204
37	112	16.5	191	3.32.3-4	124
		16.6-8	191	3.32.7	62
Instructor				3.32.8	125
1–2	61	*Diogn.*		3.34	62
2	86, 202	11.1	60, 147	3.36.3	127
3	61, 86, 202			3.36.4	107
		Epiphanius		3.37.1-2	62
5	86, 202	'Treatise on Weights and		3.37.1	124
9	202	Measures'		3.37.2	87, 89, 147, 204
		14B–15B	147		
Strom.				3.37.3	62
1	123, 147	Eusebius		3.37.4	112, 114, 164
1.1	111, 218	*Hist. Eccl.*			
1.10	111	1.1	61, 127	3.39.1	60
2.9	202	1.1.1	172	3.39.2-4	11, 151
2.11	182, 202	1.2.27	164, 179	3.39.2-3	148
2.18.91	188	1.7.14	173	3.39.2	127
3.4	155	1.8.3	87, 89, 204	3.39.4	5, 61, 196
6.5	127	1.10.2	204	3.39.7-8	109, 112
6.7	127	1.10.6	87, 204	3.39.7	150
6.15	61	1.10.11	204	3.39.11	206
6.16	111	1.11.1	87, 89	3.39.14	62, 111, 112
7.16-17	61	1.12.1	87, 89		
7.17	111, 149, 154	2.1.1	62	3.39.15	149, 172, 173, 175, 176, 204, 205
		2.1.8	204		
Cyprian		2.1.13	62		
Treatise		2.6.5	204	3.39.16	174
4	61	2.9.4	204	4.7.3	157
		2.15.1-2	205	4.14.3	112
Did.		2.15.1	62, 114, 148, 204	4.14.7	147
1.2	208			4.21	111
1.3	94, 208	3.1.1	112	4.22.5	157
2.1	94	3.3.1	204	4.22.8	87, 89
6.1	94	3.3.2	204	4.23.6	205
7.3	109	3.3.7	204	4.23.12	201, 204
8.2	85	3.4.3	62, 87, 89	4.29.3	156
9.5	191	3.4.7	87, 89, 180, 183, 203	4.29.5	205
11	157			4.30.1	157
11.3	85			5.1.5	114
11.4-6	191	3.7.8	123, 142	5.8.1	112, 204
12	192	3.10.11	123	5.8.2	174
13.3	119	3.11.1	123	5.8.3	204
15.3-4	85	3.24.3	205	5.8.8	165
15.3	191	3.24.5	164	5.10.1	62, 155
15.3b	191	3.24.6-7	174, 204	5.10.2	173

5.10.3	174	5.2	85	John Chrysostom	
5.11.1-5	155	7.2	85	*Hom.*	
5.11.2-5	155-56	8.2	60, 85, 190	20	174
5.11.3	164				
5.11.4-5	125			Justin	
5.16.2–17.4	197	*Pol.*		*1 Apol.*	
5.19.2	157	6.1	172	8	60
5.20.4-8	204			14	78, 193
5.20.5	147	*Smyrn.*		38	127
5.20.6-7	150	3.2-3	190	42	127
5.23.1	109			66	163, 173, 180
5.24.16	150	*Trall.*			
5.28.8	205	2.3	172	67	193
5.28.13-14	205	11.1	189		
6.2	203			*2 Apol.*	
6.14.5-7	112, 148	Irenaeus		3	193
6.14.7	151	*Adv. Haer.*			
6.25.3-4	202	1.3.6	197	*Trypho*	
6.25.13	154	1.6	197	8	157, 194
6.26.4	174	1.8	197	10	193
6.36.1	156	2.4.1	86, 212	38	134
6.38.1	202	2.10.2	61	100	86
7.14.1	156	2.22.2	86	103	148, 164
7.15.4	204	2.27	197	105	164
7.18.1	87	3	126	107	164
7.19.1	61, 62	3 preface	127, 197	109	127
7.32.25	156	3.1	61, 86, 126		
Fragments of Caius		3.2.1	107, 197	Kerygma Petrou	
3.1-4	151	3.2.2	61	1.1-3	142, 174
		3.2.3-4	127		
Gospel of Thomas		3.2.9	86	*Mart. Pol.*	
9	199	3.3.1-2	111	1.1	85
75	26, 199	3.3.4	150	4.1	85
		3.4	107	5.28	61
Hippolytus		3.4.1	86, 107, 111, 173	5.32	61
Treatise on Christ and Anti-Christ				5.44	61
67	203	3.5.1	111	5.46	61
		3.11.7	86	6.3	61
Ignatius		3.11.9	124	22.1	61
Eph.		3.15.3	147	22.2-3	150
5.3	189	3.19.9	197	22.2	173
6.1	189	3.19.11	197		
14.2	189	4.14.3-4	150	Novatian	
		4.27	197	*On the Trinity*	
		4.32	153	16	61, 204
Mag.		4.32.1	147		
6.2	94	11.7	86	Origen,	
12.1	189	11.9	86	*Contra Celsus*	
		28	156	5.63	61
Phld.		33	196	6.6	86
3.1	189			27	86

Index of Ancient Sources

De Principiis		Shepherd of Hermas		28	111
4.1	202	*Mand.*		36	203
4.9	202	4.1.6	194		
		11	157	*Against Marcion*	
Pistis Sophia		11.9	119	4.3	86, 180,
42	174	12.6.3	194		203
				4.4	61, 124
Polycarp		*Sim.*		4.5	86, 123,
Phil.		5.2.6	194		127, 149
2.3	195	9.20.2-3	194		
6.3	86	9.22.3	194	*On Idolatry*	
7.1-2	59, 60,	9.25.2	60	5	203
	227	9.31.2	194		
7.1	195			*The Treatise on the*	
11.3	188	*Vis.*		*Resurrection*	
12.1	195	4.2.6	194	48.8	85
Ps.-Clement		Tertullian		Theophilus of Antioch	
Recognitiones		*Against Heresies*		3.14	86
2.1	165	21	127		
		22	125		

OTHER ANCIENT AUTHORS

Homer		*1 En.*		Josephus	
Od.		89.55	192	*Ant.*	
14.152-153	82	89.66	182	17.6.2	
		89.67	192	§§149-154	134
Lucian					
The Passing of Peregrinus		Philo		*War*	
11	173	*Vit. Cont*		1.33.2	
		25	164	§§648-650	134

INDEX OF AUTHORS

Addis, W.E. 107
Allon, G. 135
Althaus, P. 19
Anderson, H. 214
Arnold, T. 107
Aune, D.E. 65, 110, 111, 116-19, 141, 144, 153, 157, 170, 215

Bagatti, B. 145
Baillie, D.M. 19, 22
Baird, J.A. 12, 20, 24-34, 36, 38, 39, 47, 55, 64, 65, 67-69, 72-75, 78, 80, 83, 85, 93, 97, 99-101, 103, 116, 121-26, 131, 137-40, 142-47, 161, 163, 167-71, 195, 200, 205, 212-16, 222, 224-29, 232, 233, 235, 236, 239-41, 243-45, 247-49, 251, 252, 254
Baltzer, K. 64, 65
Barbour, I.G. 42-44
Barnett, A.B. 183, 214
Barrett, C.K. 15, 139, 142, 247, 248
Bauer, W. 157, 234, 254
Bethune-Baker, J.F. 108
Betz, H.D. 173
Black, M. 31, 134, 168
Boccaccini, G. 131
Boman, T. 25, 26, 118, 169
Boring, M.E. 108, 116, 117
Bornkamm, G. 19, 128
Bousset, W. 130
Bowman, J.W. 19, 118, 170
Braaten, C.E. 21
Brandon, S.G.F. 142
Braun, H. 220
Buber, M. 53, 85
Bultmann, R. 17-19, 21-26, 30, 35, 37, 42, 72, 231, 238, 249
Burridge, R.A. 62
Buswell, G. 220
Butterfield, H. 22
Buttrick, G.A. 94, 181, 183

Calvin, J. 16
Carrington, P. 174
Charlesworth, J.H. 78, 131
Chilton, B. 28, 78
Collingwood, R.G. 22, 23
Collins, A.Y. 66
Conant, J.B. 33
Conzelmann, H. 19
Cross, Jr, F.M. 134
Cullmann, O. 19, 149
Culpepper, A. 150

Dahl, N.A. 214
Davids, P.H. 139
Davies, W.D. 135, 142
Denny, J. 177
Dibelius, M. 17, 152
Dihle, A. 65
Dobschütz, E. von 152, 170, 174
Dodd, C.H. 15, 19, 22, 70, 81, 93, 109-11, 177, 210, 223
Donaldson, J. 109
Dungan, D. 105

Easton, B.S. 19
Ebeling, G. 19, 21
Edwards, R.A. 144
Eichhorn, J.G. 16
Ellison, J.W. 12
Evans, C.A. 21, 28, 78

Farmer, W. 236
Fascher, E. 19
France, R.T. 139
Friedrich, G. 82
Fritsch, C.T. 134
Fuchs, E. 21

Gealy, F. 181

Index of Authors

Gerhardsson, B. 102, 107, 112, 131-36, 139, 140, 142, 143, 161, 165, 169, 186, 222, 224, 245-48
Gillespie, T.W. 117
Godet, F. 179
Grant, F.C. 167
Grant, R.M. 108
Grobel, K. 141
Groh, D.E. 108
Gundry, R.H. 196
Gunkel, H. 17, 25

Hadas, M. 248
Hall, D.R. 12, 20, 237
Hanson, R.P.C. 108, 111, 114
Harnack, A. 231
Harrisville, R.A. 21
Harvey, V.A. 21
Headlam, A.C. 177
Hengel, M. 20
Hennecke, E. 55, 67, 78, 82, 112, 123, 147, 148, 151, 167, 174, 199, 212
Herder, J.G. 169
Hick, J. 35
Higgins, A.J.B. 110
Hill, D. 117
Hunter, A.M. 178
Hurtado, L. 130

Jacobson, A.D. 144
Jeremias, J. 19
Jewett, R. 108
Johnson, L.T. 36
Jülicher, A. 28, 29

Kähler, M. 20
Käsemann, E. 19, 21, 108
Kelber, W. 65, 130, 139, 165-67, 169, 215, 245, 248
Kilpatrick, G.D. 152
Kingsbury, J.D. 153
Kleist, J.A. 196
Kloppenborg, J. 144
Knight, G.W. 115
Knox, W.L. 167
Koehler, L. 19
Koester, H. 84, 85, 127, 135, 169, 188, 189, 191, 192, 194, 200, 201, 207
Kuhn, T. 42, 43
Kümmel, W.G. 220
Küng, H. 169
Kurzinger, J. 196

Lake, K. 173, 190, 195, 205
Lawler, H.J. 205
Lehmann, P.L. 109
Long, Jr, E.L. 109
Lonning, I. 219
Lord, A.B. 169
Luther, M. 16

Mack, B.L. 18
MacRae, G.W. 116
Manson, T.W. 167
Manson, W. 214
Marxsen, W. 220
McArthur, H.K. 167, 214
Meagher, J.C. 51, 53, 55, 70, 81, 98, 105, 110, 111, 175, 223, 231
Meeks, W.A. 108
Melamed, E. 137
Metzger, B.M. 155-57, 185, 188, 189, 194, 195-97, 199, 206, 216, 219-21, 236
Meyer, B.F. 28
Meyer, E. 167
Miller, R.J. 117
Moore, G.F. 26, 135
Moule, C.F.D. 115, 177

Neill, S. 22
Neirynck, F. 144
Neusner, J. 135, 147

Ogden, S.M. 21, 214
Ong, W.J. 165
Oulton, J.E.L. 205

Perrin, N. 142
Powell, M.A. 22

Quasten, J. 203

Redlich, B. 19
Reicke, B. 183
Renan, E. 64
Rengstorf, K.H. 130
Resch, A. 169
Richards, K.H. 144
Riesenfeld, H. 47, 48, 117, 214, 223
Riesner, R. 139
Roberts, A. 109
Robertson, W. 177
Robinson, J.M. 19, 21, 36, 135, 155, 169

Sanday, W. 177

Scannel, T.B. 107
Schillebeeckx, E. 215
Schmidt, K.L. 17
Schmithals, W. 121, 125, 128
Schneemelcher, W. 55, 67, 78, 82, 112, 123, 147, 148, 151, 167, 174, 199, 212
Schoeps, H. 125
Schürmann, H. 108
Scott, E.F. 27
Scroggs, R. 147
Shuler, P. 65, 66
Smith, D.M. 142, 150
Smith, M. 64, 134-39, 248
Smith, R.H. 147
Stanton, G.N. 174
Stather-Hunt, B.P.W. 167
Stendahl, K. 130, 142, 143, 152, 153, 163, 170, 171, 220
Stewart, J. 169
Strack, H.L. 26
Strecker, G. 157

Streeter, B.H. 144, 145
Stuhlmacher, P. 65, 82, 83
Suggs, M.J. 96, 122, 128, 171

Talbert, C.H. 64
Taylor, R. 170
Taylor, V. 19, 117, 167
Tolbert, M.A. 66

Vermes, G. 71, 215
Vincent, J.J. 169
Vorster, W.S. 64, 65
Votaw, C.W. 64

Wellhausen, J. 17, 20, 36
Wendling, A. 167
Wenham, D. 139
Wikgren, A. 214
Wilder, A.N. 94, 142
Witherington, B. 130, 139
Wrede, W. 17, 18, 20, 35-40

JOURNAL FOR THE STUDY OF THE NEW TESTAMENT
SUPPLEMENT SERIES

110 Mark L. Strauss, *The Davidic Messiah in Luke–Acts: The Promise and its Fulfillment in Lukan Christology*
111 Ian H. Thomson, *Chiasmus in the Pauline Letters*
112 Jeffrey B. Gibson, *The Temptations of Jesus in Early Christianity*
113 Stanley E. Porter and D.A. Carson (eds.), *Discourse Analysis and Other Topics in Biblical Greek*
114 Lauri Thurén, *Argument and Theology in 1 Peter: The Origins of Christian Paraenesis*
115 Steve Moyise, *The Old Testament in the Book of Revelation*
116 C.M. Tuckett (ed.), *Luke's Literary Achievement: Collected Essays*
117 Kenneth G.C. Newport, *The Sources and Sitz im Leben of Matthew 23*
118 Troy W. Martin, *By Philosophy and Empty Deceit: Colossians as Response to a Cynic Critique*
119 David Ravens, *Luke and the Restoration of Israel*
120 Stanley E. Porter and David Tombs (eds.) *Approaches to New Testament Study*
121 Todd C. Penner, *The Epistle of James and Eschatology: Re-reading an Ancient Christian Letter*
122 A.D.A. Moses, *Matthew's Transfiguration Story in Jewish–Christian Controversy*
123 David Lertis Matson, *Household Conversion Narratives in Acts: Pattern and Interpretation*
124 David Mark Ball, *'I Am' in John's Gospel: Literary Function, Background and Theological Implications*
125 Robert Gordon Maccini, *Her Testimony is True: Women as Witnesses According to John*
126 B. Hudson Mclean, *The Cursed Christ: Mediterranean Expulsion Rituals and Pauline Soteriology*
127 R. Barry Matlock, *Unveiling the Apocalyptic Paul: Paul's Interpreters and the Rhetoric of Criticism*
128 Timothy Dwyer, *The Motif of Wonder in the Gospel of Mark*
129 Carl Judson Davis, *The Names and Way of the Lord: Old Testament Themes, New Testament Christology*
130 Craig S. Wansink, *Chained in Christ: The Experience and Rhetoric of Paul's Imprisonments*
131 Stanley E. Porter and Thomas H. Olbricht (eds.), *Rhetoric, Scripture and Theology: Essays from the 1994 Pretoria Conference*
132 J. Nelson Kraybill, *Imperial Cult and Commerce in John's Apocalypse*
133 Mark S. Goodacre, *Goulder and the Gospels: An Examination of a New Paradigm*
134 Larry J. Kreitzer, *Striking New Images: Roman Imperial Coinage and the New Testament World*
135 Charles Landon, *A Text-Critical Study of the Epistle of Jude*

136　Jeffrey T. Reed, *A Discourse Analysis of Philippians: Method and Rhetoric in the Debate over Lierary Integrity*
137　Roman Garrison, *The Graeco-Roman Context of Early Christian Literature*
138　Kent D. Clarke, *Textual Optimism: A Critique of the United Bible Societies' Greek New Testament*
139　Yong-Eui Yang, *Jesus and the Sabbath in Matthew's Gospel*
140　Thomas R. Yoder Neufeld,*Put on the Armour of God: The Divine Warrior from Isaiah to Ephesians*
141　Rebecca I. Denova, *The Things Accomplished among Us: Prophetic Tradition in the Structural Pattern of Luke–Acts*
142　Scott Cunningham, *'Through Many Tribulations': The Theology of Persecution in Luke–Acts*
143　Raymond Pickett, *The Cross in Corinth: The Social Significance of the Death of Jesus*
144　S. John Roth, *The Blind, the Lame and the Poor: Character Types in Luke–Acts*
145　Larry Paul Jones, *The Symbol of Water in the Gospel of John*
146　Stanley E. Porter and Thomas H. Olbricht (eds.), *The Rhetorical Analysis of Scripture: Essays from the 1995 London Conference*
147　Kim Paffenroth, *The Story of Jesus According to L*
148　Craig A. Evans and James A. Sanders (eds.), *Early Christian Interpretation of the Scriptures of Israel: Investigations and Proposals*
149　J. Dorcas Gordon, *Sister or Wife?: 1 Corinthians 7 and Cultural Anthropology*
150　J. Daryl Charles, *Virtue amidst Vice: The Catalog of Virtues in 2 Peter 1.5-7*
151　Derek Tovey, *Narrative Art and Act in the Fourth Gospel*
152　Evert-Jan Vledder, *Conflict in the Miracle Stories: A Socio-Exegetical Study of Matthew 8 and 9*
153　Christopher Rowland and Crispin H.T. Fletcher-Louis (eds.), *Understanding, Studying and Reading: New Testament Essays in Honour of John Ashton*
154　Craig A. Evans and James A. Sanders (eds.),*The Function of Scripture in Early Jewish and Christian Tradition*
155　Kyoung-Jin Kim, *Stewardship and Almsgiving in Luke's Theology*
156　I.A.H. Combes, *The Metaphor of Slavery in the Writings of the Early Church: From the New Testament to the Begining of the Fifth Century*
157　April D. DeConick, *Voices of the Mystics: Early Christian Discourse in the Gospels of John and Thomas and Other Ancient Christian Literature*
158　Jey. J. Kanagaraj, *'Mysticism' in the Gospel of John: An Inquiry into its Background*
159　Brenda Deen Schildgen, *Crisis and Continuity: Time in the Gospel of Mark*
160　Johan Ferreira, *Johannine Ecclesiology*
161　Helen C. Orchard, *Courting Betrayal: Jesus as Victim in the Gospel of John*
162　Jeffrey T. Tucker, *Example Stories: Perspectives on Four Parables in the Gospel of Luke*
163　John A. Darr, *Herod the Fox: Audience Criticism and Lukan Characterization*
164　Bas M.F. Van Iersel, *Mark: A Reader-Response Commentary*

165 Alison Jasper, *The Shining Garment of the Text: Gendered Readings of John's Prologue*
166 G.K. Beale, *John's Use of the Old Testament in Revelation*
167 Gary Yamasaki, *John the Baptist in Life and Death: Audience-Oriented Criticism of Matthew's Narrative*
168 Stanley E. Porter and D.A. Carson (eds.), *Linguistics and the New Testament: Critical Junctures*
169 Derek Newton, *Deity and Diet: The Dilemma of Sacrificial Food at Corinth*
170 Stanley E. Porter and Jeffrey T. Reed (eds.), *Discourse Analysis and the New Testament: Approaches and Results*
171 Stanley E. Porter and Anthony R. Cross (eds.)*Baptism, the New Testament and the Church: Historical and Contemporary Studies in Honour of R.E.O. White*
172 Casey Wayne Davis,*Oral Biblical Criticism: The Influence of the Priniples of Orality on the Literary Structure of Paul's Epistle to the Philippians*
173 Stanley E. Porter and Richard S. Hess (eds.), *Translating the Bible: Problems and Prospects*
174 J.D.H. Amador, *Academic Constraints in Rhetorical Criticism of the New Testament: An Introduction to a Rhetoric of Power*
175 Edwin K. Broadhead,*Naming Jesus: Titular Christology in the Gospel of Mark*
176 Alex T. Cheung,*Idol Food in Corinth: Jewish Background and Pauline Legacy*
177 Brian Dodd, *Paul's Paradigmatic 'I': Personal Examples as Literary Strategy*
178 Thomas B. Slater, *Christ and Community: A Socio-Historical Study of the Christology of Revelation*
179 Alison M. Jack, *Texts Reading Texts, Sacred and Secular: Two Postmodern Perspectives*
180 Stanley E. Porter and Dennis L. Stamps (eds.),*The Rhetorical Interpretation of Scripture: Essays from the 1996 Malibu Conference*
181 Sylvia C. Keesmaat,*Paul and his Story: (Re)Interpreting the Exodus Tradition*
182 Johannes Nissen and Sigfred Pedersen (eds.), *New Readings in John: Literary and Theological Perspectives. Essays from the Scandinavian Coference on the Fourth Gospel in Århus 1997*
183 Todd D. Still, *Conflict at Thessalonica: A Pauline Church and its Neighbours*
184 David Rhoads and Kari Syreeni (eds.), *Characterization in the Gospels: Reconceiving Narrative Criticism*
185 David Lee, *Luke's Stories of Jesus: Theological Reading of Gospel Narrative and the Legacy of Hans Frei*
186 Stanley E. Porter, Michael A. Hayes and David Tombs (eds.), *Resurrection*
187 David A. Holgate, *A Prodigality, Liberality and Meanness: The Prodigal Son in Graeco-Roman Perspective*
188 Jerry L. Sumney, *'Servants of Satan', 'False Brothers' and Other Opponents of Paul: A Study of those Opposed in the Letters of the Pauline Corpus*
189 Steve Moyise (ed.),*The Old Testament in the New Testament: Essays in Honour of J.L. North*
190 John M. Court,*The Book of Revelation and the Johannine Apocalyptic Tradition*

191 Stanley E. Porter, *The Criteria for Authenticity in Historical-Jesus Research. Previous Discussion and New Proposals*
192 Stanley E. Porter and Brook W.R. Pearson (eds.), *Christian–Jewish Relations through the Centuries*
193 Stanley E. Porter (ed.), *Diglossia and other Topics in New Testament Linguistics*
195 Stanley E. Porter and Dennis L. Stamps (eds.), *Rhetorical Criticism and the Bible: Essays from the 1998 Florence Conference*
196 J.M. Holmes, *Text in a Whirlwind: A Critique of Four Exegetical Devices at 1 Timothy 2.9-15*
197 F. Gerald Downing, *Making Sense in (and of) the First Christian Century*
198 Greg W. Forbes, *The God of Old: The Role of the Lukan Parables in the Purpose of Luke's Gospel*
199 Kieran O'Mahony, O.S.A., *Pauline Persuasion: A Sounding in 2 Corinthians 8–9*
200 F. Gerald Downing, *Doing Things with Words in the First Christian Century*
202 Gustavo Martín-Asensio, *Transitivity-Based Foregrounding in the Acts of the Apostles: A Functional-Grammatical Approach*
203 H. Benedict Green, CR, *Matthew, Poet of the Beatitudes*
204 Warren Carter, *Matthew and the Margins: A Socio-Political and Religious Commentary*
206 David Edgar, *Has God Not Chosen the Poor? The Social Setting of the Epistle of James*
207 Kyu Sam Han, *Jerusalem and the Early Jesus Movement: The Q Community's Attitude toward the Temple*
208 Mark D. Chapman, *The Coming Crisis: The Impact of Eschatology on Theology in Edwardian England*
209 Richard W. Johnson, *Going Outside the Camp: The Sociological Function of the Levitical Critique in the Epistle to the Hebrews*
210 Bruno Blumenfeld, *The Political Paul: Democracy and Kingship in Paul's Thought*
211 Ju Hur, *A Dynamic Reading of the Holy Spirit in Luke–Acts*
212 Wendy E. Sproston North, *The Lazarus Story within the Johannine Tradition*
213 William O. Walker Jr, *Interpolations in the Pauline Letters*
214 Michael Labahn and Andreas Schmidt (eds.), *The Teaching of Jesus and its Earliest Records*
215 Barbara Shellard, *New Light on Luke: Its Purpose, Sources and Literary Context*
216 Stephanie L. Black, *Sentence Conjunctions in the Gospel of Matthew kai, de, tote, gar, ou)n and Asyndeton in Narrative Discourse*
218 Paul L. Danove, *Linguistics and Exegesis in the Gospel of Mark: Applications of a Case Frame Analysis and Lexicon*
219 Iutisone Salevao, *Legitimation in the Letter to the Hebrews: The Construction and Maintenance of a Symbolic Universe*
224 J. Arthur Baird, *Holy Word: The Paradigm of New Testament Formation*

BS
2315
.B26
2002